Discover
the
Hidden
New Jersey

R

*RUTGERS
UNIVERSITY
PRESS*
New Brunswick
New Jersey

Discover the
HIDDEN
New Jersey

RUSSELL ROBERTS

Library of Congress Cataloging-in-Publication Data

Roberts, Russell, 1953–
    Discover the hidden New Jersey / Russell Roberts.
      p.   cm.
    Includes bibliographical references and index.
    ISBN 0-8135-2252-8 (alk. paper)
    1. New Jersey—History—Miscellanea.   2. New Jersey—History—
Anecdotes. I. Title.
F134.5.R6   1995
974.9—dc20   95-4571
                                                          CIP

British Cataloging-in-Publication information available

974.9
Rob

To Megan—because without her I am nothing

CONTENTS

Preface

THERE'S a lot more to New Jersey than I realized.

Like the proverbial thunderbolt from the sky, this thought struck me one day while researching my last book for Rutgers University Press, *Down the Jersey Shore*. As a lifelong resident of the state, I always assumed that I had somehow soaked up a lot of New Jersey knowledge, purely by the osmosis of being here for so many years.

I soon found out, however, that I had been sadly mistaken. As I worked on the Shore book, I continually discovered tidbits of information about the rest of New Jersey, making me keenly aware of how little I actually knew about my native state. The more I found, the less I knew; the less I knew, the more I *wanted* to know. Finally, one day I made the fatal pronouncement: "What I don't know about New Jersey would fill a book."

So now it has.

I began this book by wracking my brain (a painful process that is best not tried without the assistance of trained professionals) for all those miscellaneous pieces of New Jersey information that had been stuck in there for years, like scraps of cloth thrown into a sewing box in the vague hope that someday they might be stitched together into something worthwhile. I examined these bits of information in the cold light of a book deadline, to see if they really were interesting, or if they'd just been taking up space all those years. Fortunately, many of them proved worthwhile, and provided me with initial leads that eventually lead to bigger and better things.

Usually it would be just a few words plucked from my mental shorthand that would send me on a quest to find out more ("Napoleon's brother—didn't he live in New Jersey?"). Other times ideas would take on a more substantive nature, as images and memories lodged for years deep in my subconscious swam to the surface and demanded to be heard: ("The 1962 Nor'easter, remember? Remember how the wind howled and the rain hammered on the windows, and you huddled up against your mother and father, so scared that at any moment the entire house was going to float away on a raging sea of water?").

And then there were those special moments, the moments that all writers love the most, when, out of the blue, I would come upon something so interesting, and so utterly fascinating, that I would laugh out loud with delight, like some maniacal miner who has just found a nugget of gold hiding amidst the gravel. (Unfortunately, these moments of epiphany often seemed to occur in a library, where loud chuckling and whoops of glee are not looked upon too kindly by the other patrons.)

Early on, I determined to write longer about fewer subjects, rather than shorter about many things. Short little essays about topics bother me, for, like just a few potato chips, they always leave you wanting more. There are literally scores of topics that could be covered in each chapter, but in attempting to cover everything I felt that I would really be covering nothing, so cursory and brief would the writing be. Thus I opted to pick a few topics that I found particularly interesting, and elaborate on those, in the hopes of providing you with a sit-down dinner rather than a quick snack.

A writer is, by necessity, a reader (and hopefully by choice too, or a serious career change is in order). As such, I've tried to fill this book with information that I would have enjoyed reading in a book of this type, had the shoe been on the other foot and it was me instead of you perusing this volume in a store, wondering if it was worth my time and money. I hope you feel that what I found, and what I wrote about, was worth it for both of us.

If this book has a central theme, it is this: New Jersey is a fascinating place. It's the state where baseball began and from which the movies fled, where two of our nation's Founding Fathers fought over a theory and the winner was subsequently killed in a duel, where a monster lives deep in an untamed wilderness in the most urbanized state in the union. It's been the home of heroes, like the young girl who gave her life so that millions of others could live, and the final resting place of scoundrels, such as the man who tried to rip apart the country for his own glory. It's the place where dinosaurs were first found, and it's the place where the last camp meeting community still survives along the shore. New Jersey is all this and more, and this book celebrates that uniqueness.

As far as what this book contains, I make no pretense about being a historian or a folklorist, attempting to document all I've found for scholarly purposes. I'm merely a conduit, passing along what I hope are some cracking good stories, facts, trivia, and nuggets of information that I discovered on my voyage of discovery throughout New Jersey, which took me to every corner and county of the state, and most points in-between.

I hope you feel that the journey was worthwhile.

Acknowledgments

I T ' S probably been said before but I'll say it again: Writing a book is like having a baby. For months you can think of nothing else; you worry about it, lay awake at night thinking about it, and have a thousand hopes and dreams for it. Then suddenly it's over: The baby is born or the book is delivered to the publisher (hopefully not the other way around), and you are left with a deep emptiness inside.

Without the kind and generous assistance of the following people, this book would never have been delivered. To all of them, all I can say is a heartfelt "Thank you." These kind souls are, in no particular order: Joy Peto Smiley, Marguerite Loretangeli, David Taylor, Leeanne Schmidt, Kathy Clark, Sara Watson, Charles Webster, Mike Fowler, Rita Altomara, Darci Harrington, Angus Gillespie, Roy Schlische, Jim Albertson, Dave Robinson, Ed Skipworth, and Suzanne Merighi. I would also like to extend my gratitude to the "nameless mass" of tour guides, curators, and others who helped me find the truth. Some were only a voice on the phone, but human kindness always transcends machinery.

As always, special thanks go to Marilyn and David, for once again feeding and helping to guide a poor, misbegotten writer in the initial stages of his quest. I would also like to thank Rutgers University Press for giving me the opportunity to write this book, and to all those hard-working folks at the press who took a bewildering mass of pages and photographs and turned them into something publishable. Special thanks go to Marlie Wasserman and Karen Reeds for their help and understanding.

Thanks as well to Kelly for his loyalty and support. I'm going to miss you, old friend.

A big tip of the writing cap to Peter and everyone at Computer Vision Technology, who resurrected my computer when it died five days before deadline. Machines may be the servant of humanity, but they sure like to make it difficult sometimes.

Last but not least, I would be remiss if I did not individually thank all my friends at the Bordentown Library. This is the place where the search often started, and their continued help and support was, and is, greatly appreciated: Annemarie Edinger, Agnes Julie Gray, Jackie Lennon, Beverly Jacob Turczyn, Ellin C. Leder, Jane E. Snow, Doris T. Rule, Leona Lee, Muriel Hartman, Jessica Gyarfas, and Al Addis.

CHAPTER ONE

New Jersey Firsts

GEORGE WASHINGTON may have been "first in war, first in peace, and first in the hearts of his countrymen," but New Jersey has been first in a lot of things as well.

The vast number of "firsts" that have occurred in the state, from technological breakthroughs and important scientific discoveries to more whimsical achievements—such as the invention of the first drive-in movie theater—would fill a book by themselves. Those who put down New Jersey should remember that without this state, there would be no baseball, college football, movies, electric lights, boardwalks, public libraries, condensed soup, or a multitude of other things both important and enjoyable. All these got their start in New Jersey—the "first state" of innovation and ingenuity.

The first Jersey "first" may or may not be true, but it's a heckuva story, and too good to pass up.

One day in the 1820s, Col. Robert Gibbon Johnson strode up the court house steps in Salem. With a confident smile at the huge crowd that had gathered around, Johnson reached down into a basket at his feet and picked up something that everyone agreed was poisonous. As people in the audience watched in disbelief, Johnson proceeded to eat first one "poisonous" object, then a second, and, incredibly, even a third, and was still very much alive when he finished.

The crowd gasped in disbelief. How could Johnson have done it? How could he have eaten those things and survived? Finally, someone said aloud what was on everyone's minds: "Colonel Johnson is the first person to eat a *tomato* and live!"

A tomato? Poisonous? Indeed, according to local legend, in the early days of the United States, tomatoes were considered quite harmful. Just one bite would make a person sick, while eating a whole one was tantamount to calling the undertaker. Johnson, a farmer and learned man who knew better, finally decided that drastic action was the only way to disprove the "killer tomato" theory.

Unfortunately, even though this story has a long and glorious history in New Jersey (supposedly it was even dramatized on a radio broadcast), it's probably not true. After all, Spanish colonists in the New World were eating tomatoes for many years before Johnson's supposed demonstration on the court house steps. Still, it's a great story, and certainly one of the most unusual New Jersey firsts—real or imagined—ever recorded.

Around 1930, night after night, in the driveway of his home in Riverton, a New Jersey man sat in his car, intently watching a movie screen that he had nailed to a tree, on which was playing a film from a projector perched on top of the automobile. Sometimes, he would even turn on the lawn sprinkler while the movie was going on and sit there, in the car, watching the movie while the water poured down around him. Anyone who saw him might well have shaken their head, and that's perfectly understandable. What they could not possibly know was that what they were witnessing was not the actions of a raging eccentric, but rather the birth of an American icon: the drive-in movie theater.

The man sitting in his car and watching movies "in the rain" was Richard M. Hollingshead, Jr. His father, Richard Hollingshead, Sr., owned the Whiz Auto Products Company, which had correctly anticipated the switch from the horse to the horseless carriage by dumping their line of harness products for a full line of automobile soaps, polishes, etc., thus becoming quite successful. Born on February 25, 1900, Hollingshead junior joined his father's company after completing his education. It was a

1   Richard M. Hollingshead, Jr., "Father of the Drive-In." (Courtesy of Quigley Photographic Archive, Special Collections Division, Georgetown University Library/Motion Picture Herald/Better Theatres)

job for life, as are most jobs in a family business, but the young man was restless. He wanted to make his own mark in the world.

Hollingshead took his first steps on the path that would lead to the drive-in when he realized that cars and movies were two things that

people refused to surrender, no matter how tight money became. He then analyzed the reasons why people didn't want to go to the movies: "The mother says she's not dressed; the husband doesn't want to put on his shoes; the question is what to do with the kids; then how to find a baby sitter; parking the car is difficult or maybe they have to pay for parking; even the seats in the theater may not be comfortable to contemplate."

Having defined the problem, Hollingshead next sought the solution. In the driveway of his home, he set a 1928 Kodak projector on the hood of his car, nailed a makeshift movie screen onto a nearby tree, and placed a radio behind the screen to provide sound. Then the erstwhile inventor sat in his car and watched the film unwind. No matter what he did—including using the lawn sprinkler to simulate rain—he liked it. The car was convenient, roomy, and private; no more annoying loud mouths talking behind you, no more people crinkling candy wrappers during a crucial scene, and no more tight, uncomfortable theater seats.

Over the next few months, Hollingshead worked out the bugs in his idea. He figured out that by elevating each row of cars slightly, those in the back would be able to see as well as those in the front. He found a company that would build a 50-foot wide projection screen. For adequate sound he contacted RCA Victor in Camden, which devised "controlled directional sound," basically a fancy name for three centrally located speakers (the infamous in-car speaker did not appear until the late 1940s) that would blast the sound all at once throughout the entire theater lot.

Having solved these problems, by spring 1933, Hollingshead was ready to unleash his invention on the world—or at least on New Jersey. A crew of workmen, many taken off the relief rolls, descended on a site on Crescent Boulevard in Pennsauken Township (most reports erroneously give the location of the first theater as the Admiral Wilson Boulevard in Camden) on May 16, 1933, to begin building the outdoor theater. Construction took a mere three weeks, and cost an estimated $30,000. On June 6, the world's first "Automobile Movie Theater" opened for business.

"Sit In Your Car—See and Hear MOVIES" trumpeted the huge sign outside the theater. The cost was twenty-five cents per person, or $1 for an entire carload. The first film was *Wife Beware*, starring Adolphe Menjou.

The grand opening was a glorious success. The lot was jammed, thanks in part to a clever marketing campaign by Hollingshead. Besides giving out passes to many Philadelphia and Camden media outlets, he also ran ads targeting particular groups that he thought the drive-in concept would appeal to. One of the ads, for example, showed a rather large woman trying to squeeze into a tiny indoor theater seat (much to the dismay of the surrounding patrons).

"The world's first Automobile Theatre opened on Crescent Boulevard last night with more than 600 motorists attending the initial performance," announced the next day's *Camden Courier* under a headline reading "600 Motorists See Open-Air Movies." The story went on to say that "beer and lunches" would be on sale the following week and that features with "all dull or uninteresting parts omitted" would be shown three times nightly.

Unfortunately, business died off quickly after that triumphant first night. Hollingshead ultimately sold the theater to a man who "moved" it to Union, New Jersey. In later years, Hollingshead contended that his biggest problem was getting movie distributors to give him first-run films (a problem that forever plagued drive-ins, which always seemed to be playing *Attack of the Killer Tomatoes* while the local indoor theater was showing the latest blockbuster).

In reality, several factors contributed to the demise of the first drive-in: The sound was poor, and often not synchronized with the film; many cars were situated at odd angles to the screen, which made viewing difficult; and, the price was high for what was, essentially, a novelty experience. Most importantly, with the windows rolled up, cars quickly became steam baths on New Jersey's humid, sticky summer nights; with the windows down, the state's other hot weather terror—the voracious Jersey mosquito—snacked on theater patrons with a vengeance. (Realizing that heat would be a problem, Hollingshead had planted over 200 trees around the theater.)

Nearly twenty years later, fueled by the mass migration to the suburbs, the lack of indoor theaters there, and cheap gas, the drive-in came into its own. During the 1950s, drive-ins almost single-handedly enabled films to stave off the onslaught of television. For Hollingshead, however, there were no laurels, even belated ones, from Hollywood. The inventor of the drive-in died on May 13, 1975, ignored by the industry to which he had contributed so much.

Today, New Jersey is one of just four states in the entire country that does not have at least one drive-in theater (Delaware, Alaska, and Rhode Island are the others). So, ironically, the state that gave birth to an American institution is also one of the few in which you cannot see such cinematic classics as *Mad Monkey Kung Fu* in the comfort of your own car—and that's sad (or is it?).

DID YOU KNOW?

What are the top drive-in movies of all time?

Texas Chain Saw Massacre
Basket Case

The Beast Within
I Dismember Mama
Mad Monkey Kung Fu

Today, *E Pluribus Unum* (which means, roughly, "from many, one") is found on all United States coins. The first state to adopt that motto was New Jersey, back in 1786, when it placed the saying on so-called "horse head" cents. Other states didn't follow suit until several years later.

Hot-air ballooning has become an extremely popular pastime all over the world. It's especially widespread in France, where the large, colorful balloons are a common sight floating over the countryside. Indeed, it was a Frenchman who made the first airborne passenger flight in the Western Hemisphere—right here in New Jersey!

On January 9, 1793, a farmer working in his field in Deptford Township looked up to behold a wondrous sight. Floating down at him from out of the sky was a huge, round object with a wicker basket underneath. Even more amazing was that inside the wicker basket was what appeared to be a man, who was shouting something at him in a language the farmer had never heard before.

As the object settled down in his field, thoughts of witches, devils, and the like must have raced through the farmer's mind. Yet, pushing these fears aside, he ran toward the strange object to see for himself what had landed so unceremoniously in his field.

Seeing the farmer approaching, the man in the wicker basket climbed out and tried talking to him, but neither could understand a word that the other said. Then the man showed the farmer a letter, which also had little effect, since the farmer couldn't read. Finally, the man reached into the wicker basket and pulled out the universal communicator: wine. Soon he and the farmer were toasting each other's friendship—which was fortunate, because other people were arriving who had also seen the strange object, and one of them had a gun.

Luckily, the man with the gun could also read. He took the letter from the man and read it to the small group. The letter identified the balloonist as a Frenchman named Jean-Pierre Blanchard, and guaranteed him safe passage wherever he landed. It was signed by President George Washington.

With the mention of Washington's name the mood in the field instantly changed from wariness to friendliness. Blanchard later recorded in his journal: "In the midst of profound silence was it [the letter] read with a loud and audible voice. How dear the name of Washington is to this people! With what eagerness they gave me all possible assistance, in consequence of his recommendation."

Blanchard had taken off from Philadelphia earlier that day, in the midst of bands playing, people waving handkerchiefs, and cannons booming. President George Washington had been on hand to wish the balloonist good luck and to give him a letter of safe conduct.

At a few minutes past ten o'clock in the morning, Blanchard's balloon lifted off from the yard of the Walnut Street Prison. Taking a southeasterly course, the balloon floated over the Delaware River and the surrounding countryside until coming to rest in Deptford. The 15-mile trip would have taken several hours by horseback or carriage, but the French adventurer had made the journey in less than sixty minutes.

The small group brought the flying Frenchman and his balloon to a nearby farmhouse. There they wrote down what they had seen: "These may certify, that we the subscribers saw the bearer, Mr. Blanchard, settle in his balloon in Deptford Township, County of Gloucester, in the state of New Jersey, about fifteen miles from Philadelphia, about ten o'clock 56 minutes, A.M. Witness our hands the ninth day of January, Anno Domini, 1793." It was signed by Everard Bolton, Joseph Griffith, Joseph Cheesman, Samuel Taggart, Amos Castell, and Zara North.

Later, after he returned to Philadelphia, Blanchard went to Washington's home, where he presented the president with the unusual two-country flag (the French tricolor was on one side, the Stars and Stripes on the other) that he had carried on his trip.

The young Frenchman had hoped that the fanfare of this trip would be the start of a successful career for him demonstrating his ballooning skills in the United States, where the sport was unknown. Unfortunately, his hopes were doomed to failure. Although Blanchard had sold tickets to spectators of his historic flight at the then-stratospheric price of $5 apiece, he failed to make money on the venture and returned to Europe. There he continued to support himself through ballooning until he had a heart attack while on a flight over Paris in 1808. Although he managed to land safely, he died the following year.

This is a first that most drivers in New Jersey probably wish would have been a "last"—the invention of the first traffic circle.

Today, of course, traffic circles are distinguished mainly by the amount of expletives muttered by approaching drivers. But in 1925, when they were first unveiled to the general public in Camden County, the traffic circle was hailed as a wonderful innovation that would—get ready to laugh—help reduce bottlenecks and accidents.

The first traffic circle in the United States was Airport Circle in Camden County. It was named for Central Airport, which was then located on the north side of Route 130. When the circle was opened, much of Camden and Burlington counties were farmland, and the roads were not heavily traveled. The circle, modeled after the roundabouts and rotaries of Great Britain, was considered a marvelous alternative to traffic signals as a way to manage traffic.

But ingenuity soon gave way to inanity. Just as the opening of Philadelphia International Airport in the early 1950s sounded the death knell for Central Airport, so did the post–World War II building boom that swept through New Jersey mean the end of a traffic circle's effectiveness. By the 1960s, as farmland was replaced by homes, offices, and retail outlets, and the vehicles these spawned poured onto the highways, traffic circles had become the very thing they were supposed to guard against: traffic bottlenecks. All those cars piling willy-nilly into circles became reminiscent of mice racing around a maze with no exit and no hope.

In the 1980s, the New Jersey Department of Transportation began to phase out the once-revolutionary traffic circle. By mid-1994, approximately thirty of the sixty-seven circles in the state had been eliminated.

The next New Jersey first concerns a man with a broad face and a little round belly that shakes when he laughs like a bowl full of jelly. No, it's not your Uncle Fred after Thanksgiving dinner, but Santa Claus, who looks the way he does today thanks to the artistic talents of a Morristown resident named Thomas Nast.

Nast was born in Landau, Bavaria, in 1840. When he was six his parents emigrated to the United States, where they settled in New York. Young Thomas displayed his artistic ability at an early age; after just two years of formal schooling, he got an illustrator's job with *Leslie's Illustrated*

Newspaper, in 1855, at age fifteen. His first published drawing showed a crowd boarding a ferry for Elysian Fields in Hoboken.

In 1862, Nast moved to the leading periodical of the day, *Harper's Weekly*. This was the second—and one of the bloodiest—year of the Civil War; thousands upon thousands of Americans lost their lives in places with names like Antietam, Gaines' Mill, and Shiloh. The war was never far from anyone's thoughts and was certainly the major story at *Harper's*. To Nast fell the job of illustrating the war for *Harper's* readers, through drawings of battles, the soldier's life in camp, and other scenes. He did his job well; his drawings kept Northern sympathies for the war strong during those dark days when Confederate victories were causing the Union flame to flicker uncertainly. (Ulysses S. Grant later said that "[Nast] did as much as any man to preserve the Union and bring the war to an end.")

Drawing battles, death, and man's inhumanity to man was a wearying, depressing chore, so one supposes that Nast jumped at the chance to inject a little joy into his work. This opportunity came during late December 1862; Germans have always had a strong Christmas tradition, and so it was natural for Nast to draw, for the first time, the symbol of Christmas—Santa Claus—in a cartoon that appeared on the cover of the January 3, 1863, issue of *Harper's*. The drawing is entitled "Santa in Camp," and shows St. Nicholas dispensing gifts to Union soldiers. Inside this same issue, Nast drew a few Santa scenes to help counter-balance the generally depressing pictures throughout of lonely soldiers stuck in cold and snowy camps, aching for the warmth of home and hearth during the holiday season.

The Santa Claus that Nast drew (and soon began to refine, in other holiday issues of *Harper's*) was a far cry from what had been done before. Previously, the jolly old elf had been shown as a short, stumpy man with a thin, hawklike face, and sharp features. (In fact, one drawing in 1837 verges on being outright scary, depicting Santa with coal-black eyes and a sinister smile, leering over his shoulder at the reader from the fireplace.) The beard, when one was present, was usually short and scruffy, and Santa's garb ran the gamut from an overcoat and pants to an Arabian prince-type of suit, complete with puffy sleeves.

Nast gave Santa a complete makeover. He made Santa friendlier by rounding and softening his features, and by putting the now-famous twinkle in his eye. He lengthened Santa's beard to modern-day levels, and gave him the large, portly (or, as we would say in today's politically correct world, "weight-challenged") frame that is so familiar today. For his clothing, the artist dressed Santa in a furry suit with a large black belt around the middle.

Nast continued to draw Santa Claus for years to come, even after his political cartoons, which established such symbols as the Republican elephant and the Democratic donkey, made him famous. His Christmas sketches were a phenomenal success, not just because of Santa Claus, but because the artist captured the joy and excitement of the holiday so perfectly.

As time went on, Nast gave Santa a few more contemporary characteristics, such as his toy-making workshop and a large book in which he recorded the names of good and bad children. The final touch came when, for a series of color paintings for a book about Santa, Nast depicted him in a red suit, which he trimmed in white fur to add a little contrast. (Before this, Nast had always drawn Santa in black and white, and had assumed that his suit was fawn-colored.)

Nast was a firm believer in politics as an instrument of national self-improvement. His beautiful three-story Morristown home, known as Villa Fontana, played host to numerous important personages from both the United States and abroad. Although internationally famous, Nast did not hesitate to use his talent to aid his home town. He drew huge cartoons showing scenes from the Revolutionary War and Washington's life for the Centennial Celebration at Washington's Headquarters in Morristown. Nast also provided scenery for local theater productions and contributed a self-portrait for the cover of a cookbook that was sold to benefit Morristown Memorial Hospital.

Sadly, Nast did not find the happiness in later life that he had given so many others through his art. Disgusted by the political corruption spawned in the wake of the Civil War, he left *Harper's* in 1886, although his influence had diminished considerably before that. During his final years a series of financial crises plagued him, and he was forced to give up his home. In 1902, down on his luck, he gratefully accepted the consular post in Guayaquil, Ecuador. But on December 7, 1902, after just six months in residence there, he died of yellow fever at the still-young age of sixty-two.

There's nothing unique anymore about being served food in your car, thanks to car hops and those ubiquitous and incomprehensible drive-through speakers found at virtually every fast food restaurant. But here's a New Jersey first that puts them all to shame. In 1762, the Seven Stars Tavern in Salem County had what was almost certainly the first "drive-through" window in history. A horseback rider could canter up to the window, order food and drink, get served, and pay the check—all without dismounting his or her faithful steed.

Although it may sound incredible, considering their popularity, blueberries owe their broad acceptance and use today entirely to one New Jersey woman, who developed the first cultivated blueberry. The woman was Elizabeth White.

Born in New Lisbon on October 5, 1871, Elizabeth Coleman White spent virtually her entire life working in the sandy soil of the Pinelands. She wasn't one to sit on the porch drinking tea while others did the work; she personally dug up and transplanted so many blueberry bushes, and picked so many blueberries, that her hands were permanently stained with dirt and blueberry juice.

In 1910, White and her father, J. J. White, were searching for a companion crop to the cranberry—one which would grow well in the sandy, acidic soil of the Pinelands. In November of that year she read a bulletin about blueberry culture by Dr. Frederick V. Coville, a botanist. Intrigued, she invited Dr. Coville to visit her at Whitesbog. The two hit it off, and White began concentrating on trying to develop the first cultivated blueberry. (Prior to this, the only blueberries on the market were wild ones, which were just as likely to be small and bitter as they were fat and sweet.)

The best way to approach the task, she felt, was to enlist the aid of the Pinelands residents in finding the heartiest wild blueberry bushes. White developed a network of agents and friends who were always scouring the Pinelands for a wild bush with large, tasty berries. She also used handbills to spread the word: "I will pay for Huckleberry Bushes, from one to three dollars a bush, when the largest berries on it will not drop through holes the size of the blue spots [on an accompanying illustration]" read the flyers.

After securing a bush that met her standards, White would cross-pollinate it with others to try and develop the ultimate blueberry plant. Hundreds and thousands of hours of work went into the tedious, time-consuming process of cross-pollination. By 1916, however, White had successfully marketed the first cultivated blueberry in history.

A generous woman, White was quick to give credit to those who had found the bushes. She dubbed a blueberry developed from a bush found by Ruben Leek the "Rubel," and called another blueberry the "Sam," after Sam Lemon, who brought her the bush.

White continued working with her blueberry bushes, always seeking the next best bush and berry. Her standards were exacting: between 1912 and 1928 approximately 25,000 plants were sent to Whitesbog. Only fifteen cross-pollinated varieties met White's requirements.

For decades she continued to work with blueberries, developing newer and better varieties. At age eighty-three, when most people have long since settled into their easy chairs, Elizabeth White turned over blueberry development to others and began propagating various varieties of holly. By the time she died, on November 27, 1954, this tireless woman had not only left behind a mountain of achievement in the fields of cranberry cultivation and holly propagation, but she had single-handedly launched the entire domestic blueberry industry.

On the morning of July 17, 1933, two black men boarded a Fairchild 24 monoplane in front of hundreds of cheering spectators at Atlantic City's Bader Field. What they were about to attempt was incredibly risky—and historic.

The men, C. Alfred Anderson and Dr. Albert E. Forsythe, were trying to become the first African-Americans to make a transcontinental flight. Their goal was to fly nonstop across the United States to Los Angeles, then fly back to New Jersey.

Even under normal conditions, a nonstop cross-country trip was fraught with risk. However, the two men had decided to make the trip as difficult as possible. Thus the plane carried no parachutes, lights, or even a radio. The only instruments on board were a compass and an altimeter.

"The trip was purposely made to be hazardous and rough," Forsythe later said, "because if it had been an ordinary flight, we wouldn't have attracted attention." What made this decision easier was that both pilots were broke. "We had no radio, no lights, and no parachutes because we didn't have the money to buy those things," Forsythe said.

Both men deserved credit for even being at Bader Field in the first place. Blacks were not welcomed in aviation during this time, and almost no one would teach a black how to fly a plane. Forsythe, however, didn't let this invisible color barrier stop him. Born in Jamaica, he had always dreamed of flying. After establishing a medical practice in Atlantic City, Forsythe began turning his dreams into reality. Discovering that Anderson had gotten his pilot's license at a flight school outside of Philadelphia, he headed there himself.

However, getting a license and flying were two different things. Even with his license, Anderson had been unable to find work, and Forsythe knew that opportunities for blacks in the air were minuscule at best. He hoped that a successful transcontinental flight would prove that African-Americans could compete with whites in aviation.

Thus, when Anderson and Forsythe boarded their plane, called "The Pride of Atlantic City," at Bader Field, they were carrying not only their own hopes, but the hopes of an entire race with them.

Without instruments of any kind, the men used a Rand McNally road map as their guide. This worked fine—until it blew away. From then on, for the rest of the 2,500 mile trip, they were on their own. Losing the map, however, was the least of their problems. On their journey, the plane was buffeted by high winds, heavy rain, and hail, the engine overheated over the Mojave Desert, and the craft had barely enough power to scale the Rocky Mountains. Just to make things interesting, at night they were forced to use flashlights to help guide them along.

But they made it.

Two thousand people greeted the pioneer pilots when they landed in Los Angeles two and one-half days later. However, when they returned to Atlantic City, their accomplishment was barely noted by the *New York*

---

2   *C. Alfred Anderson* (second from left) *and*
Dr. Albert E. Forsythe (fourth from left) *during a visit to Tuskegee Institute. (Courtesy of New Jersey Aviation Hall of Fame)*

Times, which ran a small story well off the front pages headed "Negroes End Flight." This was despite the fact that Wiley Post's attempt to set a new record for around-the-world flying was plastered all over the front page. "First of Race to Span Nation Land at Atlantic City," read a secondary headline above the three-paragraph story, which noted that it was the "first airplane flight to the Pacific Coast and back ever undertaken by two Negro flyers," but carried no details about the trip itself.

New Jersey, however, made up for the newspaper's excuse-me story. A cheering crowd of 1,000 greeted the pioneer pilots on their return to Atlantic City. A few days later, 15,000 exuberant people lined the streets of Newark for a parade in the two men's honor. Forsythe and Anderson were not only heroes, and the owners of another New Jersey first, but they had delivered another stinging blow to that destroyer of dreams known as prejudice.

DID YOU KNOW?

And now, for something completely different, here's a New Jersey first that is not really a New Jersey first!

New Jersey is often credited with having the first brewery in America. Sometime around 1640, so the story goes, a man named Aert Teunissen Van Putten established a brewery in "Hoboquin" (Hoboken), which was in an area known as Pavonia, named after Michael Pauw, who owned the land. An industrious man, Van Putten cleared the land, started a farm, planted fruit trees, and also built a brewhouse.

However, while Hoboken has been quite prominent in New Jersey history, and owns a distinguished first as far as being the true birth place of baseball, this seems like one of those instances in which legend has replaced fact. Several sources point to a brewery in a log house built on Manhattan Island by Adrian Block and Hans Christiansen in 1612 as the actual site of the first brewery in America. Brewing went on here for twenty years, until another brewery was established on the island in 1632 by Peter Minuit—still a decade ahead of Van Putten. In fact, it seems as if there might even have been a brewery at the famous lost Colony of Virginia as early as 1587.

3 Samuel Colt in front of the Connecticut State Capitol Building (Courtesy of Colt Manufacturing)

"God created men, but Colt made them equal."

Since the invention of gunpowder, no single weapon has played such a pivotal role in a nation's history as Samuel Colt and his ingenious multiple-shot revolver. It was the gun that Won the West; as the above phrase suggests, it put men of unequal ability on the same terms, enabling the weaker to hold their own against the stronger and allowing men more

interested in farming than fighting to establish a foothold on the rugged frontier. It was a weapon, and a concept, that Colt tried desperately, but unsuccessfully, to sell to the U.S. government for years. It was also a weapon that was first developed and manufactured in New Jersey.

Before Sam Colt, guns were simple: They shot one bullet at a time. After the gun was discharged, the weapon had to be reloaded—a time-consuming process that could seem like an eternity if an enemy was bearing down on you with a loaded weapon of their own.

But then came young Colt (born in Hartford, Connecticut, on July 19, 1814), who displayed a wooden model of a pistol with a revolving cylinder that fed fresh bullets into the chamber automatically. He had whittled the model at age sixteen, during an 1830 sea voyage. According to the story, Colt got the idea of the revolving cylinder while watching the ship's wheel spin around and seeing how it could be stopped in any position by means of a clutch.

The voyage had been an early attempt by Colt to seek his fortune. When this didn't work out he organized, upon his return to dry land, a traveling sideshow under the name Dr. Coult, expert on "practical chemistry." His knowledge of chemicals, however, was limited to demonstrating to his audiences how silly people act after inhaling laughing gas.

But underneath Colt's sideshow demeanor there still burned a desire to produce an automatic weapon. He continued to have mechanical models built of his "repeating pistol." Each brought him a little closer to success. Finally, on February 25, 1836, after numerous failures, Colt was granted a United States patent.

Now all that Colt needed was a factory in which to begin production. He turned his attention to Paterson, New Jersey, the nation's first planned industrial city, where other members of the Colt family were in charge of the Society for Useful Manufacturers (SUM), the agency that ran the manufacturing sector. Colt's relatives found financial backers for his factory, who used their influence to steer his request for a charter through the New Jersey legislature. By the summer of 1836, the Patent Arms Manufacturing Company of Paterson was in business.

Never a believer in doing anything halfway, Colt's four-story resplendent factory had a weather vane shaped like a gun and was surrounded by a white fence with pickets in the form of pistols. Here Colt began producing the first automatic weapons ever built in the United States.

To Colt's way of thinking the game was already won, but in reality his troubles were just beginning. Figuring that the best way to generate business was to impress those with the power to dispense it, he built fancy guns with silver and gold handles and engraved barrels, and sent them to world leaders. These were universally ignored. He tried interesting two presidents, Andrew Jackson and Martin Van Buren, in his guns, but they wouldn't listen either. The United States Army, always on top of the latest technical innovations, denounced Colt's revolvers as worthless.

Without orders, Colt had nothing but his dogged belief to sustain him, and soon even that wasn't enough. In 1841 the Patent Arms Manufacturing Company went bankrupt, and the following year it ceased to exist. Colt left Paterson penniless, an apparent failure.

Fortune, however, has a strange way of smiling on a person. Some of Colt's weapons had gotten into the hands of Texans, who were fighting for their independence from Mexico. The reputation of the guns began to spread. In 1846, many Texans were serving in the American Army with Zachary Taylor during the Mexican War. They still had their Colt revolvers with them—at least as many as were still in service, since Colt had been out of business for several years and the guns were showing their age. Their enthusiastic endorsement of the weapon impressed Taylor, who sent Capt. Samuel Walker north to find Colt and get as many more of the guns as possible. Walker negotiated a deal with Colt for one thousand revolvers at $25 apiece. (Interestingly enough, after Colt made the agreement with Walker he tried to buy one of his former guns as a model, since he had given all his away. Nobody had one, and Colt was forced to sketch the pistol's design from memory and his patents.) Colt arranged for Eli Whitney to build these pistols for him, and subsequently established a new factory in the town of his birth, Hartford, Connecticut. The rest, as they say, is history.

Because it was the first firearm that could be used effectively by a rider on horseback, Colt's pistols soon spread throughout the land. When he died in 1862, Samuel Colt, the man who had departed from Paterson virtually penniless, left an estate of $15 million.

The man's name was Alexander Boardman, and he had a problem: How to stop visitors to Atlantic City's beach from tracking sand all through his hotel and the train on which he was conductor.

As anyone who has ever lived at the Jersey Shore knows all too well, beach sand is nearly impossible to clean up. The insidious little grains seem to hide in every nook and cranny of every chair, sofa, floor, and rug, and even after hours of sweeping and scrubbing, they can still be felt. It's enough to make even Mr. Clean throw in the towel.

As a conductor on the Camden & Atlantic Railroad, Boardman spent a lot of time sweeping out sand tracked into his cars by riders returning from a day of walking on Atlantic City's beaches. If this wasn't bad enough, as the owner of the Ocean House Hotel in Atlantic City he also had to deal with sand tracked all over his fine carpets and left on his furniture by guests and visitors.

Desperate to save both his hotel and his railroad cars, Boardman conceived of the idea of a boardwalk—a wooden walkway of planks over the sand that would enable people to walk on the beach without actually stepping on it.

Another hotel owner in Atlantic City, Jacob Keim, heard about Boardman's idea. The two met, discussed the pros and cons, and decided to present the idea to the other hotel owners in town. At that gathering, held in the spring of 1870, Boardman summed up his and the other owner's predicament: "Our carpets and even stuffed chairs are being ruined by the sand tracked into our places from the beach."

The group liked the idea of a boardwalk, and petitioned the city council to build one. Finding no opposition the council agreed, and, after issuing script to finance the project (the city treasury was nearly bare), the first boardwalk was built quickly. It was dedicated on June 26, 1870, with parades, celebrations, and speeches.

This initial boardwalk bore little resemblance to today's Disneyland-like extravaganzas of sight and sound. It was noncommercial, since buildings were not permitted within thirty feet of it; the plank walk itself rose just a foot-and-one-half above the beach. The pathway was constructed of twelve-foot sections of boards one-and-one-half inches thick, that were nailed to joists set crosswise under the boardwalk every two feet. Most unusual of all was that the first boardwalk was portable; at the end of the season, each twelve-foot section was removed and stored away in anticipation of the next summer.

Although it hadn't been intended as such, the first boardwalk was a rousing success as a tourist attraction. People came to Atlantic City from all over to see this clever innovation, and many of those who came liked what they saw and stayed. During the next five years, the number of new people moving into Atlantic City exceeded the town's total population of the previous sixteen years. The boardwalk had launched Atlantic City on its way to becoming the premier resort town of the entire East Coast.

Thanks to Alexander Boardman's dislike of sweeping up sand, one of the Jersey Shore's most enduring symbols had been born.

(Incidentally, the first boardwalk also had its share of firsts: salt water taffy, picture postcards, and rolling chairs all made their debut on the Atlantic City Boardwalk.)

New Jersey has had many other firsts as well. Although space doesn't permit all these stories to be told, here's a list of some of the others:

☐ The first baseball game played under modern rules (see the sports chapter for the full story).

☐ The first collegiate football game (again, see the chapter on sports).

☐ Edison's astounding legacy: the first incandescent light bulb, phonograph, commercially viable film projector, and hundreds of other firsts.

☐ The first log cabin, built in Swedesboro in the 1640s.

☐ The nation's first planned industrial city: Paterson (see the chapter on town histories).

☐ The first public library in its own building was in Burlington in 1757.

☐ The first air conditioner, built by Willis Haviland Carrier in Newark in 1911.

☐ The first national historic park: Morristown, dedicated in 1933 (see the chapter on day trips for more information).

☐ The first Episcopal Church in the country, built in Perth Amboy in 1698.

☐ The first frozen food, produced by Charles F. Seabrook in 1933.

☐ The first Indian reservation, located on a 1,600-acre tract of land in Evesham Township (Burlington County) on August 29, 1758.

☐ The first United States flag made from an American loom, made by John Rule of Paterson.

☐ The first transistor, developed by a team of scientists from Bell Laboratories in Murray Hill and patented in 1948.

CHAPTER TWO

The Rocks, the Land, and Other Things

ALTHOUGH it is a small state, ranking forty-sixth in the country in terms of size, New Jersey's geologic characteristics are large. In stark contrast to our Midwestern cousins, New Jersey has several different geologic regions, plus a wide diversity of rocks and landscapes. New Jersey also has some areas not found anywhere else in the world, such as at Franklin in Sussex County, which contains over 300 different types of minerals and is the home of the well-known Franklin Marble. Spicing up New Jersey's geologic stew even further are several hidden yet fascinating characteristics of the state's natural makeup, such as the existence of a major earthquake fault line in the north. It seems that, just like in everything else, there's much more to New Jersey's geology and landscape than meets the eye.

To understand New Jersey's geology, you have to go back hundreds of millions of years, when all the continents were attached in one giant land mass with Africa as the approximate center. North America was on the outer fringe of this gigantic conglomeration, with the eastern portion of the United States roughly attached to the upper portion of what is today eastern Africa.

Gradually, the continents separated and drifted apart; as they did, the Atlantic Ocean filled the gap between North America, Europe, and Africa. (However, if you think that by walking on Jersey Shore beaches you're treading on land that was once part of Africa, think again; the actual "connection" is well offshore. However, much of present-day Florida was once part of Africa and got carried away by North America during the big break-up.)

During this period the eastern edge of North America was experiencing what geologists call an active continental margin. This is similar to what is happening along the western coast of the United States today, with earthquakes, volcanism, and other upheavals occurring.

(To understand just how long ago this was occurring, the Appalachian Mountains—which are today low peaks worn down by erosion and are classified as "old" geologically—were as high and awesome-looking as the Himalayan Mountains are today.)

For millions of years, the land that would eventually become New Jersey buckled and bubbled along with the rest of North America, as frequent earthquakes, volcanic eruptions, and other often-violent episodes shaped the landscape. As the continent went through its birthing throes, creatures began to appear, first in the seas and then on land. After many more millions of years had passed, time and evolution produced one of the most spectacular species ever to walk the earth: dinosaurs.

Dinosaurs first appeared on earth at the end of the Triassic period, approximately 200 million years ago. The great beasts flowered during the Jurassic and Cretaceous periods, then abruptly died out about 65 million years ago, for reasons still not understood. They then remained hidden underground for hundreds of millions of years, until a discovery in New Jersey helped bring the age of dinosaurs to light.

One day in 1838, John E. Hopkins was digging marl (a type of soil used for fertilizer) on his farm near Haddonfield. Suddenly his plow struck something large and hard in the ground. Mystified, he dug it up, only to find that what he had uncovered was a giant, ebony-black bone. Plainly, it was too large to be from any animal known in existence at that time. Subsequently, Hopkins found more bones of similar size and appearance.

Word of Hopkins's unusual discovery spread. When people stopped by to marvel at the strange find, Hopkins sometimes gave them pieces of the bones as souvenirs. No one suspected the enormity of the discovery that Hopkins was giving away as casually as Halloween treats.

Two decades passed. Then, in 1858, W. Parker Foulke, a fellow at the Academy of Natural Sciences in Philadelphia, was vacationing in Haddonfield when he heard of the discovery and hurried over to Hopkins's farm. Foulke knew of the controversial theories put forth by British paleontologist Richard Owen some years earlier that an entire race of extinct creatures had ruled the earth for millions of years before humans arrived. After receiving Hopkins's permission to dig for more bones, the Philadelphian came upon a cache of fossils, many of them quite large. Foulke's pulse quickened: He knew that something of immense scientific value had been unearthed.

Assisted by Hopkins, Foulke and Joseph Leidy, the director of the

Academy of Natural Sciences and a professor of anatomy at the University of Pennsylvania, continued the excavation, and found many more of the odd-looking bones. The two scientists brought them back to the Philadelphia institute, where Leidy examined them. Finally he announced that Foulke had indeed discovered what Owen had called "Dinosauria," or "Terrible Lizards." Then Leidy, Foulke, and others painstakingly assembled the bones into a dinosaur skeleton that the director called Hadrosaurus foulkii, after the town and the discoverer. The creature was twelve-feet high and thirty-feet long, and probably had to eat 200 pounds of plant material per day to sustain its body weight.

Hadrosaurus was the first complete dinosaur skeleton discovered in the United States. Of equal significance was that Leidy concluded that the creature was bipedal, because the hind limbs were larger than the forelimbs. Indeed, when he constructed the skeleton he showed the dinosaur standing on its hind legs only. This was a clear contradiction of popular theories of the time, which had dinosaurs plodding about on all fours.

The unearthing of Hadrosaurus opened the door for a frenzy of dinosaur discoveries in the later half of the nineteenth century (two scientists were such bitter rivals that their competition was dubbed the "bone wars"), and went a long way toward improving the understanding of these strange and fascinating creatures. Today a replica of the skeleton of the "original" Hadrosaurus is still on display at the Academy of Natural Sciences in Philadelphia.

Hadrosaurus is not the only dinosaur discovered in New Jersey. Another is Deinosuchus, a gigantic, meat-eating fifty-foot long crocodilelike creature guaranteed to be no day at the beach. Dryptosaurus, whose bones have also turned up in the state, was another nasty-looking meat-eater with daggerlike teeth and eight-inch foot claws. By contrast, Nodosaurus, a relatively peaceful plant-eater, and Quetzalcoatlus, the largest of all the Pterosaurs (its wing span was between forty and fifty feet), seem tame.

One of the most fascinating things about dinosaurs is that new discoveries occur constantly. Will the next big dinosaur "event" happen in New Jersey? It's entirely possible.

Although New Jersey is a relatively small state in area, it boasts several different geologic provinces, or regions where its natural formations are markedly different from each other.

4 Joseph Leidy, Director of the Academy of Natural Sciences, was the man who put together the bones found on the Hopkins farm and named the creature Hadrosaurus foulkii. (Courtesy of the Academy of Natural Sciences)

In the Northwest part of the state (mainly Sussex and Warren counties, although parts of Passaic and Morris are also included) is the valley and ridge province. This region takes up approximately one-twelfth of the state's area. New Jerseyians call these ridges "mountains," although time and erosion have worn them down to little more than bumps on the face of the earth. The Wallpack and Kittatinny mountains, part of the Appalachian chain, are typical New Jersey ridges—or "mountains," if you prefer. One of the most famous natural landmarks in this province is the Delaware Water Gap. Another is High Point State Park, which, as its name suggests, is the highest elevation in New Jersey (1,496 feet above sea level; High Point Monument on Kittatinny Mountain raises this to over 1,800 feet.)

Moving south, the second geologic province in the state is the New Jersey Highlands. Approximately forty miles long and taking up about one-eighth of the state, the Highlands extend across northwestern Passaic, Morris, and Hunterdon counties, and southeast along Sussex and Warren counties. The Highlands contain the oldest rocks in the state—some are over a billion years old—as well as the mineral deposits at Franklin, which

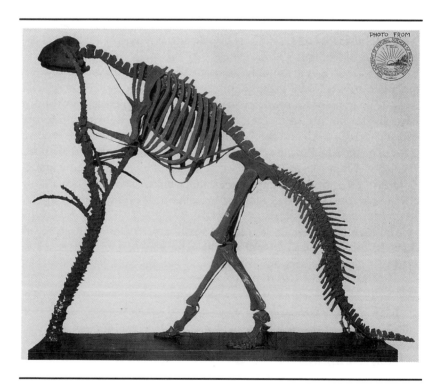

most geologists consider one of the most spectacular concentrations of minerals in the entire world.

Franklin's geologic fame began early in the nineteenth century when Dr. Samuel Fowler discovered zinc ore deposits on his land. Fowler subsequently developed a process for making zinc-based paint, and for years Franklin provided zinc oxide for use as a paint additive. After Fowler's death the New Jersey Zinc Company ran the mine for over a century, mining 500,000 tons of zinc ore annually until the mineral was finally exhausted in 1954. (The Franklin Mineral Museum now sits on the site of the former zinc mine.)

Today Franklin is known more for its incredible variations of minerals than for its proclivity with zinc. Some of the over 300 different minerals uncovered at Franklin are found nowhere else in the world, and geologists seem to be constantly discovering new ones to add to the list.

The Highlands have played a major role in the history of New Jersey, as well as that of the United States. The ridges are a continuation of the famed Green Mountains of Vermont and Massachusetts fame, and this is appropriate indeed. During the Revolutionary War, Ethan Allen's Green Mountain Boys gave the American cause for independence a lift by capturing Fort Ticonderoga. In New Jersey, the Highlands provided Washington's often outnumbered forces with a perfect defensive position from which to observe and harass the British during much of the war. The valleys paralleling the ridges acted as ideal supply lines for the Continental troops during the cold winters at Valley Forge and Morristown.

A bit further down the state is the third geologic province, known as the Newark Basin (also called the Piedmont Lowlands). This region extends across New Jersey in a broad 1,500-mile swath (constituting approximately one-fifth of the state in area). All of Union, Essex, Hudson, and Bergen counties are in this region, as are large chunks of Mercer, Somerset, and Middlesex and portions of Hunterdon, Morris, and Passaic. Towns in the Newark Basin differ widely in appearance, such as Princeton, Newark, New Brunswick, Lambertville, Frenchtown, and Morristown, yet are alike in geologic characteristics.

The Newark Basin has an extremely diverse geography. The Watchung Mountains, which extend from Bound Brook to Passaic, are one of the most distinguishing features of this region. (Watchung comes from the Native American words *Wach Unks*, which means "high hills.") The Palisades Sill, part of which are those large rock outcroppings covered with

5   *Nineteenth-century Mount of the Hadrosaurus foulkii
(Courtesy of the Academy of Natural Sciences)*

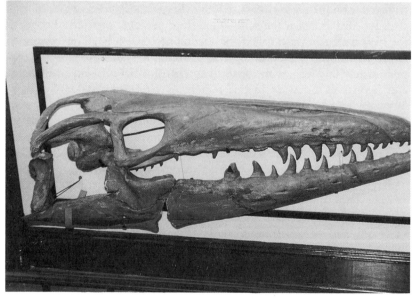

graffiti that everyone stares at as they travel on major highways in northern New Jersey, are also part of the Newark Basin. However, the soft, marshy area of the Hackensack Meadowlands, home to the Meadowlands Sports Complex among other things, is also part of the Newark Basin.

In geologic terms, the remaining portion of the state (everything southeast of a line running from New Brunswick to Trenton, and south along the Delaware River to the Atlantic Ocean), is considered the Coastal Plain. This is indeed surprising news to people who live in Chatsworth, New Egypt, Vineland, and other towns far away from the coast, but the soil and rock that underlie their communities are the same as those that are underneath Atlantic City, Wildwood, Point Pleasant, and other shore-based towns.

The Coastal Plain is divided into two areas: the Inner Coastal Plain, which is a thin strip from approximately Perth Amboy down to Freehold, and then in a swath across the state to just above Salem, and the Outer Coastal Plain, which constitutes the rest of the region. One of the distinguishing characteristics between the two "plains" is that the Inner Coastal region has much more fertile soil than its counterpart, where the soil is mainly sand and gravel.

The entire Coastal Plain province is a low-lying region, without the hills and mountains of northern New Jersey. There are exceptions, however, such as at Crawfords Hill in Monmouth County, which rises almost 400 feet into the air, and at the Navesink Highlands, whose elevation is 276 feet.

The Pinelands lie in the Outer Coastal Plain, which helps explain much about the unique characteristics of the region. The principle geologic formation found at the surface throughout most of the Pinelands is known as Cohansey Sand. The composition of a soil determines how many nutrients and water it can hold; soils that have a relatively equal mixture of sand, clay, and gravel are much more fertile than those composed primarily of coarse particles such as gravel and sand. Since soil in the Pinelands primarily developed from the Cohansey Sand, it was sandy soil, and thus unable

---

6　*A male mastodon found in Salem County in 1869.*

7　*The skull of a mosasaurus found in New Jersey. These meat-eaters, which could reach forty-five feet in length, inhabited the ocean off New Jersey about 65 million years ago.*

to retain moisture and nutrients. This poor soil inhibited plant growth, which lead to the region being dubbed the Pine Barrens by frustrated farmers who tried to grow crops there and failed.

Obviously, since it constitutes such a huge chunk of the state—occupying three-fifths (4,500 square miles) of territory—the Coastal Plain is the largest geologic region in New Jersey. Amazingly, the Coastal Plain was once more than double its present size.

Approximately 18,000 years ago, the last great Ice Age, known as the Wisconsin Glaciation, was at its peak. (In New Jersey, the ice came down as far south as Newark.) The presence of these large sheets of ice over large sections of the earth drew so much water from the world's oceans that sea level ultimately dropped a staggering 425 feet. Since the reduced water level meant that more land was exposed, New Jersey's shoreline was more than eighty miles further east than it is today, and the land behind it was all part of the Coastal Plain.

When the glaciers began melting and retreating northward, the water released flowed back into the oceans, which caused sea level to rise. From around 7,000 years ago to 2,500 years ago, the oceans rose at an extraordinarily rapid rate of around two millimeters per year. Even when the increase slowed to a more modest .75 millimeters per year, land—such as New Jersey's Coastal Plain—was still being drowned at a steady pace.

Although it may seem as if the Wisconsin Glaciation happened a long time ago, in geologic terms 18,000 years is barely a speck on the great clock of the earth. To get a better idea of how quickly rising sea levels are impacting New Jersey, consider that in the seventeenth century—just a few hundred years ago—deeds were issued for land that is today underwater, almost a mile off the coast. Sea level is rising today at a rate of about four millimeters per year (twice as fast as during the conclusion of the Wisconsin Glaciation). Some scientists estimate that this rate will more than double to 8.5 millimeters per year by the year 2100. Considering all this, one has to wonder what New Jersey's Coastal Plain will look like in another geologic wink of an eye.

The glacial ice also affected New Jersey's geology in other ways. In some northern regions, the advancing ice scraped off the cover of soil, exposing the bedrock underneath. As the ice retreated, it formed large glacial lakes in areas like Passaic and Hackensack. (The modern-day Hackensack Meadowlands owe their existence to the presence of these glacial lakes.) Unless they were maintained by sediment dams, most of these lakes did not survive the ice's retreat. Great Swamp is an example of a glacial lake that has survived until modern times, although on a much smaller scale.

Indeed, one of the things that attracts geologists and other scientists to

New Jersey is the fact that ancient lake deposits in the state exhibit some of the best recorded evidence of global climate changes, dating back 200 million years, of anyplace in the world. A two-year, multimillion dollar effort to retrieve these rocks from the Newark Basin concluded in 1993. (New Brunswick, Princeton, and Pennington were three of the sites where drilling took place.) Certain areas along the Delaware River, such as near Lambertville, also show evidence of these climate changes.

As might be expected New Jersey, during the last great Ice Age, experienced great changes in climate and vegetation. In marked contrast to the dinosaur era, when warm temperatures and abundant plant life were the rule, the time of the Wisconsin Glaciation was like one long, silent winter. Many scientists feel that the region of the state not covered by ice—primarily the Coastal Plain—was a windswept, treeless land mass much like modern-day Siberia.

Across this desolate, snow-covered land roamed a variety of animals (the dinosaurs, of course, had died out millions of years before). Chief among them in this era (known as the Pleistocene Epoch in scientific terms) were the great woolly mammoths and the large mastodons.

The woolly mammoths were truly impressive creatures, with their shaggy coats of fur and large, curving tusks that resembled huge fishhooks. These great beasts were about fourteen-feet tall and had tusks extending more than fifteen feet in length. Mastodons, which were much more common in New Jersey, were somewhat smaller, averaging between eight- and ten-feet tall.

A superb fossil find of the Pleistocene Epoch was made in Hackensack in 1962. Two high school students exploring an area where a road was being built found three mastodon teeth. Subsequent excavation by scientists unearthed almost an entire mastodon skeleton, which was promptly christened the "Hackensack Mastodon."

But, like the dinosaurs before them, the woolly mammoths and the mastodons would not last. Extinction claimed them along with other Pleistocene creatures, opening the way for the arrival of yet another species to claim dominance of the earth: human beings. Their history is still being written.

What does New Jersey's geologic future hold? Some geologists feel that what goes around comes around, and that the state will once again enter an active phase. This means earthquakes, volcanoes, and other natural occurrences that will make things in the state much more unpredictable than they are today. (Don't start planning a move to Kansas, however; this isn't going to happen in our lifetime.)

If earthquakes do become more common in New Jersey in the future, one triggering mechanism will likely be the ancient Ramapo Fault. This

1 billion-year-old major fault line in the northern part of the state was once quite active, but has been relatively quiet for many millions of years. (Part of I-287 lies almost directly on the Ramapo Fault.) The fault extends southwesterly from New York State, running through parts of Passaic, Bergen, Morris, and Somerset counties.

Although most of the quakes that emanate from the Ramapo Fault are relatively minor, there have been some occasionally larger jolts. On August 10, 1884, an earthquake measuring five on the Richter scale occurred along the fault. The Ramapo Fault was also responsible for a three-magnitude quake that happened in July 1978.

However, even though the Ramapo Fault does kick up its heels every now and then, the magnitude of the earthquakes that this activity produces is barely enough to register on extremely sensitive seismographs, never mind turn the entire state into a mini-California. Hopefully, the Ramapo Fault will continue to be just a source of study for geologists, and not a source of concern for New Jerseyians.

Human beings are relatively recent arrivals on this planet, having been on this earth for just about 10,000 years. Geologic time, on the other hand, is measured in the millions and billions of years. Despite this disparity, the future of both is now intermixed: human activity affects the

state's geology, while any geologic activity affects people. Whether the next change is measured in millions of years, or thousands of years—or even hundreds of years—it's obvious that the geologic history of New Jersey is still being written.

DID YOU KNOW?

One of the best places in the entire state to learn about New Jersey's geology is at the Rutgers University Geology Museum. Located in Geology Hall on the Cook College campus in New Brunswick, the museum was built in 1872 by George Cook, founder of Cook College, who raised the entire $70,000 cost. For more than 100 years the building was used for the entire geology department, until rocks, professors, and students were transferred to the Busch Campus in 1976. Currently the museum is used as a research and teaching facility, and also hosts school groups and other organizations. Besides a wide assortment of New Jersey rocks and minerals, the museum also contains a mastodon skeleton, Indian artifacts, sea shell fossils, and even an Egyptian mummy!

8   The Rutgers University Geology Museum in New Brunswick.

CHAPTER THREE

Interesting People

A L T H O U G H you'd never get a comedian to admit it, New Jersey's history is filled with an incredible array of fascinating men and women. People, of course, see only what they want to see, and so to someone who thinks of New Jersey as nothing more than turnpikes and toxic waste dumps, the idea that the state boasts a roster of interesting and noteworthy people is akin to trying to make a four year old eat their vegetables: no way, no how.

Yet the fact is that New Jersey has always played an important role in the history of the United States. Although Benjamin Franklin was being coy when he described New Jersey as "a barrel tapped at both ends" because of its proximity to New York City and Philadelphia, it is precisely this nearness to these major urban centers that has drawn the rich, famous, and just downright interesting here. The result is a historical pedigree that New Jersey can match against any other state in the union.

So throw out those turnpike jokes. It's time to meet some of the most interesting people in New Jersey's history.

The Battle of Waterloo in 1815 not only destroyed the last hopes of Napoleon for European domination, it also sent members of the Bonaparte family scurrying out of France to seek asylum and escape the wrath of the allies. Many stayed in Europe; others, however, sought to put as much distance between themselves and their conquerors as possible, and so naturally they looked to the United States, separated by an entire ocean from the reach of European vengeance. One of those who sought refuge in the

United States was Joseph Bonaparte, Napoleon's older brother, and he found it in Bordentown, New Jersey.

Today Bordentown is a small community nestled along the Delaware River just south of Trenton. Little in the town's typical small-town appearance suggests its former heavyweight status as an important link in the chain of travel between New York City and Philadelphia from the mid-eighteenth through the early nineteenth centuries. The town is virtually equidistant between the two major cities, and both stage and boat passengers frequently used Bordentown as a rest stop before continuing their journey. The town has had its share of famous residents, including Thomas Paine, Francis Hopkinson (a signer of the Declaration of Independence), and Commodore Charles Stewart, of "Old Ironsides" fame.

Nothing, however, could have prepared Bordentown residents for the adventure that began on June 16, 1816, when Dr. William Burns of Bordentown encountered two men approaching the town in a carriage. The pair inquired whether there were any properties for sale in the area. Burns led the two men—one of whom was Joseph Bonaparte, and the other his American interpreter, James Carret—to the Point Breeze estate, which was currently on the market. Two months later Bonaparte "owned" the huge estate. (A law at that time forbade aliens to own property in New Jersey, and so title to Point Breeze was actually in the name of George Reinholdt, an American friend.)

How did the older brother of Napoleon Bonaparte wind up in quiet little Bordentown? According to one story, during the waning days of his empire Napoleon took out a map of America and said to Joseph: "If I am ever forced to fly to America, I shall settle somewhere between Philadelphia and New York, where I can receive the earliest intelligence from France from ships that arrive at either point." Joseph supposedly selected Bordentown on the basis of that conversation.

A more likely reason, however, is that Joseph was seeking privacy. Before buying Point Breeze, he had lived in New York City and Philadelphia, and had tried unsuccessfully in both places to blend into the crowd. He was, after all, a fugitive from the European allies and as such a marked man; he never knew whether the next knock on his door would be that of foreign agents, ready to drag him back across the water. Perhaps it was an incident on Broadway, when in full view of hundreds of people a Frenchman dropped to his knees in front of Joseph, and sobbed out his devotion to the Bonaparte family, that convinced Joseph he could not hide in a city of thousands.

Who was this mild-mannered, aristocratic Frenchman? At the time he bought Point Breeze for $17,500, he was forty-eight years old, one year older than Napoleon. Lacking his brother's thirst for power, Joseph might have used his considerable financial acumen to enjoy a quiet life as a

successful businessman. But you can hardly run a dry goods store when your brother wants to be King of the World. Napoleon thrust Joseph into a series of military and political jobs for which the elder Bonaparte was badly suited, including reigns as the King of Naples (1806–1808) and King of Spain (1808–1813).

After Waterloo, both Napoleon and Joseph prepared to flee to the United States. However, Napoleon changed his mind at the last moment, leaving Joseph to sail alone for the United States on July 29, 1815, aboard the *Commerce*. Napoleon was captured and exiled to St. Helena. The two brothers never saw each other again.

Joseph's Point Breeze estate initially consisted of a house and 211 acres. After the New Jersey legislature repealed their objections to aliens owning property in January 1817, Joseph went on a buying spree that eventually enlarged his holdings to approximately 1,000 acres.

The land that Joseph purchased was pure wilderness, shot through with marshes, thorn bushes, and ravines. He quickly turned the land, however, into an estate fit for a former king. In a biographical sketch of Joseph in *Frank Leslie's Popular Monthly* of February 1894 (in which Bordentown was called "The American St. Helena"), the transformation of Point Breeze was described as follows: "A tract of marshy land . . . [was] turned into an artificial lake; the forest was intersected with walks and drives; open spaces here and there were cleared for lawns; rustic bridges were thrown over rocky-sided ravines, summerhouses were erected in sequestered spots, flowers bloomed in the parterres and rare exotics in the conservatories."

The house also reflected Bonaparte's fondness for things regal. Described by *Leslie's* as "a palace," it was built of brick and covered with white plaster. Inside, said the magazine, "was a grand staircase, flanked by great reception and dining rooms. The huge fireplaces had marble mantels with marvelous bas-reliefs. The bedchambers were hung with rare tapestry. The walls were decorated with still rarer paintings, more or less dishonestly acquired, and statuary of similar beauty."

It took Joseph several years, and much money, to finish both the grounds and the house—one contemporary account said that the house alone cost him $20,000—but by January 1, 1820, the French exile could look forward to the coming year with the knowledge that the work was finally done.

Two days later, the entire house burned to the ground.

---

9 A portrait of Joseph Bonaparte in his royal robes. (Photo by Pat King-Roberts; Painting courtesy of the Bordentown Historical Society)

Joseph was in Trenton on business on the afternoon of January 3 when word of the fire came. He rushed back to find his home a blazing inferno. Despite the best efforts of the citizens of Bordentown—including the ladies, who formed a bucket brigade—the home was destroyed.

The people, however, did manage to save many precious statues, paintings, books, and papers from the flames. Joseph, used to the pillaging and looting that routinely occurred during European wars, was astonished when the residents returned these valuable items to him. In gratitude, he addressed a letter to them, saying that the incident showed him that "Americans are, without contradiction, the most happy people I have known."

Undeterred by this disaster, Joseph quickly converted his stable into a new home. Soon this house too was filled with paintings, sculptures, gold tapestries, chandeliers, and other objects of nobility. Upon his arrival in America he had adopted the name the "Count de Survilliers" (the name of a village on his estate in France), and he continued to use this title at Point Breeze.

Yet despite his obvious wealth, lofty title, and aristocratic manner, Bonaparte was clearly liked by his Bordentown neighbors. He used local labor in every endeavour he undertook, such as clearing his land and building his house. When there was no work to do, Joseph often invented jobs for residents who wanted to earn some money. In the book *Bonaparte's Park and the Murats*, written in 1879 when the memory of Joseph was still fresh, author E. M. Woodward said: "The count was a great benefit to Bordentown . . . besides liberally patronizing the shops, he gave employment to all who asked for it. He always paid most liberal wages; cash each day, and in hard money."

Bonaparte let the locals wander freely over his vast estate, where peacocks strutted across immaculate lawns, swans glided over the lake, and deer gamboled in the thicket. In the winter Bonaparte allowed ice skating on the lake, and he would often go down and watch the action, frequently rolling apples and oranges onto the ice for the skaters. On the day before Christmas, Joseph's daughter Zenaide would drive along the length of the lake in a sleigh made in the shape of a swan, throwing out sugarplums and toys as holiday treats.

Visitors to his home were always warmly welcomed and given a tour that highlighted the many *objects d'art*. Joseph particularly enjoyed showing his strait-laced American visitors his many nude and seminude female paintings and sculptures, and watching his guests' "blushes and giggles." In the April 1845 edition of *Goodey's Lady's Book*, the walls of Bonaparte's sleeping quarters were described as covered with oil paintings of young women "with less clothing about them than they or you would have found comfortable in our cold climate."

Although Joseph's wife remained in Italy and never joined him at Point Breeze, claiming she was too ill for the ocean voyage, he did have the company of many friends and relatives, including his daughters Zénaïde and Charlotte, his devoted secretary Louis Mailliard, and others. A steady stream of famous personages also came to Bordentown, including Henry Clay, Daniel Webster, John Quincy Adams, and the Marquis de Lafayette.

The many French expatriates who came to Point Breeze gave rise to tales that Joseph was plotting a revolution that would once again place a Bonaparte on the throne of France. On the surface, these rumors seem unfounded; Joseph, finally free from his brother's ambition, seems to have genuinely enjoyed playing country squire. In 1820, when Mexico revolted against Spanish rule and Joseph was offered the Mexican crown, he turned it down with the comment: "I have worn two crowns. I would not take a step to wear a third."

Yet, suspicions still linger about Joseph's true intentions at Bordentown. Was Point Breeze supposed to be a government-in-exile for the Bonapartes, while they plotted their return to power in France? The French considered the Mexican offer as part of a plot to help Napoleon escape. Indeed, reports of plots to free Napoleon from his St. Helena exile were as numerous then as JFK assassination conspiracy theories are today.

What gives these theories an extra pinch of intrigue is the network of underground tunnels that Joseph built at Point Breeze. One led directly to the Delaware River and was wide enough to allow a boat with an eighteen-foot sweep of oars to be rowed from the river directly to the basement of Joseph's home. Other tunnels led from nearby Crosswicks Creek to the house, while still others connected different buildings on the estate.

The "official" version is that the tunnels allowed family members to pass from one building to another during bad weather. Adolph Maillard, son of Joseph's trusted secretary, wrote that "when Joseph built the lakehouse for his daughter Zénaïde and her household, he connected it by an underground gallery, with the main house, for the facility of service, and for her own use in bad weather."

In 1914, *The World Magazine* came up with the best tunnel theory yet: The real Napoleon, it said, did not die at St. Helena in 1821, but escaped his rocky exile and wound up in New Jersey.

"And if Napoleon did get away from St. Helena, where did he go?" the magazine asked. "There is but one reasonable answer . . . Bordentown, N.J. He could have been rowed from the Delaware River directly into his brother's house. And during the years that he was watching for a chance to return to power, he could have had the freedom, through a labyrinth of secret underground passages, of one of the most beautiful estates in America."

Was this pure fantasy, or did one of the world's most notorious men once live in New Jersey, emerging from his hiding place only in the darkest hours of the night to walk the deserted streets of Bordentown and dream of glories past? We'll never know for sure.

By the mid-1830s the European political climate had changed, and Joseph was able to travel to England in 1832, where he stayed for five years. He returned to the United States in 1837, but just to settle his affairs. He left for Europe again in 1839 and was finally reunited with his wife in Italy. It was there, in Florence, that he died on July 28, 1844, at age seventy-six.

In March 1847, a correspondent for the Massachusetts newspaper *Daily Herald* visited Point Breeze and found the "broad roads covered with weeds . . . the deer all departed . . . the once favorite home a dreary, tenantless pile of bricks and mortar."

The days of royalty in Bordentown were over.

They called James Still "The Black Doctor of the Pines." But he was more than just a country doctor with an encyclopedic knowledge of herbs and plants; in an age when the shackles of slavery had given way to the bonds of uncertainty for blacks, James Still was a symbol of hope to African Americans everywhere.

"I was born in Washington Township (now Shamong), Burlington County, State of New Jersey, April ninth, one thousand eight hundred and twelve, at what was called the Indian Mill," writes Still in his 1877 autobiography, *Early Recollections and Life of Dr. James Still.* His parents were Levin and Charity Still, former slaves in Maryland who bought their freedom and came north to live.

At the age of three, Still had a moment of epiphany: A doctor came to his home to vaccinate the children. Still was deeply impressed by the doctor's mastery of the healing powers.

"From that moment I was inspired with a desire to be a doctor," Still wrote. "It took deep root in me, so deep that all the drought of poverty or lack of education could not destroy the desire."

Still began playing doctor, using a thin piece of pine bark for a needle. His thoughts were always of the time when he, like the doctor, could travel around, "healing the sick and doing great miracles."

It is fortunate that Still's desire to be a doctor ran so strong, because it was sorely tested in his early life. The family experienced bouts of extreme poverty, times when things were so desperate that Still had to wrestle a piece of meat out of the mouth of the family cat in order to have something to eat.

Education was a hit-or-miss proposition for the young boy. Still went to school only in bad weather, because on good days he had to work around the house. Even when he did go to school, the teacher was so poorly trained that the students were taught incorrect grammar and pronunciation. Sometimes, Still would contemplate the enormity of the obstacles standing in the way of his becoming a doctor: There were no black doctors, no white doctor would teach him, and he couldn't afford to go to college. But the dream did not die.

When he was eighteen years old James was bound-out for $100 by his father to Amos Wilkins for three years. As part of the agreement, James received one month's schooling each year.

Although Still worked at the Wilkins farm without complaint, he had attacks of extreme loneliness. These were moments when his hope of becoming a doctor seemed nothing more than a cruel joke. "I had no books, no money or friends, no one with whom to keep company," he wrote. "I often thought myself the most desolate person in the State—no one with whom to commune of my future hopes."

When his servitude expired, Still, now twenty-one, packed his meager belongings into two handkerchiefs, collected $9.50 from Wilkins, and prepared to face the world. He walked to Philadelphia—fearful that he would be picked up as a runaway slave along the way—to visit his sister Keturah, and promptly got a job in a glue factory.

For the next several years Still experienced life's typical ebb and flow. He worked a succession of jobs that ranged from good to awful. He married Angelina Willow in 1835, and had a daughter named Beulah, only to lose both wife and child to illness within a year of each other (1838 and 1839, respectively).

In 1843, after remarrying, James bought a small still. With this he began distilling sassafras roots and various herbs, and selling the mixtures to druggists in Philadelphia. The old dream of becoming a doctor, which had retreated to the back of his mind, now came to the fore once again. Obtaining some books on medical botany, he began making medicines from the plants that he found in Burlington County. He used one of these mixtures to cure his neighbor's daughter of scrofula (a form of tuberculosis). Unknown to Still, he had begun fulfilling his long-cherished dream.

"I thought it [curing the girl] no great thing, for it always seemed to me that all diseases were curable, and I wondered why the doctors did not cure them," he wrote.

Word of Still's medical expertise spread, and soon so many people were coming to see him that he had to hire someone to dig and distill roots and herbs, which remained his only source of income. Then Still took the case of a young girl who was so severely ill with scrofula that all the doctors had given up on her. In ten weeks time she was nearly well, and Still's reputation as a healer took a giant leap. People began calling him "Doctor" Still.

Giving up his distilling business to concentrate full-time on his practice, Still built a small wagon out of pine. Using a cigar box as a medicine chest, he traveled around the area, dispensing his homemade medicines. Physicians laughed at the uneducated black man driving around in his homemade wagon, derisively calling him "Black Jim," but his patients never laughed at the results.

"My calls were many, and I rode continually," Still said. "The cases under my care I cured."

Although his usual charge was just $1 for medicine and advice, Still and his family soon grew prosperous. The man who once had to wrestle a cat for supper acquired property at the old Cross Roads section of present-day Medford, built a large home there, and was able to keep his growing family (eventually numbering seven children) properly fed and clothed. Yet he changed little; he still traveled great distances to visit patients and took a keen interest in all his cases. On Sunday he tried to rest, but so many people would come to his office then that he didn't even have time to eat.

Still practiced under difficult circumstances. Often he took so-called hopeless cases, knowing that if the patient died under his care he would be blamed by prejudiced people just waiting for this successful black man to stumble. Since he was not a licensed physician, he had to tread carefully. He learned that if he sold his homemade medicines, instead of giving prescriptions and charging for medical services, that he could continue his practice without obtaining a license.

As might be expected, the medical community was not fond of Still's success. "Oh, they will soon be well now; Black Jim has been there!" was the contemptuous cry often hurled at those Still treated. Families were pressured by doctors to ignore Still's advice—sometimes with disastrous results. Once Still advised a girl that he was treating for cancer not to have the tumor cut out, or she would die. But upon hearing that, a physician assailed the girl's father: "Why are you taking your daughter to Medford, to that old nigger?" He told the father to have the tumor surgically removed. The man did just that, and his daughter was dead within two weeks.

Still was supremely confident of his healing powers. "I can say assuredly that I have found no disease but that I have also found a remedy for it in some stage of it."

Besides medicine, Still also gave his patients the power of positive thinking. Often he would visit the bedside of someone seriously ill and give them what amounted to a "pep talk" that seemed to have amazing results.

One such case was that of a girl named Mary Sooy. When he arrived at the girl's home, it was filled with grieving men and women on a death watch. Undaunted, Still went to the girl, took her hand, and said: "Miss Sooy, you are not dying, and will not die this time. I know that you and everyone must die sometime, but you will not die now." The girl recovered completely under Still's care.

In 1872, his rigorous schedule finally caught up with him, and Still became seriously ill. Although he recovered, in the next year he suffered a slight stroke. This made him stop traveling, and he could treat only patients who came to his Medford office. But this didn't stop the flood of patients, and he remained busy up to the day he died. On March 9, 1882, James Still died, one month short of his seventieth birthday.

Still was survived by his wife, Henrietta, three sons and four daughters. Though he had at one time wrapped all his worldly belongings into two handkerchiefs, Still left an estate valued at $19,921.

He also left, in his autobiography, his philosophy, which stands as a lasting tribute to this decent, humble man:

> Be kind to all. Do not speak disparagingly of your neighbors. Treat your enemies with all the courteousness you can command. Let not wordly riches be your chiefest goal, for you cannot take them with you when you exchange time for eternity. The race is not to the swift or the battle to the strong, but to those who honestly contend until the warfare is ended.
>
> Aspire to greatness.

DID YOU KNOW?

Medical advice from Dr. Still:

For fevers [at a time when most physicians did nothing for fevers, preferring to let them run their course]: "Moderate the violence of the arterial excitement and prevent local inflammation and congestion. Support the powers of the system, relieve urgent symptoms, and restore the suppressed evacuations."

For rheumatism [arthritis]: "By giving sudorific medicine to promote perspiration, and bathing the feet in tepid water with ashes added at night before retiring to bed, drinking freely of catnip or other herb tea, and applying stimulating liniment to the affected parts, relief is obtained by the sufferer."

For coughs: Eight ounces of spikenard root, comfrey root, horehound tops, elecampane root, bloodroot, skunk-cabbage root, and pleurisy root. All bruised. Boil in two gallons of soft water down to one gallon. Express and strain the liquid, until you have one gallon. Add ten pounds of white sugar, and boil to form a syrup. Strain again. When nearly cool take two drachms oil anise and four ounces alcohol, mix and pour into the balsam. Also one pint tincture of lobelia. Let the whole stand twenty-four hours. Dose: one teaspoon three, four, or five times a day.

Antibilious Powder: Take four ounces of pulverized jalap root, eight ounces of pulverized alexandria senna, three drs. of pulverized cloves, and 1/2 ounce of cream of tartar. Mix and rub well in a mortar. Dose: one teaspoonful in warm water, sweetened, on an empty stomach.

Emetic Powder: Take four ounces of ipecac, four ounces of lobelia, and two ounces of bloodroot. Pulverize separately, mix, and rub well with a mortar. Dose: teaspoonsful given every thirty minutes in warm boneset tea.

Artist John Frederick Peto found nothing in New Jersey but heartbreak and frustration. Yet today he is recognized as one of the finest still-life painters in American history. The story of Peto's posthumous rise to greatness is a tale of detective work that unearthed the secrets buried in a small Ocean County town.

Peto was born in Philadelphia on May 21, 1854. As a boy he sketched pictures of local scenes, animals, birds, and flowers. By the age of twenty, Peto had decided to become an artist; his first known picture is dated 1875. Besides painting, his creativity found outlets in photography and coronet playing.

For over a decade Peto worked as an artist in Philadelphia. Then, in 1887, two important things happened to him: he married Christine Pearl Smith from Ohio, and he began visiting Island Heights, New Jersey.

Located just outside Toms River in Ocean County, Island Heights today still displays the charm and serenity it had in the 1870s, when it was founded as a Methodist camp meeting town. As a coronet player, Peto was in great demand at the camp meetings, and the young painter found himself spending more and more time there. For a few years he continued working in Philadelphia, but Peto had fallen under the spell of the raw

---

10   John F. Peto in the studio of his Island Heights home.
(Courtesy Joy Peto Smiley)

natural beauty that the Jersey Shore possessed at that time. In 1889 he decided to move to Island Heights.

Peto built a sweeping Victorian house at 102 Cedar Avenue, in what was then an open field. The home commanded an unobstructed view of the broad Toms River, less than a half-mile away. At the rear of the house was a two-story art studio. Into this large but cozy room Peto crammed

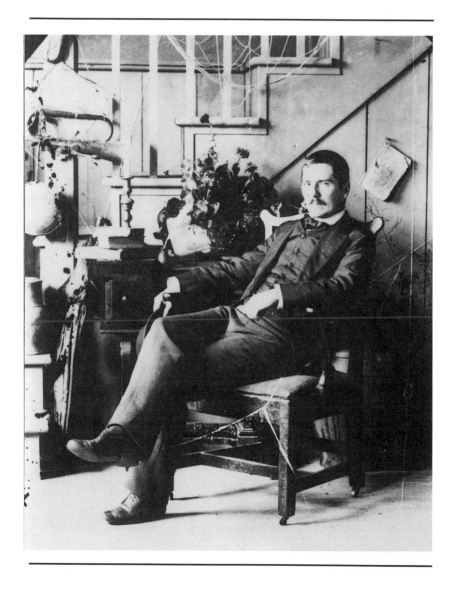

his canvases, paints, piano, and the countless objects that he loved to depict in his still-life paintings, such as books, envelopes, photographs, candles, lanterns, knives, musical instruments, and door hinges.

Peto's still-life paintings are examples of the *trompe-l'oeil* school of painting, which means, literally, "trick the eye." His paintings look so realistic that, for example, a picture of a wall, with playing cards and pictures pinned to it, seems so real that one is tempted to reach out and pluck the items off. Peto's uncanny ability to alter perspective make his paintings some of the finest examples of *trome-l'oeil* ever produced.

In 1888 Peto's only child, Helen, was born. The artist seemingly had it all: a beautiful home, lovely wife, adorable child, and monumental talent.

But appearances can often be deceiving. Although his home was indeed gorgeous, moving to Island Heights removed him from Philadelphia's mainstream art world. The difficulty of any creative person in trying to support him or herself solely through their work has been a recurring theme since prehistoric man first scratched a picture on the cave wall, and Peto was no different. Without any standing in the art world, he was forced to sell his paintings for whatever money they would bring, usually a few dollars at most.

As the economic pressures grew, his home life became more turbulent. Peto had been brought up by his maternal grandmother and her four unmarried daughters. When he moved to Island Heights, two of his aunts came to live with him. One was extremely demanding, causing tension between Peto and his wife. In her later years, this woman became senile and had to be locked in her room. There she spent hours rattling the doorknob, while below, in earshot, Peto tried desperately to concentrate on his painting.

Peto also suffered from Bright's disease, a painful condition of the kidneys. His daughter remembered being sent out of the house when the doctor came to examine her father. Often Peto would cry out in anguish as the doctor performed some type of treatment. There was also a long legal battle over the estate of one of his great-aunts that further spent Peto's time and emotional resources.

11 Peto's studio today. (Photo by Pat King-Roberts; Courtesy of Joy Peto Smiley)

12 Another view of Peto's studio today. (Photo by Pat King-Roberts; Courtesy of Joy Peto Smiley)

Because of his mounting troubles, the paintings that Peto produced during his final years, while some of his best work, have been described by art historian John Wilmerding as being "tinged by an air of sad exhaustion."

In November 1907, Peto went to see a doctor in New York City, possibly to get treatment for his kidney ailment. After the procedure, however, he fell ill and was feverish when he arrived at his sister's apartment in the city. A few days later, John F. Peto died at age fifty-three.

Normally, this would be the end of the story. Instead, it's just the beginning.

In Philadelphia at the same time as Peto was a still-life painter named William Harnett. Peto was a friend and admirer of the slightly older artist, and paintings by the two are often remarkably similar. Unlike Peto, however, Harnett remained in Philadelphia throughout his career, and his body of work became well-known, unlike Peto's.

Perhaps inevitably, the work of the two became intertwined, and the more famous Harnett was credited with many Peto paintings. This confusion was helped along by an unscrupulous Philadelphia art dealer, who forged Harnett's name on some of Peto's works. Thus, Peto suffered the indignity of not only being obscure in life, but in death as well.

This was the situation for decades, even though paintings credited to Harnett were wildly divergent in style: one style was tight, jewellike, and rational, while the other was softer and more romantic. This, however, was chalked up to different "periods" that Harnett had gone through. Of Peto there was nary a thought.

Then, on July 21, 1947, an art expert named Alfred Frankenstein left New York for a trip to Philadelphia. On the way he intended to stop for a few minutes at Island Heights to see Peto's daughter, Helen, who had converted the family home into a boarding house. Frankenstein, who had been researching United States still-life painters, was troubled by the stylistic differences in Harnett's work. But he wasn't looking for the answers in Island Heights. He wanted only to gather some biographical information about the forgotten Peto from the artist's daughter.

As Frankenstein wrote in his 1953 book *After the Hunt*: "Nothing was known about John Frederick Peto beyond the fact that a number of still lifes bearing his name had for some years been kicking around the galleries

---

13   This painting by Peto, entitled **Still Life: Hat, Umbrella and Bag,** *shows Peto's remarkable ability to trick the eye into thinking that it's looking at a photograph. (Courtesy Philadelphia Museum of Art; The Albert M. Greenfield and Elizabeth M. Greenfield Collection)*

of various New York dealers. Peto was . . . one of a large, completely unexplored group of painters whom the art world casually accepted and casually dismissed as 'Harnett imitators.'"

After locating Helen, Frankenstein explained his purpose. Helen agreeably led him into her father's former studio. Frankenstein described what happened next: "Up to this point, it was clear that she thought me rather strange; as soon as I stepped into Peto's painting room, however, she must have thought me violently insane. For on ledges, shelves, and wall-brackets in Peto's workshop were the very candlesticks, pistols, lamps and other objects represented, over and over again, in paintings by William Michael Harnett."

The secret had been discovered. Intending to stay at Island Heights only a few hours, Frankenstein remained there for the next five days, questioning Helen and her husband, and examining Peto's models, photographs, and other evidence. At last, he could arrive at only one conclusion: "The 'hard' style, and the 'hard' style alone, was Harnett; the 'soft' style was Peto concealed under forged Harnett signatures." Frankenstein also noted that the Petos with Harnett's signature were very popular and were in some of the country's most important public and private collections. Forty years after his death, John Frederick Peto had finally been vindicated.

Today, the artist's granddaughter, Joy Peto Smiley, runs a bed and breakfast in the elegant red Victorian house in Island Heights that is still called The Studio in Peto's honor. Joy remembers her mother telling her how Frankenstein reeled back in shock upon first entering Peto's studio, seeing not only the artist's models, but also stacks of Peto paintings lying about.

The walls of Peto's former studio are still adorned by some of the objects he used in his paintings, and when you look at them, you get a feel for Peto the artist. But to discover something of Peto the man, you need look no further than two iron hooks sunk into a ceiling beam. From these Peto, the devoted father, hung a swing for his daughter Helen. This is how they would spend hours together, she swinging, he painting, and neither one of them ever dreaming that one day, the work he was creating in a tiny studio in New Jersey would be considered genius.

Today she's not very well known. No one speaks of her in the same breath as Eleanor Roosevelt, Amelia Earhart, or other famous women. Even though there's a hospital named in her honor in Belleville, many are unaware to whom the name refers.

At the beginning of the twentieth century, however, millions of people in the United States knew the name Clara Louise Maass. She was a genuine hero; people everywhere praised the courage and selflessness of the young New Jerseyan.

Born in East Orange on June 28, 1876, Clara was the oldest child of German immigrants Robert E. and Hedwig Maass. After emigrating from Germany the Maasses, like so many others, found that the streets of the New Land were paved not with gold, but sheer hard work. Without skills, Robert Maass was forced to toil in the local hat mills. His tiny wage was barely adequate for the needs of his growing family, which soon numbered nine children.

Because money was tight, Clara began working while still in grammar school. This helped her mature emotionally at an early age. At fourteen, she was an intelligent-looking girl, with honey-blond hair hanging in bangs over her forehead and eyes already filled with the burdens of adulthood.

Two years later, after leaving school for a full-time job, Clara's appearance had changed even more. Now her hair was bound in a tight knot atop her head, and her expression was thoughtful and serious. Clara Maass had left childhood behind forever.

In 1893, at age seventeen, Maass took a step that would change her life, and ultimately the lives of millions of people. She enrolled in the nursing school of Newark German Hospital.

Built in 1870 to ensure that the city's large German population received proper medical care, Newark German Hospital had been advertising for nursing candidates between the ages of twenty and forty. But the years of responsibility had paid off for Clara; she looked and sounded much older than her seventeen years. Hospital officials could tell that she was a woman used to hard, thankless work, and long hours, which was just what nursing offered back then. (Nursing was so difficult that the hospital would graduate just one nurse from its program in 1894—everyone else dropped out.) Maass was accepted into the nursing program.

Hard work, however, was no stranger to Clara. She threw herself into her studies with her customary determination, and was rewarded in 1895 when she, along with three other girls, received her nursing cap and pin. Just three years later, Clara was named head nurse at German Hospital. The young girl with the serious smile was rising rapidly in her profession.

Then, abruptly, Clara took a detour off the straight-ahead road of job, home, and family that she had been expected to travel: She applied to become a "contract nurse" for the United States Army in the Spanish-American War.

Viewed today through the prism of history, it's easy to recognize the Spanish-American War as a jingoistic exercise forced upon an unsuspecting

populace by the patriotic exhortations of William Randolph Hearst and other newspaper publishers. But back then, the war was very simple: Spain was the bad guy that was bullying her Cuban colony, and the United States was the good guy, riding to the rescue of our small southern neighbor.

As wars go, the Spanish-American War was more period than paragraph; the fighting, which took place entirely in Cuba and the Philippine Islands (another Spanish territory), was over in less than four months, with the United States victorious. Seven hundred U.S. soldiers died in battle.

But the United States was fighting two enemies during that war: Spanish soldiers and the deadly disease yellow fever—called "Yellow Jack" by sailors (because when it struck a port city a yellow quarantine flag was flown alerting incoming ships to avoid the area) and *el vomito negro* (the black vomit) by the Spanish.

Of all the diseases to plague humanity throughout the ages, yellow fever was one of the worst. Between 1668 and 1893 there were 135 major yellow fever epidemics in United States port cities, including one terrible bout in Philadelphia in 1793 that killed one out of every ten citizens. Yellow fever's symptoms—headaches, backaches, chills, nausea, fever, swollen lips, inflamed eyes, discoloration of the tongue, and dark vomit colored by blood—were among the most terrible of any disease. Worst of all, no one knew what caused yellow fever.

Then, in the mid-1890s, British Army surgeon Sir Ronald Ross discovered that the *Anopheles* mosquito was the carrier of malaria. Medical researchers began to consider insect hosts as the cause for other diseases, including yellow fever. As more and more soldiers on both sides died of yellow fever during the Spanish-American War, the idea of an insect host gained momentum.

This was how things stood when Clara Maass volunteered for duty as a contract nurse for the army. However, by the time her offer was accepted, the brief war was over. Instead of Cuba, Clara was ordered to the field hospital of the 7th U.S. Army Corps at Jacksonville, Florida, to help nurse soldiers suffering from typhoid, malaria, and other diseases. From there she was sent to Savannah, Georgia, and then to Santiago, Cuba. On February 5, 1899, her contract with the army expired, and Clara returned to the United States and German Hospital.

She would not remain there long, however. When U.S. troops were

14   Clara Louise Maass. (Courtesy Clara Maass Medical Center)

sent to the Philippine Islands to put down a revolt, Clara again volunteered her services.

"I am in excellent health and I have a good constitution, and am accustomed to the hardships of field service," she wrote the Surgeon General on November 9, 1899.

Her answer quickly arrived. On November 20, she received a telegram ordering her to board the U.S. Army transport *Logan* for the trip to Manila, the capital of the Philippines.

She arrived at Manila in the midst of a yellow fever epidemic. For the first time, Clara saw the terrifying speed and destructive force of Yellow Jack as infected soldiers rolled violently back and forth in their cots, and the doctors looked on helplessly.

After seven months of nursing the sick, Clara was stricken with dengue, an illness that produces severe pain in the joints and muscles. When she took a long time to recover, the army sent her home in the summer of 1900.

By then, a team of physicians in Cuba led by Dr. Walter Reade were zeroing in on the cause of yellow fever. In August 1900, the doctors had targeted the *Aedes Aegypti* mosquito as a likely carrier of the disease. They began experiments to see if people bitten by the insect would catch yellow fever.

At the same time, Havana was in the grip of a horrifying yellow fever epidemic. A new wave of Spanish immigrants had provided *el vomito negro* with fresh victims, and dozens were dying every day. Dr. William Gorgas, one of the team involved in the mosquito experiments, issued a call for nurses to administer to Havana's sick. One of those who answered was Clara Maass.

By then—the autumn of 1900—the life of the twenty-four-year-old nurse was settling into a more typical pattern. She was engaged to be married to a New York businessman (who has never been identified). Yet she immediately responded to Gorgas's call. By November she was in Havana, and working at a tree-shaded hospital called Las Animas.

At the hospital, Clara learned from Doctor Juan Guiteras about the yellow fever research going on. Still searching for definitive proof that the *Aedes Aegypti* mosquito was to blame for the disease, the United States Army in the spring of 1901 offered $100 to anyone who volunteered to be bitten by a mosquito suspected of carrying yellow fever, and $200 if the person got the disease. Six Spanish immigrants submitted to the test; two died.

These were the odds facing Clara early in 1901, when she volunteered for the experiment. At first the doctors resisted her offer, but Maass quietly and firmly insisted. Finally she was accepted into the program, the only woman and only American among nineteen participants.

Maybe she volunteered for the dangerous experiment because she believed herself immune after having worked with so many yellow fever victims, or possibly she did it for the money. Most likely, however, is that Clara Maass saw an opportunity to serve yet again, and in the spirit of nurses everywhere, could not refuse.

Maass was bitten by ten mosquitoes on five different occasions between March and June 1901. The results were negative. She insisted that the doctors try again. They did—at nine A.M. on August 14 with two mosquitoes already suspected of having caused the disease.

The suspicions were correct. Yellow fever ripped through the young woman's body, battering her with violent headaches, extreme muscle pain, intense vomiting, and a high fever. This time there would be no escape.

As Yellow Jack closed in on her, Clara wrote a final letter home: "Goodbye, Mother," it said. "Don't worry, God will care for me." In a line that summed up the brave young woman's life, she said: "You know I am the man of the family but do pray for me."

On August 24, 1901, Clara Maass died of yellow fever.

Her death ended the yellow fever experiments. She was the only American, and the only woman, to die in the research. Her death proved that the bite of an infected mosquito could not be used to provide immunity from the disease, and also showed that the mosquito was the carrier. Dr. Gorgas began a swift, systematic extermination of the insect. His success was nothing short of spectacular: not a single case of yellow fever was reported in Havana from October, 1901 to June of the following year. This was after a period of 140 years—from 1762 to 1901—when not a single day had gone by without at least one case of yellow fever being reported.

As for Clara, her death was widely reported in the New York City newspapers. "Trained Nurse, Sacrifice to Duty, Dies from Yellow Fever In Cuba," said the *New York Herald*, which featured a picture of Clara with the story. The *New York Times* carried the story on the front page. Two days later, the *Times* eulogized the brave young woman under the heading "The Martyrs of Science:" "Miss Maass . . . was willing to incur the risk of infection if thereby she might assist in establishing a scientific hypothesis of first importance," the paper said. "The annals of medicine are full of the records of the noblest and most disinterested self-sacrifice for the sake of truth. No soldier in the late war placed his life in peril for better reasons than those which prompted this faithful nurse to risk hers."

In time, however, the story of Clara Maass was forgotten. A burst of publicity occurred in the early 1950s, but that too faded away. In 1976, the United States issued a thirteen-cent stamp with Clara's picture to commemorate the one hundredth anniversary of her birth. What made this action significant was that it took place during the nation's bicentennial year, when names like Washington and Jefferson were on everyone's lips. A nurse from New Jersey had upstaged the Founding Fathers.

Today, the former Newark German Hospital is named in her honor. And even though not many people know her name, or what she did, the supreme sacrifice of Clara Maass will always stand tall in the annals of the human race.

So far, this chapter has dealt with topics of considerable weight. Thus it seems only fitting that we conclude on a lighter note—a considerably lighter note—with the story of Sam Patch.

Who was Sam Patch? He was a celebrity of the type later perfected by Evel Knievel, Bobby Riggs, and others of that ilk, people who achieve notoriety by making up in hustle, guts, and showmanship what they lack in ability. Sam blazed the trail for all the P. T. Barnums who were to follow—and he did it by "merely" jumping over waterfalls.

Sam was born in 1807 in Rhode Island. After a few years spent at sea, he found work at the Hamilton Mills cotton works in Paterson. Since his wages supported both himself and his widowed mother, it seemed likely that Patch would spend his life as so many others did then, toiling long, hard hours in industrial obscurity.

But Sam Patch had other ideas.

In 1827, near his twentieth birthday, Sam announced that he was going to jump over the Passaic Falls. Upon hearing this, his coworkers undoubtedly laughed; the falls, while no Niagara, were still extremely dangerous. A person would have to be crazy to willingly jump into those swirling waters.

Patch, however, persisted in his claim, and set the date as September 29, the same day that a new span of the Chasm Bridge was going to be dropped across the falls.

On that Saturday, a large crowd, including Sam, gathered to watch the new bridge being installed. Having heard what Patch intended to do, the police followed him around most of the day, until he gave them the slip.

When he reappeared, Patch was on a precipice eighty feet above the falls. After a brief speech about how the bridge engineer, Mr. Crane, had done a great thing, and how he was about to do another, Sam launched himself into the air.

The stunned crowd watched as the young man disappeared into the foaming water. Seconds later a thunderous cheer arose when Sam poked his head up and swam to shore. He had proved the nay-sayers wrong.

Patch's leap was considered so momentous that *The Saturday Evening*

Post, one of the country's leading periodicals, carried the following item about it on Saturday, October 6, 1827: "It is stated that on Saturday last a man by the name of Samuel Patch leaped from a rock at Patterson's [sic] Falls, New Jersey, which is from seventy to eighty feet high, into the water, merely for the vanity of performing a surprising feat. He escaped unharmed."

Thus was born "Jumping" Sam Patch.

First Patch solidified his national fame by jumping over the Passaic Falls a few more times. Before he jumped, according to one local report, he would remove his coat, vest, and shoes, and "lay them carefully by, as if debating the question whether he should want them again." Then, after a brief speech in which either one or both of his favorite expressions were used ("Some things can be done as well as others" and "There's no mistake in Sam Patch"), Sam would dash forward and leap over the falls.

Although spectators thrilled to Jumping Sam's exploits, others were not so easily impressed. The *Providence Cadet* sniffed that "water passing down the falls accumulates a large quantity of air and renders it almost impossible for a person to sink to any considerable depth." The paper likened the water at the bottom of the falls to landing on "an ocean of feathers."

The *Elizabeth Town Journal* was even more cold-hearted: "Our informant states that Patch is a mechanic connected with one of the factories in Patterson [sic]—that he is perfectly sane and that his object in the hazardous enterprise is gain."

Patch didn't argue with that last remark. The money was indeed good; at one jump he had cleared $13, and at another $15, primarily by passing the hat among spectators.

People, however, didn't care why he was doing it; they just wanted him to continue doing it. Thus Sam began what would today be called "The Jumping Tour." His wanderings took him all over the eastern part of the United States. He jumped from cliffs, bridges, masts, and virtually any other object high enough to make it look dangerous. As Patch's fame grew so did the crowds, and so did his income. Somewhere along the way he picked up a fox and a small bear. Occasionally, he was able to persuade the bear to jump with him.

For an opera singer, the ultimate is performing at the New York Metropolitan Opera. For a waterfall jumper, the ultimate could only be Niagara Falls. In October 1829, the now-famous Sam Patch was invited to Niagara Falls by a committee that was planning to make a day of it at the falls by also blowing up part of a huge rock that had become unsafe. Patch obligingly showed up on the big day, October 6, but after inspecting the preparations (and realizing that he would have to share top billing with the explosion), announced that he would not jump. Come back tomorrow, he advised everyone.

They did—and on October 7, 1829, Sam became the first person to ever jump over Niagara Falls. The *Colonial Advocate* filed this enthusiastic report of the event: "The celebrated Sam Patch actually leaped over the Falls of Niagara into the vast abyss below. A ladder was projected from Goat Island about 40 feet down, on which Sam walked out clad in white, and with great deliberation put his hands close to his sides and jumped from the platform. . . . While the boats below were on the look-out for him, he had in one minute reached the shore unnoticed and unhurt, and was heard on the beach singing as merrily as if altogether unconscious of having performed an act so extraordinary as almost to appear an incredible fable. Sam Patch has immortalised himself."

These words were heady praise indeed for the former Paterson mill-worker. Just to prove that his feat was no fluke, Patch did it again, jumping over Niagara Falls a second time on October 17.

By now Sam had no detractors, only supporters. His jumping exploits had captured the country's attention, and made him a star. On November 14, 1829, *The Saturday Evening Post* raved about the Jersey Jumper: "The now distinguished name of Samuel Patch, which erst had never been pronounced out of the little town of Patterson [sic], is rapidly running the honorable circle of newspaper eulogy, from Maine to Georgia. Wherever Sam goes, he meets with welcome! The good people of every town anticipate his arrival, and not a man, woman, or child, are content, till they hear from his own lips that *there is no mistake*." In closing, the paper offered this poem:

> Hail to the hero, Samuel Patch!
> Who knows not any equal—
> In jumping, Sam can find no match
> Among ten million people.

Little did the *Post*'s editor know that by the time he printed that glowing tribute, Sam Patch was dead.

The events leading up to Sam's demise were innocent enough. After his triumphant return from Niagara Falls, Sam announced that he would "astonish the natives of the west before returning to the Jerseys" by jumping over Genesee Falls at Rochester, New York. In a newspaper ad, Sam said that he was "determined to convince the citizens of Rochester that he is the real 'Simon Pure' . . . by jumping off the falls . . . from the rocky point in the middle of the Genesee River into the gulph [sic] below, a distance of 100 feet!"

On Friday, November 6, with 10,000 people looking on, Sam dove off the falls. An eyewitness wrote that Sam, after gravely examining the "abyss below him," suddenly "sprang from the cliff . . . and . . . descended like an arrow." Upon surfacing, he was "received with exultation by the crowd." It was, said the witness, an "imposing spectacle."

Perhaps it was the warmth and affection of the Rochester crowd that made Sam declare he would jump the Genesee Falls again on the following Friday—Friday the Thirteenth.

Whether you're superstitious or not, it's never a good idea to knowingly tweak the nose of Fate. Yet that was precisely what Sam was doing when he arrived at the falls on that unlucky Friday. At first when he jumped, everything seemed fine; he "descended about one-third of the distance, as handsomely as ever." But then, without warning, his body began to droop. With arms extended and legs separated, he hit the water with a loud smack and immediately sank. "Sam Patch is no more!" said the *Post*.

Although it has been erroneously reported throughout the years that Sam's body was not recovered until several months later, "frozen in a cake of ice" like some long-lost cave man, in reality Sam's body was found two days later. According to the *Post* of December 5, 1829, "it floated ashore a few rods below the spot where he came in contact with the water." After several surgeons examined the Jersey Jumper's corpse, it was found that Sam had suffered "the rupture of a blood-vessel, caused by the sudden chill of the atmosphere through which he passed to the water." Another report said that both of Sam's shoulders were dislocated.

Death, however, could not erase the memory of Sam Patch. For years afterwards, two plays—*Sam Patch* and *Sam Patch in France*—toured in the United States, with an actor named Danforth Marble in the title role. By coming such a long way in a short time, and by doing exactly what he said he'd do despite the odds and the dangers, the former millworker from Paterson had proven that there was, indeed, "no mistake in Sam Patch."

CHAPTER FOUR

The Sporting Life

S P O R T S has always played an important role in New Jersey. The history of athletic competition in the Garden State is a long and proud one, filled with many memorable events, including the extraordinary fact that both the first baseball game and the first college football game were played in New Jersey.

There was little in New Jersey's early history to indicate that it would become a sportsperson's paradise. In fact, the state frowned on virtually every type of sporting activity. Card playing and shooting dice were declared public nuisances in New Jersey by virtue of a 1748 law. In 1787, the faculty at Princeton College prohibited a play in which balls and sticks were used because they thought it unbecoming for gentlemen (this was when only men went to college) to behave in such an outlandish manner.

But people's craving for sports remained unabated. A popular New Jersey event in the early nineteenth century was "Training Days," which featured local troops performing military maneuvers in front of the public. Gradually, Training Days became like holidays, and other events, such as horse racing, gambling, and games of chance, were held in conjunction with the military exercises.

DID YOU KNOW?

Another popular public activity of the early nineteenth century was inhaling nitrous oxide. On October 24, 1809, at the Academy in Newark, twenty gallons of "exhilarating gas" was prepared for public consumption. The most common effects of this rather unusual "sport" was giddiness, sudden bursts of inspiration, and a sudden desire for physical activity. Similar exhibitions were later held in New York and Philadelphia.

Before too long, sports were booming in New Jersey. Cricket matches were popular in the mid-nineteenth century; the Philadelphia Cricket Club played its matches in Camden, and Hoboken's Elysian Fields was the site of an international contest between the United States and Canada in 1856. It would be another sport, however, that would capture the public's fancy at Hoboken.

The sport was baseball, and it was born right on the Elysian Fields. Unfortunately, due to the international baseball conspiracy—a cover-up rivaling any political-military intrigue of modern times—any link between baseball's birth and Hoboken is purely coincidental.

To find out if you've been a victim of the international baseball conspiracy, ask yourself: Who invented organized baseball? If your answer is Abner Doubleday, then you too have been hoodwinked.

According to the "official" version of baseball's birth, Doubleday conceived of the game in 1839, in Elihu Phinney's cow pasture in Cooperstown, New York. In reality, in 1839 Abner Doubleday was a second-year cadet at West Point, whose family had moved out of Cooperstown two years before. When he graduated in 1842, Doubleday said that he was opposed to outdoor exercise and that his favorite sport was chess! And, despite having "invented" the famous game, not once in his life—*never* in a distinguished career as a soldier, writer, and public speaker—did Doubleday publicly mention baseball.

Indeed, the Doubleday story has been so thoroughly discredited by baseball historians and sportswriters that it's become little more than a joke. For the real story of baseball's birth, think not of Cooperstown, but of Hoboken.

By 1845, the once tree-filled and gloriously green city of New York was growing up fast. Buildings, sidewalks, and streets were rapidly replacing the thigh-high fields of rye and barley and glades of blossoming trees laden with sweet-smelling flowers that had characterized New York in its infancy. As urbanization swept inexorably across the city, it destroyed many of the recreation areas that New Yorkers enjoyed. While for some this was just an inconvenience, for others, such as the New York Knickerbockers baseball club, it deprived them of a place to play their game. Fortunately, someone thought of Hoboken.

Although its name comes from the Indian words "Hoboran-Hackingh" (meaning "land of the tobacco pipe," from when the Indians would make bowls for their pipes out of stones found at Hoboken), by 1845 Native Americans had vanished from Hoboken. Instead, this pleasant small town (consisting of just one square mile of land) was known primarily as a recreation center.

Hoboken's chief relaxation attraction was the sprawling greenbelt called Elysian Fields, named for the place of paradise and forgetting in Greek mythology. And paradise is what it truly was: shade trees lined the walkways, flower gardens bloomed with eye-popping color, and refreshing breezes from the nearby Hudson River wafted throughout it. On Sundays, hundreds of people, including many New Yorkers, would pack this pastoral place, picnicking, drinking the cool spring waters that flowed from the earth, and watching cricket matches, foot races, and the miniature railroad that rambled over the green fields.

So it was to Hoboken that the Knickerbockers came, in the early autumn of 1845, to play the first game of modern baseball, which they had adapted from the older and more common game of town ball. On the ferry with them from New York was Alexander Cartwright—the real "Father of Baseball."

When Abner Doubleday was proclaimed the founder of baseball, it effectively buried the pivotal role that Alexander Joy Cartwright played in the formation of the game. Born on April 17, 1820, in New York City, Cartwright in 1845 was a twenty-five-year-old teller at the Union Bank

who was married to the attractive Eliza Ann Gerrits Van Wie, and living at the fashionable address of 76 Eighth Street. The black-whiskered, burly volunteer fireman was forced to change professions in July 1845, when a fire at the bank forced Cartwright to become a bookseller. Nothing, however, could quench his passion for playing town ball with his friends.

But as much as Cartwright enjoyed town ball, he knew it needed refinement. After all, being struck by a thrown ball in order to be put out while running the bases was certainly no fun, nor was it very exciting to stand in the field with dozens of other players and fight for the right to catch the occasional ball that came your way. Cartwright's orderly, analytical mind began devising new rules for town ball, rules that would make the game faster and more exciting for both players and spectators. By mid-summer 1845, he had shown some of his fellow players his ideas, which they enthusiastically accepted. They began recruiting members for a new club called the New York Knickerbockers, which was the name of Cartwright's volunteer fire-fighting organization.

DID YOU KNOW?

Cartwright devised twenty rules for his version of baseball. Among the most significant were:

- Limiting a team to three outs per inning, rather than allowing an entire team to bat.
- Throwing to bases to make outs, rather than throwing the ball at runners.
- Stationing the bases 90 feet apart.
- Limiting the number of outfielders to only three, instead of the unlimited number that used to be allowed.
- Inventing the new position of short stop.
- Establishing fair territory and foul lines.
- Restricting teams to nine men on each side, instead of an unlimited number.

15   Members of the New York Knickerbockers. Alexander Cartwright is in the middle, rear row. (Courtesy National Baseball Library & Archive. Cooperstown, N.Y.)

It has long been thought that the first game of organized baseball was played on June 19, 1846. However, as James M. DiClerico and Barry J. Pavelec, reveal in their book *The Jersey Game*, the first game was actually an intra-squad contest between the Knickerbockers in late September or early October 1845, at Elysian Fields.

On that historic day, the Knickerbockers took the Hoboken Ferry from the city to New Jersey. Once it docked in Hoboken, the team walked up Hudson Street and along the river, past the famous rendezvous spot for lovers known as Sybil's Cave, until they came to Elysian Fields. There, at what is today the approximate intersection of Twelfth and Hudson, they found a large, grassy field, and immediately began laying out what Cartwright called a "diamond." Before long, the game was underway.

No one knows the particulars of this game, since no scorebook was kept. It has been reported that forty-two runs were scored, although this was a recollection made years after the fact. However, the most important thing was that the new rules worked fine. On October 6, armed with a scorebook, the Knickerbockers split into two teams and played the first recorded modern baseball game. The score was 11–8, with Cartwright's team losing.

During the next few weeks, the Knickerbockers played several more games at Elysian Fields. Then, flushed with success, and excited by the brisk pacing and new excitement of their game, the Knickerbockers challenged the Brooklyn Base Ball Club to a match. The game was set for two in the afternoon on Tuesday, October 21, 1845, at Elysian Fields.

On that day, the *New York Herald* carried this day-late notice: "The New York Baseball Club will play a match of baseball against the Brooklyn Club tomorrow afternoon [actually, that same day] at 2 o'clock, at the Elysian Field, Hoboken."

No one knows how many spectators were there to see this historic contest, the first game between two teams using modern baseball rules. How-

16 Alexander Joy Cartwright in later years, in fire-fighting regalia. (Courtesy National Baseball Library & Archive. Cooperstown, N.Y.)

ever, what is certain is that while Cooperstown and Abner Doubleday were doing whatever it is they were doing on that October day, baseball history was being made in New Jersey. The Knickerbockers won the game, although the score is unknown.

By now there should be little doubt that Hoboken's Elysian Fields was the place where a game remarkably similar to modern-day baseball was first played. From these contests there exists such tangible evidence as newspaper accounts and scorebooks; from Cooperstown there is . . . nothing. But Cooperstown and Doubleday have been appointed the home and creator of the game, and it has been a legend too stubborn to repudiate. Thus today Cooperstown reaps the benefits of the glory that should have been Hoboken's.

On March 1, 1849, Cartwright, lured by the discovery of gold in California, headed west. Along the way, he sowed the seeds of the game that he and the Knickerbockers had played in New York like a baseball Johnny Appleseed, still using the original ball that had begun it all at Elysian Fields. According to one source, he taught the game to "enthusiastic saloonkeepers and miners, to Indians and white settlers along the way," and at "nearly every frontier town and Army post where his wagon train visited."

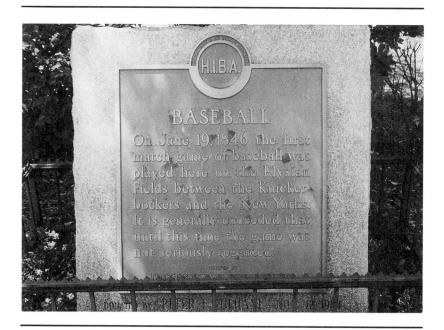

Improbably, Cartwright wound up in Hawaii, where he died on July 13, 1892. Before he went to the great stadium in the sky, however, Cartwright spread baseball throughout the Hawaiian Islands. In 1939, when organized baseball celebrated its "centennial" with much hoopla about Doubleday, Hawaii indignantly struck off a plaque honoring Cartwright and sent it to Cooperstown, demanding that it be placed in the Hall of Fame.

The Knickerbockers played baseball until the early 1870s, when they built a clubhouse at Elysian Fields. Then they vanished into history, drowned by a burgeoning tide of baseball clubs that played the game for money, not sport.

Sadly, Elysian Fields are also no more. Thanks to urbanization, all that remains of this once-glorious greenbelt is a tiny park where children play and parents gather in the shadow of New York City's imposing skyline, which looms within shouting distance just across the river. Rows of brownstone apartment buildings and an abandoned coffee factory occupy the ground where a group of men changed the face of organized sports throughout the world.

Hoboken has tried valiantly to stake its claim for baseball immortality, but the Doubleday legend is strong, and the name "Cooperstown" deeply ingrained in the public consciousness. Except for a plaque at the intersection of Eleventh and Washington streets, there's nothing in Hoboken to commemorate the city's historic role in the creation of our national pastime. Like Alexander Cartwright, Hoboken's place in baseball history seems destined to be forgotten.

DID YOU KNOW?

New Jersey is the only state in the union that can say "Here's Mud in Your Eye" to organized baseball—and mean it! For over a half-century, mud from the Pennsauken Creek (or somewhere close by) has been used by all major league baseball teams to remove the shine from new baseballs before they're put into play. The product is called "Lena Blackburne's Baseball Rubbing Mud," and fifteen pounds' worth is sent in a single coffee can to each

17 This plaque in Hoboken commemorates the birth of baseball in the town (Photo by Pat King-Roberts)

team before the start of the season. However, as far as where the company is located, who owns and operates it (although there once was a Lena Blackburne, who introduced the mud to the game and died in 1968 in Riverside, New Jersey), and, especially, where the mystery mud comes from, no one in major league baseball is telling. (This isn't just some dirty story either: a can of Lena Blackburne mud is on display in the Baseball Hall of Fame.)

On a cold Saturday afternoon in November 1869, passersby of a large field in New Brunswick were shocked to see a large group of male college students from the colleges of Princeton and Rutgers engaged in what appeared to be a massive and often violent free-for-all that had no purpose other than to kick a small rubber ball through a couple of upright poles. As the people watched the young men rolling, jumping, and running about,

they must have shaken their heads in bewilderment, thinking: What was the younger generation coming to these days?

What those people didn't know, however, was that they were witnessing a birth—the birth of college football.

Today, college football is an immensely popular sport in the United States. Not only bragging rights but millions of dollars go hand-in-hand with having a top collegiate team.

But dreams of charting the future of college football weren't the motivation that brought students from both schools together on that November afternoon in 1869. The reason was far more basic: revenge.

During the War of 1812, Princeton had loaned the town of New Brunswick a cannon for protection against a possible British invasion. In 1859, obviously figuring that since the war had been over for four decades the cannon had served its purpose, a Princeton militia company reclaimed—or stole, depending on whose side you're on—the cannon and gave it to Princeton students. Then, in May 1866, the men from Nassau Hall added insult to injury by shellacking Rutgers 40–2 in baseball. Stung by these setbacks, Rutgers cast about for a means of revenge. What they came up with was football.

It was an unusual choice. In those days, football wasn't exactly a national institution. More of an organized brawl than a sport, some colleges had even banned the game, because upper classmen used it as a way of kicking hapless newcomers around the field. By the 1860s, the game was being played sporadically by groups of college students among themselves, using a round rubber ball that resembled a miniature basketball. To advance the ball, the teams—with as many as twenty-five players per side—kicked and dribbled it with their feet, much like soccer. The object was to get the ball through the opponent's goal, usually by kicking.

This was the game that Rutgers challenged Nassau Hall to, a challenge that was immediately accepted by the Princetonians. A series of three matches were agreed upon: the first and third at New Brunswick, the second at Princeton. The first game was set for Saturday, November 6.

Rutgers's new student newspaper, *The Targum*, described the morning of that fateful day: "The strangers came up in the 10 o'clock train, and brought a good number of backers with them. After dinner, and a stroll around the town, during which . . . billiards received a good deal of attention, the crowds began to assemble at the ball ground, which . . . is a lot

---

18   This small park is all that's left of once-glorious Elysian Fields. In the background is New York City. (Photo by Pat King-Roberts)

about a hundred yards wide, extending from College Avenue to Sicard-street."

Prior to the game, team captain William J. Leggett of Rutgers (history's first intercollegiate football captain) had corresponded with his opposite number at Princeton, William S. Gummere, in order to agree upon the rules. Now, as their colleagues roamed New Brunswick, Leggett and Gummere huddled again. Although the two teams used different rules, courtesy prevailed over competition; Gummere agreed to abide by his host's rules. (This stunned *The Targum*, which wrote: "The Princeton captain, for some reason or other, gave up every point to our men without contesting one.")

It was now nearly three o'clock in the afternoon. The time for socializing was over; the time for settling matters on the field had arrived. "Grim-looking players were silently stripping, each one surrounded by sympathizing friends," reported *The Targum*, "while around each of the captains was a little crowd, intent upon giving advice, and saying as much as possible."

By "stripping," the players removed their hats, coats, and vests, and rolled up their pants. There were no uniforms; to distinguish the teams, Rutgers players wore hats or turbans made of scarlet, while the Princeton-

ians played bare-headed. (One Rutgers player, D. D. Williamson, misunderstood the instructions, and wore both a turban and shirt made of bright scarlet.)

In 1930, Rutgers's John W. Herbert, one of the last surviving participants in that historic contest sixty-one years earlier, wrote in *The Sunday World Magazine*: "To this day I remember the moment that preceded the whistle. Each team had two 'captains of the enemy's goal,' who took and more or less kept posts directly before their opponents' goal. The rest of each team was divided into two parts, one of eleven and the other of twelve men. The players in one were assigned to cover their own section of the field . . . they were called fielders. The men in the other section of each team were rovers [also called bulldogs], their assignment being to rush up and down the whole field, kicking the ball toward the enemy's goal."

As the players lined up, approximately 100 spectators craned forward anxiously. Those who had arrived early were perched on top of a wooden fence that enclosed part of the lot; the rest sat on the ground or watched from horse-drawn buckboards lolling idly on the dirt roads alongside the field.

The winner would be the first team to score six goals. Princeton, which had the bigger and stronger players, kicked first, but the ball went wide, and Rutgers pounced on it. Immediately the New Brunswick players surrounded the ball, blocking any Nassau Hall student from touching it. Then they began moving the ball down the field via a series of quick kicks and dribbles. This primitive version of the flying wedge was highly successful; within minutes the ball was kicked through Princeton's goal. Rutgers had scored the first point in college football history.

But if the New Brunswick students thought that they were in for a quick victory, they were mistaken. Seeing the effectiveness of the flying wedge, Gummere quickly whispered instructions to a "veritable Goliath of a man" on the Princeton team named Jacob E. (Big Mike) Michael. When Rutgers received the ball again, they formed their wedge, hoping to duplicate their first success. However, they had reckoned without Big Mike; ignoring the ball, the young giant plowed into the players, scattering them like bowling pins. "Time and again Rutgers formed the wedge and charged," wrote Herbert. "As often, Big Mike broke it up." Spurred on by Michael's efforts, Princeton scored the next goal to tie the game.

This is how it went all afternoon: Rutgers would pull ahead, only to

19 Artist's rendition of the first collegiate football game. (Courtesy Special Collections and Archives, Rutgers University Libraries)

have their rivals come storming back. "Every game was like the one before," said *The Targum*. "There was the same headlong running, wild shouting, and frantic kicking." Herbert remembered that "It was difficult to distinguish . . . between friend and foe in the ever shifting change of players on the field of battle."

At one point during play, the Princeton rooters began yelling "Sis Boom Ah!" Startled, the Rutgers spectators asked what that meant. It was explained that the 7th Regiment of the New York National Guard had shouted this out as they marched through Princeton during the Civil War. The Princetonians liked the sound of it, and adopted it as their own. Thus was the first college cheer born.

Not all the shouting, however, was positive. During the action, an elderly Rutgers professor pedaled up on his bicycle. After watching fifty college students pushing, pulling, mauling, kicking, and tackling one another, the professor became college football's first heckler by yelling in disgust: "You men will come to no Christian end."

The old man's words went unheeded, however, as the competition rose to white-hot intensity. At one point, the ball was kicked toward the wooden fence that served as the first grandstand. Streaking after the ball went George H. Large of Rutgers and the freight train–like Big Mike. All at once, it became apparent that the players could not stop in time; the audience tried to scramble off the fence, but they were too slow. Both players smashed into the fence, knocking it to the ground and spilling the spectators into a "seething mass" on the ground.

Eventually both players and nonparticipants sorted themselves out, and the game resumed. With the contest knotted at four goals each, Rutgers's Leggett instructed his team to use low, short kicks to get the ball past the taller Princetonians. The strategy worked; Rutgers scored the next two goals, and won the game six goals to four.

After the game, the combatants resumed their cordial ways. *The Targum* reported that "the players had an amicable 'feed' together," and Herbert recalled it as "an epicurean feast. Stories were told, songs sang, and good fellowship abounded."

The game did not exactly garner rave reviews in the press. The November 9, 1869, edition of *The New York Times* carried the following laconic lines: "A picked twenty-five of the students of Rutgers College played the

---

20 Members of the Rutgers team that won the first intercollegiate football game in the world. (Courtesy Special Collections and Archives, Rutgers University Libraries)

---

same number of Princeton a game of foot ball, on Saturday. After an exciting contest of one hour, the Rutgers were declared the winners, the score standing six to four. On returning from the ball ground the Princeton boys partook of the hospitalities of the Rutgers."

The editor of the *Bergen County Gazette* was much harsher, terming the game a "jackass performance." Sounding a theme that still echoes on college campuses, the editor called for the students to "construe correctly a page of Homer or of Virgil [rather than] be able to kick a football powerfully."

The next Saturday, November 13, 1869, the two teams met again, this time on a Princeton field near where Palmer Stadium stands today. Unlike the first game, this contest was all Princeton; the Nassau Hall students swamped Rutgers 8–0. Enthusiasm for the rubber match ran at a fever pitch on both campuses, but the contest never took place. Fearful that things were getting out of hand, administrators from both schools banned the game.

It didn't matter. The two schools had begun something that couldn't be stopped. As word of the game spread to other campuses, other schools began playing each other, and rules became more standardized. Just seven short years after Rutgers and Princeton met, representatives of Yale and

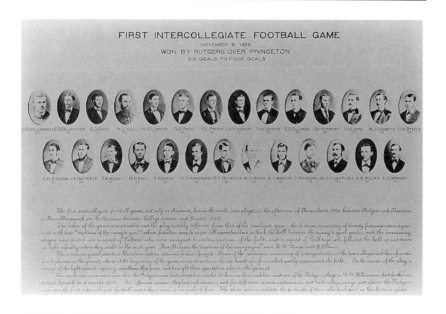

Harvard formed the first Intercollegiate Football Association. The game was on its way.

After its initial victory, it would take Rutgers almost three-quarters of a century to enjoy another triumph over its arch-rival. On November 5, 1938, sixty-nine years after their win in the first game ever, Rutgers beat Princeton 20–18 at the dedication of the new Rutgers Stadium. Ironically, that same day, Col. William Preston Lane, the last survivor of Princeton's first team, died at Hagerstown, Maryland. He was to have been a guest of honor at the stadium dedication.

DID YOU KNOW?

Football was not exactly an immediate hit. Many decried the brutality and violence of the game, such as in this poem, entitled "The Noble Game," authorship of which was credited only to "J." It appeared in the Rutgers *Targum* in November 1870:

In the Name of the Prophet—Football.

Heaven have mercy—what do I hear?
Is a civil war in progress here?
A dusty field before me lies,
From which come shrieks and groans and cries.
As if some folks from a "warmer clime"
Were bent on having a jolly good time.
Fifty young men—with lives to lose—
Fifty young men—with canvas shoes—are lustily kicking a rubber ball
And sometimes kicking each other; that's all.
And though some are half and others are lame,
They all agree—it's a "noble game."

21 Years later, no longer the boys of autumn that they once were, some of those who had participated in that historic first game returned to Rutgers, to acknowledge the cheers of the crowd one more time. (Courtesy Special Collections and Archives, Rutgers University Libraries)

Here comes a victim: What's the matter?
What occasions this horrible clatter?
Football, my boys, is making the row.
The noblest game on earth, I vow.
And really, there's nothing the matter with me,
Only broken my arm and strained my knee;
My chum got kicked in the abdomen,
And hasn't been out of his bed since then.
Two of our class have gone home to die,
And five are under the doctor's eye.
But doctor or not—it's all the same;
I tell you, sir, it's a "noble game."

See how the dust their faces begrimes
Look at that mass of writhing limbs.
Really, I think, if they come this way,
'Twould be highly impolitic here to stay.
Oh, murder! They're here! I'm down and alack,
The football is lying upon my back.
Kick after kick is all I can feel,

My neck bears the weight of one big villain's heel.
Get off! Let me up! Don't you hear me shout?
Let me up! Let me up! Let me out! Let me out!
My soul is quitting its earthly frame,
I'll be choked if I think it's a noble game.

This is the story of two Newarks, two baseball teams, and two entirely different worlds—yet just one final outcome.

The first story is about the Newark Bears. The Bears were the crown jewels of the New York Yankee farm system. Bought by Yankees owner Col. Jacob Ruppert for $350,000 on November 12, 1931, the Bears were Ruppert's first step toward building a farm system similar to that of the St. Louis Cardinals. The Bronx Bombers had not won the pennant in three years, and Ruppert had decided that developing ballplayers through a minor league system was the way for the Yankees to return to their former glory. To run the Bears, Ruppert picked George Weiss, who had been performing a similar function for the minor league Baltimore Orioles.

"I have faith in Newark," said Weiss. "It has always been a wonderful baseball city as well as a leading industrial center and noted for its civic enterprise."

That statement—crisp, formal, to the point—was typical of Weiss. With an eye for both talent and the bottom line, he was the rarest of baseball executives. In time, he would go on to become the guiding force behind the powerhouse New York Yankee teams of the 1940s and 1950s, as well as to lay the groundwork for the New York Mets "Miracle Season" of 1969. For now, however, Weiss was responsible for rejuvenating a lackluster Newark franchise that generally performed poorly at the box office and on the field. He would do his job quicker than anyone could imagine.

The previous season, Newark had shown signs of life, fighting for the pennant all season before finishing second. In 1932, with a dozen players on the team who had either been on the Yankees or were sent there by the parent club, the Bears roared to the International League pennant, winning 109 games while losing just 59. Boasting such future major leaguers as Dixie Walker (soon to be "The People's Cherce" at Brooklyn), George Selkirk, and Red Rolfe, the Bears won thirteen of their first seventeen games before ending fifteen and a half games ahead of the second-place Orioles. In the Little World Series they beat the Minneapolis Milers four games to two.

All this was just a prelude, however, to the 1937 team, considered to be the greatest minor league baseball team of all time. This Bears team was so good it was frightening; with a won-loss record of 109–43, and a winning percentage of .717, they won the pennant by a staggering twenty-five and one-half games. The Bears' players led the league in virtually every offensive category. In the playoffs leading up to the Little World Series they swept both the Syracuse Chiefs and the Baltimore Orioles. Then, in dramatic fashion, the Bears lost the first three games of the Little World Series to the Columbus Cardinals before storming back to win four in a row.

What makes the Bears' awesome season so much more amazing is that there were no future baseball superstars on the team; their roster doesn't show any names like Willie Mays or Mickey Mantle. What the Bears did have, however, was a talented group of players that, with one exception, all went on to have major league careers. This solid group included Charlie "King Kong" Keller, who would patrol the Yankees's outfield with Joe DiMaggio; George McQuinn, who led the St. Louis Browns to their only pennant; and Joe Gordon, a slick-fielding, hard-hitting second baseman with the Yanks and Cleveland Indians.

Typical of the type of uncanny season that Bears' players had in 1937 was outfielder Bob Seeds. Known as Suitcase Bob because of the many teams that he swung a bat for, Seeds had a mediocre major league career. But at Newark, in 1937, he was a holy terror; he hit .303, with 20 home runs and 112 runs batted in. In one incredible weekend, Seeds hit seven homers in ten at bats, driving in seventeen runs in the process. (In contrast, Seeds only hit twenty-eight home runs total during his nine years in the majors.) Like most of the other Newark Bears, everything came together for Seeds in 1937; it was a team that caught lightning in a bottle and never let it out.

The Bears played at Ruppert Stadium in Newark, basking in the public glow as the top farm team of the mighty Yankees. Newark was one step removed from the splendor of the majors, and Bears' games received a good deal of press. Players knew that if they showed enough at Newark, they might one day get "The Call" to the majors.

But there was another team that played in Newark, at Ruppert Stadium—and for them, The Call would never come.

The "other" team was the Newark Eagles. They were a team of African-American ballplayers forced to toil in the relative obscurity of the Negro Leagues. However, this didn't mean they were a lesser club than those in the majors; the Eagles were just as good as most, and better than some. But fate dictated that they display their talents in the shadows of organized baseball.

To baseball fans today, the idea of the Negro Leagues is incongruous. Black ballplayers are such an integral part of the game now that if they were to suddenly all go and play in a league of their own, baseball would collapse. But for years, that was exactly what black players had to do, thanks to a "gentleman's agreement" among the owners of professional baseball clubs that barred African Americans from the game. This meant that men like Josh Gibson, LeRoy (Satchel) Paige, Smokey Joe Williams, and Oscar Charleston, all prodigiously talented, were denied access to major league baseball solely because of their skin color.

Negro League ballplayers lived on a scale far below their major league counterparts. They rode buses instead of trains, played as many as four games in one day, and had to use equipment and play in ball parks that would be considered substandard in the majors.

It also meant sometimes witnessing acts of extreme human cruelty. Once, in Alabama, the Eagles' team bus stopped at a roadside cafe, so the hot, thirsty players could get something to drink. But no sooner did the players approach the cafe then the owner came out and started shaking her head.

"Why are you saying 'no,'" asked Eagles star Monte Irvin, "when you don't even know what we want?"

"Whatever it is, we don't have any," said the woman.

Finally, she agreed to let them use the drinking well out back. But after the players had all drank and the team bus was pulling away, the players saw the woman methodically smash the drinking gourd to pieces.

To their credit, the Eagles did not let these types of episodes affect their play on the field. The team was a powerhouse in the Negro National League, finishing no lower than third for eleven of their thirteen years in the league, winning the pennant twice, and the Negro World Series once.

Formed in 1935, the Eagles spent their maiden season in Brooklyn before moving to Newark the following year. The city was a logical choice; approximately 39,000 blacks—nearly one-fifth of the entire state's African-American population—lived in Newark in 1930. Despite on-going discrimination (blacks were forced to take out food from restaurants rather than eat it there and were barred from the city's municipal hospital), Newark was still a good home for African Americans. It was a "small" big city, with neighborhoods full of people who looked out for one another, and groups and organizations that helped promote family life and togetherness. Those familiar with Newark during this time, such as Irvin, remember it fondly as "just a wonderful city." In 1936, the Eagles landed in this wonderful city.

The Eagles were the dream of Abe Manley, a numbers boss in Newark. A lifelong baseball fan, Manley sat in the Eagles' dugout during home games, often traveled with them on the road, and was happier than a kid on Christmas morning just to be near the diamond.

Manley could afford to indulge his passion for the Eagles because of his wife, Effa. It was she who actually ran the ball club, keeping one eye on the bottom line and the other on the team's performance. In the man's world of Negro League baseball, Effa was an original.

Effa was born around 1900 to a multiracial Philadelphia family that contained a white mother, black father, and mulatto children. As she freely admitted, she was white—"I was this little, blond, hazel-eyed white girl always with these Negro children"—but that didn't stop her from falling in love with Manley when the two baseball fanatics met at the 1932 World Series, nor did it prevent her from quickly assuming a leadership role in the Negro League. The other owners respected her business acumen.

Effa brooked no interference with her team. Once she stopped talk of a players strike in its tracks by announcing to the militant players that "no Newark Eagle was gonna strike, period." Former players remember her

22   *The 1946 Newark Eagles. (Courtesy National Baseball Library & Archive. Cooperstown, N.Y.)*

"suggestions" to the manager during games. "She was loud, and if the pitcher was going bad you could hear 'Get him out of there,'" said former first baseman Francis Matthews. "She wanted everyone in Newark to know she was in charge."

It was this potent combination—Abe the benevolent sugar daddy, Effa the hard-nosed numbers-cruncher—that made the Eagles soar. The Manleys built the Eagles, not only into a sports powerhouse, but a potent social force as well. White politicians soon found that they had to attend both Bears and Eagles games. The Eagles became a social institution in Newark, appearing at functions in the black community and holding clinics for kids.

The two greatest Eagle players were Monte Irvin and Larry Doby. Irvin was a phenomenal New Jersey high school athlete (All-State in football, basketball, baseball, and track for three straight years) who joined the Eagles at age nineteen in 1938 and finally broke into the major leagues with the New York Giants in 1949. Doby also had a superb high school career in Paterson before landing with the Eagles. In 1947 he became the first black player in the American League when he signed with the Cleveland Indians.

The pinnacle for the Eagles came in 1946. With World War II over, the Negro Leagues were flourishing, and so were the Eagles. The team finished the season with a record of 47–16, with Irvin hitting .395 and Doby .348. In the Negro World Series, the Eagles' foe were the powerful, Yankee-like Kansas City Monarchs. In a classic seven-game series, the Eagles defeated the Monarchs to win the championship.

As they celebrated their team's triumph, however, little did Abe and Effa know that it was the Eagles' last hurrah. Once the Brooklyn Dodgers broke baseball's color line in October 1945, by signing Jackie Robinson (who, incidentally, played his first professional game at Jersey City on April 18, 1946), other teams began following suit. As black stars went to the majors, they took Negro League fans with them, and attendance plummeted. In 1947, just one year after being crowned the kings of black baseball, the Eagles lost $22,000.

Further hurting the Eagles was the tendency of major league owners to either pay Negro League owners nothing—as in the case of Jackie Robinson—or a pittance for signing their stars. In 1947, Effa negotiated the sale of superstar Monte Irvin to the New York Giants for a paltry $5,000. "If he'd have been white they'd have given me $100,000," she remarked bitterly.

By 1949 the Newark Eagles were gone, along with most of Negro League baseball. Ironically, that's the year that this tale of two Newarks comes full circle, for it was also the last season for the Newark Bears. Attendance had been steadily dropping since the miracle year of 1937; by 1949 just 88,170 fans had paid their way into once-magical Ruppert Stadium. That winter, the Chicago Cubs bought the Bears franchise and moved it to Massachusetts. All that was left for Newark was the memories.

DID YOU KNOW?

The Newark Eagles weren't the only successful New Jersey–based African-American team. Two decades earlier, the Atlantic City Bacharachs (named after the town's mayor, Harry Bacharach) were one of the top teams of several different blackball leagues. In 1926 and 1927 the Bacharachs played in that era's version of the Negro World Series, only to lose both times to the Chicago American Giants. The man considered by many to be the greatest black player of all time, John Henry "Pop" Lloyd, played several seasons with the Bacharachs.

DID YOU KNOW?

New Jersey has a long and proud history of minor league baseball. Match these cities with their team nicknames.

Camden	Skeeters
Trenton	Atlantics
Jersey City	Giants
Paterson	Merritt
Newark	Resolutes
Elizabeth	Indians

Answers: Paterson Atlantics, Camden Merritt, Newark Indians, Elizabeth Resolutes, Trenton Giants, Jersey City Skeeters

It was Saturday, July 2, 1921, and the biggest fight in the history of boxing was about to take place between scowling Jack Dempsey, the Manassa Mauler, and handsome Georges Carpentier, the urbane Frenchman. As over 90,000 people roared, Dempsey and Carpentier stepped into the ring—a ring not in the boxing mecca of New York's Madison Square

Garden, but located on a patch of land called Boyle's Thirty Acres across the Hudson River in Jersey City.

If Babe Ruth put baseball on the map and the Baltimore Colts–New York Giants' overtime struggle in the 1958 NFL title game opened the door for mass acceptance of pro football, then the 1921 bout between Dempsey and Carpentier was the match that made boxing legitimate. Long accustomed to being run out of cities and states because of public displeasure over a sport in which two grown men tried to beat each other's brains out, boxing by 1921 had at least gotten to the point where the local sheriff didn't come down and arrest the participants of every match. Still, it was because some of those old-fashioned prejudices against boxing still lingered that Jersey City was able to become the center of the sporting universe.

New York Governor Natahan L. Miller was a man who held firmly to his convictions, and one of those was that professional prizefighting was disgusting. Lost in the nineteenth century dream world of amateur athletics, when men competed just for the sport of it, he waged a vigorous campaign against professional boxing in his state despite a law that had made prizefights legal in New York.

Miller's steadfast but naive convictions threatened the plans of George L. "Tex" Rickard, the first true genius at boxing promotion. To build up interest in a fight, Rickard would pull stunts like letting the prize money remain on public display for weeks, so that even those people who didn't like boxing would finally buy a ticket just to satisfy their natural curiosity and find out who was going to win that damned money they'd been staring at for so long. Rickard didn't have to go to those lengths to publicize the Dempsey-Carpentier fight; public interest in the bout had been sky high even before the two fighters signed the contract. It was a match made in promotional heaven.

At the age of twenty-six in July 1921, Jack Dempsey was at the peak of his power. Born William Harrison Dempsey on June 24, 1895, in Manassa, Colorado, Jack Dempsey by 1921 had brawled and bludgeoned his way to boxing's top prize, the heavyweight championship. Back then boxing was much more violent than it is today, and Dempsey's savage fury was usually given full vent by referees, who normally only stopped a bout if blood made the ring too slippery. Already a forbidding-looking man, the black-haired Dempsey added to his arsenal of fear by not shaving before a fight. Opponents took one look at the stubble-bearded wild man across from them and began wondering what fool notion could have possessed them to step into a ring with such a creature. Usually the next thing they remembered was waking up in the trainer's room.

Georges Carpentier, on the other hand, was the perfect antithesis of

Dempsey. Urbane, cultured, witty, and handsome, the erudite Frenchman had won the hearts of millions by serving with distinction in World War I (a war Dempsey avoided serving in). Then, in one of the biggest upsets at the time in boxing history, Carpentier had knocked out English champion Joe Beckett, a strapping two hundred-pounder who looked as if he could snap Carpentier in two. Ever since that victory Carpentier had been regaled as the "class" of boxing, and a match between him and Dempsey set up a classic Beauty and the Beast confrontation. As Randy Roberts wrote in *Jack Dempsey—The Manassa Mauler*: "Give the masses of people some rosy-cheeked, clear complexioned Lancelot to cheer and some thick-bearded, Simon Legree to boo and jeer, and the money would roll in in waves."

Getting the fight wasn't a problem for Rickard; finding a place to hold it was another matter. Miller was firmly against having it in New York, which ruled out Madison Square Garden and the Polo Grounds, the two most desirable sites. Other cities were ruled out because Rickard wanted to be close to New York, then the publicity capital of the world.

Then in April 1921, New Jersey Governor Edward I. Edwards stepped in and offered his state as host for the bout. Rickard dove for the offer like a drowning man for a life preserver. Quickly the sites were narrowed down to a precious few: Newark, Jersey City, and Atlantic City. For reasons that probably had a lot to do with political boss, mayor, and boxing enthusiast Frank Hague, Jersey City was the winner.

The only problem with Jersey City was that it didn't have a place big enough to hold the bout in. Rickard, however, didn't let that stop him. Within days hundreds of workers were swarming all over a patch of ground called Boyle's Thirty Acres. The pinewood arena that was frantically constructed was first planned to seat 50,000. As fight fever rose, the capacity of the oval, saucer-shaped arena was increased to 70,000, then 90,000. Unfortunately, time (the workers had just over thirty days) and the repeated changes to the design to accommodate more fans made the final structure incredibly shaky. Those who sat in the expensive seats near ringside had no worries. However, for those in the hastily improvised wooden seats on the outskirts, it was like sitting on the raised section of a seesaw; whenever those on the bottom (near the ring) made noise or stamped their feet, the vibrations raced through the stands and made the top of the seesaw shake like a leaf in a hurricane.

The two fighters trained in very different ways for their upcoming clash. Carpentier set up camp in Manhasset, Long Island, an area of ritzy estates. The press and public were barred from his workouts. (Ring Lardner believed the reason for this was that he knew he was going to get killed, and so he hardly bothered to train.) Dempsey, on the other hand, trained in Atlantic City. Everyone was invited to come and see the champ, who, when he wasn't sparring or engaged in rigorous runs up and down the beach, would often talk to anyone who happened to be around.

As the fight date grew closer groups protesting the bout grew louder. The Clergymen's Community Club of Jersey City sent an official letter of protest to Mayor Hague, claiming that the fight would corrupt the moral standards of the city. Other organizations made similar pronouncements, but they were merely fanning the breeze. It would have been easier to try and stop Halley's Comet.

By the end of June the fight was making international news. (In fact, a Swiss newspaper complained that "one-tenth of the press-power concentrated upon [the fight] would have put the United States into the League of Nations.") Every scrap of information about the fight was plastered over the front page of newspapers around the world.

Naturally, local newspaper tripped all over themselves in covering the contest. Typical of the breathless coverage was this lead paragraph from a June 30, 1921 *Newark Evening News* story: "When Jack Dempsey and Georges Carpentier face each other for the world's heavyweight boxing championship in Jersey City Saturday afternoon there will be present a greater number of persons prominent in national and international life than ever before attended a pugilistic contest in the history of the sport."

However, despite its florid tone, the story was correct. Among those notables going to the fight were J. P. Morgan, Henry Ford, Vincent Astory, Payne Whitney, Al Jolson, John D. Rockefeller, Douglas Fairbanks, members of the Theodore Roosevelt family, and George M. Cohan. Even more remarkable was the number of women who bought tickets. Drawn by the dashing Carpentier, thousands of females came to see a sport that they had virtually ignored before.

Fight day—July 2—dawned hazy and humid, with a threat of rain. (In fact, just before one in the afternoon it did sprinkle a little, nearly giving Rickard a heart attack.) Thousands of people had camped overnight in the field surrounding the stadium, hoping to buy a ticket at the gate, but these were gone quickly. At nine A.M. the gates opened, and the crowd started to file in. They wouldn't stop until a record 91,163 seats had been filled. According to one contemporary source, by the time of the fight, the boxing ring looked like a small, square lump of sugar at the bottom of a bowl covered with 10,000 black flies.

The spotlight was on Jersey City that day, and the city was ready. To guard against the risk of fire in the wooden arena, barbecue equipment, old newspapers, and other inflammables were left outside the gates, and 400 firemen were on duty. For medical care, an emergency hospital was set up near the arena. Police had taken every precaution against crooks and pickpockets sneaking into the stadium; over 3,000 officers and detectives patrolled the inside and outside of the arena.

As Dempsey later wrote, promoter Rickard was so overcome with the grandeur and spectacle of it all that he rushed into the champ's dressing room, crying: "Jack! Jack! You never seen anything like it. We got a million dollars in already and they're still coming! And the people, Jack! I never seen anything like the people we got at this fight. High-class society folk—you name 'em, they're here. And dames! I mean classy dames, thousands of them!"

Those "classy dames," "high-class society folk," and everyone else got what they came for just after three o'clock that afternoon, when first Carpentier, then Dempsey, climbed into the ring. By then, the heat and humidity had caused many men in the crowd to shed clothing. (The women resisted this temptation.) Dempsey looked so menacing, and Carpentier so frail, that the wife of one sportswriter gasped and said "It's over."

The first round was tame, as both men felt the other out. The few punches Carpentier landed on Dempsey had as much effect as gnats landing on the champion's skin. The Manassa Mauler's punches, however, were more devastating; one bloodied the Frenchman's nose.

In the second round Carpentier bore in more aggressively, and hit Dempsey with a solid right on the chin. The crowd roared, feeling that Georges might have a chance to win after all, and many sportswriters later wrote that Dempsey was in danger of being knocked out at that point. The truth is, however, that the blow did little more than annoy Dempsey. "Dempsey was never in any more danger of being knocked out than I was," cracked H. L. Mencken.

By the third round Dempsey was through fooling around. Punches rained in on Carpentier from all angles, and the Frenchman wobbled back to his corner. Less than a minute into the fourth round, Carpentier lay prone on the canvas, with blood flowing from his nose and mouth. The Battle of the Century was over.

"Dempsey Knocks Out Carpentier in Fourth Round of Title Bout," screamed the front page of the *Newark Evening News* in an extra July 2 edition. "Dempsey gave Carpentier an unmerciful beating," reported the paper. "He opened up a cut under the Frenchman's eye and batted him so viciously around the head with vicious rights and lefts until Carpentier's face was swollen and bleeding."

Although the fight was not that good, everyone connected with it had reason to smile. It was the first sports event ever to be broadcast on radio, and the first to gross over $1 million. Sports history had been made again in New Jersey.

DID YOU KNOW?   ?

On the same day as the Dempsey-Carpentier fight, a historic event occurred in New Jersey that should have been plastered across the front page of newspapers all over the world: the signing of the treaty formally ending World War I. Because of all the fight hoopla, however, the occasion passed virtually unnoticed.

Because of partisan politics, the United States never signed the Treaty of Versailles, which formally ended the war for the European Allies. Technically, the United States remained at war with Germany long after the guns had stopped. Finally, after Warren G. Harding was elected president in 1920, a compromise resolution was crafted and passed by Congress on July 1, 1921. Harding had left Washington for a relaxing Independence Day weekend at the Somerset County home of his friend, Senator Joseph Frelinghuysen. On Saturday, July 2, Harding interrupted a golf game to return to the Frelinghuysen home and sign the resolution that officially ended the Great War. Just thirty people witnessed the event, and newspapers, dominated by stories of the great fight, gave the news short shrift. Even the staid *New York Times* played down the signing, putting it in a one-column story entitled "Harding Ends War" and splashing the Dempsey-Carpentier bout all over the front page. Clearly, the Great War had been superseded by the Battle of the Century.

CHAPTER FIVE

Away for the Day

A S a small state, New Jersey takes a lot of flak from those who assume that bigger is better. However, there are distinct advantages to not being the size of Texas—not the least of which is that New Jerseyians don't have to walk around wearing ten-gallon hats! However, another, more important advantage is that it doesn't take forever and a day to get someplace in New Jersey. Virtually all of the state's many attractions are within a few hours' ride. This makes New Jersey the ultimate "day tripper" state—a place where, if everyone in the entire family can't find something that tickles their fancy, they're just not looking hard enough. So pack up the car, make sure the kids have something to do (besides asking you "Are we there yet?" every five minutes), and let's head out to discover some of New Jersey's best day trips.

Popcorn Park Zoo

Humane Way, Forked River (Ocean County)

T H I S is a zoo unlike any other you've ever experienced.

After all, where else can you actually be intercepted by animals looking for a free meal as you walk around? Where else can you see a three-legged deer, a blind cow, an abused tiger, and a goat rescued from becoming part of a cult ritual? Indeed, where else can you see the one and only Parkway Porker?

The answer to all these questions is the Popcorn Park Zoo. What makes Popcorn Park unique is that it's the only federally licensed zoo in the United States that caters to the needs of sick, abandoned, injured, and abused animals. Without Popcorn Park, all the animals there would be dead. Thus, not only has the zoo given these creatures a new lease on life by rescuing them from their formerly unhappy existence, it's actually giving them life itself.

Popcorn Park was founded in 1977 by the Associated Humane Societies in order to provide a home for wildlife that, for one reason or another, simply could not survive in the wild. Eventually it was expanded to include exotic and domestic animals in the same situation. Today, over 200 of these creatures live happily on seven acres of Pinelands sand and scrub pine at Popcorn Park. (The name comes from the fact that you can purchase containers of popcorn with which to feed the animals.)

At Popcorn Park, the animals are not shy about expressing themselves. Groups of geese frequently approach you as you walk through the zoo, honking noisily to let you know that they know you have popcorn, and they want some of it. No sooner do you get past the geese than the deer take their place, tamely eating right out of your hand—and frequently sticking their noses into the popcorn box if you're not careful!

Among the animals that you'll meet at Popcorn Park are lions, tigers, pot-bellied pigs, goats, ponies, turkey vultures, snakes, foxes, raccoons, bears, monkeys, and even an African elephant. Each of them has a story,

such as the aptly named Parkway Porker, a 600-pound pig who was picked up while casually munching away along the Garden State Parkway; Orange of Orange, a deer who was hit by a car and lost a leg but does very well now, thank you; and Gatsby the Goat, who was found in Elizabeth with his horns, tail, and feet painted as if for some bizarre ritual.

Popcorn Park Zoo is a delightful place for young and old alike. If you like animals, it's hard to resist. (Note: The park is only open June through October.)

Allaire State Park

Route 524, Farmingdale (Monmouth County)

A s you will find out shortly in the chapter on the Pinelands, this region was once the home of a vast, iron-producing empire. Even though the fires for the huge blast furnaces that once belched smoke and soot throughout the Pinelands have long since been extinguished, you can relive this unique era in New Jersey history at Allaire State Park.

In 1822, businessman James P. Allaire purchased the 5,000 acre Monmouth Furnace ironworks from William Newbold for $19,000. For Allaire, owning the newly rechristened Howell Iron Works made sense; he owned a marine engine-building facility in New York City, and needed a reliable source of iron.

Within a decade the Howell Works (the name wasn't changed until after Allaire's death) was prospering. At one stretch in the mid-1830s, the blast furnace ran continuously for twenty-one months. Several hundred people lived in the little community that sprang up around the ironworks, which was typical of Pinelands bog iron towns. However, what was not typical was Allaire's munificence as an employer. He established a school, church, and stage service in his town, and built sturdy brick rowhouses for the workers to live in. The virtually self-sufficient village (it even issued its own script in place of money) contained a bakery, blacksmith shop, general store, sawmill, and other businesses. It was about as comfortable an existence as any iron worker and his family could expect.

But Allaire ran into financial difficulties in 1847, at the same time that

23 Kids can't resist feeding the deer at Popcorn Park. In the front is Orange of Orange, the three-legged deer. (Photo by Pat King-Roberts)

the bog iron industry was entering a decline that would lead to its eventual extinction. With both the industry's collapse and Allaire's money troubles occurring concurrently, there was no way the little town could survive. By 1854 just ten employees were left at the Howell Works. The era of bog iron was over, and with it the useful life of the tiny town.

Today, you can relive these days of "ore" at Allaire State Park. A walk through the quaint village nestled amid the shady trees is both relaxing and educational. Some of the buildings remain in operation, including the bakery and general store. (Building operation is seasonal, and dependent on volunteers; it's best to call ahead.) The church at Allaire is reputed to be

the only one in New Jersey with its steeple at the rear instead of in the front. A visitor's center explains the history of bog iron.

But there's more to Allaire than just old buildings. At the park you can hike, camp, ride the Pine Creek Railroad (in season), picnic, or just lay on a blanket in the sun. There is a picturesque millpond in the center of the village where children are allowed to fish. In the winter the park offers excellent cross-country skiing.

The Trash Museum/Liberty Science Center

Trash Museum
2 De Korte Park Plaza, Lyndhurst (Bergen County)

Science Center
Liberty State Park
Jersey City (Hudson County)

D I D you know that every year Americans throw away enough aluminum cans to make thirty jet airplanes? Or that we toss away so many rubber tires each day that if you stacked them one on top of each other, they'd be ten times higher than Mount Everest? Or that each person produces 2,000 pounds of garbage per year?

You'd know all these things if you went to the Trash Museum.

The Trash Museum at the Hackensack Meadowlands Developmental Commission Environment Center is especially designed for children. Bright colors, plenty of buttons to push, and cartoon characters painted on the walls make the museum a fun and educational experience for kids—and adults too!

At the Trash Museum you can walk through a giant garbage dump, which contains virtually everything that can be thrown away, including televisions, bicycles, bathtubs, furniture, tires, boxes, clocks, cans, sneakers, toys, telephones, and bottles. There are exhibits that show how to reduce trash through the use of nondisposable items, how recycling works, and examples of beautiful things that can be created from so-called "garbage," such as brightly colored suncatchers made from old soda cans.

---

24 "Psst. Hey, you there. Got any popcorn?" (Photo by Pat King-Roberts)

A popular activity for kids at the museum is playing the Composting Challenge. Children move playing pieces in the form of soup cans and juice boxes toward the finish line on a wall-sized game board, trying to be the first to create a compost heap.

Although the Trash Museum is designed for kids, there's a lot for grownups to think about there as well. It's an enjoyable, educational trip, and the only place where getting "trashed" is a lot of fun!

Since the Trash Museum only takes between sixty and ninety minutes to see in its entirety, after you're finished you may want to head down the Turnpike just a few miles and check out the Liberty Science Center in Liberty State Park.

Kids simply love the Science Center. To them, it's not science and learning, it's just fun. However, little do they know that we sneaky adults have planned it so that they can have fun and learn, all at the same time.

Each of the Science Center's three floors has its own theme: Environment, Health, and Invention. Each area contains a variety of interactive exhibits for children, such as a talking ladybug, a 100-foot-long dark tunnel that kids have to find their way through using only their tactile senses, a computer-controlled driving simulator, and a recording studio mixing booth. There's also a bug zoo, a hologram display, a salt marsh, and many other exhibits that put science into perspective in the world around us.

The highlight of the center is the Kodak Omni Theater, which features a colossal eight-story, 125-foot-high screen and multichannel sound system that practically sweeps you off your feet. At the end of a visit to the Liberty Science Center, both you and your kids are bound to be tired—and a little smarter too.

Edison National Historical Site/Glenmont

Main Street and Lakeside Avenue, West Orange (Essex County)

ALTHOUGH he was known as the "Wizard of Menlo Park," Thomas Alva Edison spent forty-four remarkable years after Menlo Park at his laboratory and home in West Orange, where he continued to plan, produce, and perfect inventions that single-handedly changed the world. The genius of the greatest inventor this country has ever produced is celebrated at the Edison National Historic Site in West Orange, which consists of both his laboratory complex as well as his spacious home, Glenmont.

In 1887, while sick and near death from pneumonia and pleurisy, Edison had a dream that he would build an invention factory that would allow him to be even more creative and productive than he had been at Menlo Park. Admittedly, after inventing the incandescent light bulb and the phonograph Edison had created a tough act to follow, even for himself, but after recovering from his illness he forged ahead with the vision he had seen in his dreams. The result was the West Orange complex, which most historians now consider the first modern research and development facility. Here, various teams worked on many different projects simultaneously, all under the influence and guidance of the great inventor himself.

When Edison wasn't at his laboratory—which wasn't often—he could be found just down the road at Glenmont. This twenty-three-room Queen Anne–style mansion was originally built by an accountant who had among his clients the Arnold Constable department store. When the store wondered how he could afford such a magnificent house on an accountant's salary, the numbers cruncher confessed that he had been skimming money from them. Using a little creative accounting of their own, company officials made him sell the house back to them for one dollar. The

25 Sonny, the African Elephant, at Popcorn Park. (Photo by Pat King-Roberts)

house was vacant when Edison came along; the inventor snapped it up for $125,000, furnishings and all.

Both the laboratory complex and Glenmont can be toured as part of the Edison National Historic Site. The National Park Service likes you to visit the laboratory first before going to Glenmont (to get into the house you need a ticket that can only be obtained at the Visitor's Center).

The laboratory tour is a fascinating journey through the mind of an authentic American legend. Among the highlights are the Phonograph Room, which displays various versions of Edison's landmark invention; the chemical labs; machine shop; and a showing of *The Great Train Robbery*, the Edison-produced film that gave birth to the modern motion picture storyline. There is also a reproduction of the Black Maria, the famous movie studio that Edison built, on the laboratory grounds. Of particular poignancy is the large wall clock in the library; the hands remain forever frozen at 3:27—the time on October 18, 1931, when Edison died.

The laboratory tour helps you discover Edison the inventor; Glenmont provides a glimpse of Edison the man. From the first room that you enter, which displays large photographs of Edison and good friends Henry Ford, Harvey Firestone, and the famous naturalist John Burroughs on camping trips (having not yet discovered L.L. Bean, the group apparently always dressed in suits and ties for these excursions), you know that you're about to see a side of Edison that has escaped the history books.

Considering that the owner gave the world electric light, Edison's house is incredibly dark. Even when viewed in the summer, when the daylight is most intense, much of Glenmont is as dark and gloomy as a haunted house. The first floor was where the Edisons gave parties and formal receptions (everybody who was anybody was always dropping in on the famous inventor). The second floor, which still contains the bed in which Edison died, was used as the living area. A National Park Service guide conducts you through both floors, spinning anecdotes about Edison (he apparently liked to spit tobacco juice on the carpets) all the while.

In a quiet, shady corner of the back yard are the graves of Edison and second wife, Mina. Even though the great man has been dead for many years, his influence is still shaping our world today, in a thousand different ways.

---

*26 The furnace stack from the bog iron works at Allaire State Park.
(Photo by Pat King-Roberts)*

BLACKSMITH SHOP

Built principally of brick in 1836, this structure replaced an earlier Smithy shop which stood between the General Store and the Furnace. At peak operation, the shop had four fires burning at once. Tools were made, horses were shod, and wagonwheels were fitted, chairs were made and repaired, and a whole host of other miscellaneous iron work was performed.

Delaware Water Gap National Recreation Area

Sussex County

I N the tumultuous decade of the 1960s, the expression "What A Rush" became a chic thing to say when something took your breath away or made you gasp in amazement. Undoubtedly, those words have been used many, many times by those seeing the Delaware Water Gap for the first time.

Millions and millions of years ago, the Delaware River began cutting its way through the quartzite rock of the Kittatinny Mountains. Although it would take a millennium to complete the task, the river had time on its side. Today we are the beneficiaries of the river's persistence with the breathtaking natural panorama on display at the Delaware Water Gap. This is one of the most spectacular scenic vistas not only in New Jersey, but in the entire country.

The park consists of 70,000 acres on both the New Jersey and Pennsylvania sides of a thirty-five-mile stretch of the Delaware River. The park was created in 1965 by Congress. (Part of the original plans called for the building of the infamous Tocks Island Dam along the Delaware to provide water and assist in flood control. The project, which was fought tooth-and-nail for years by environmentalists, is currently dormant.)

Even people whose idea of picturesque is a minimall on every corner will be stunned by the raw natural beauty of the Delaware Water Gap. Here is where Nature threw away the manual and just decided to let it all hang out, with awe-inspiring results. Over 200 miles of scenic roads wander through the Water Gap; stopping anywhere can suddenly bring you face to face with wildlife, waterfalls, or trails leading into the forest. Hikers are a common sight here, since a twenty-five-mile portion of the Appalachian Trail cuts through the Kittatinny Ridge.

Of all the vistas, however, none is more spectacular than looking down at the Delaware River from the neighboring mountains. Both the Tammany and Minsi mountains soar 1,200 feet above the river. Here the Delaware is not the shallow, sluggish river that it becomes further south, but a swift-moving engine of immense power that is sixty-feet deep in spots. Gazing down on it from a thousand feet above, it's easy to understand why the Water Gap has attracted landscape artists for centuries.

27 The blacksmith shop at Allaire State Park. (Photo by Pat King-Roberts)

As might be expected, the Delaware Water Gap is a haven for those who love the outdoors. Beside the obligatory sight-seeing, there's also camping, hiking, swimming, boating, picnicking, and fishing to enjoy. When the temperature drops the activities switch to snowmobiling, cross-country skiing, and ice skating.

One of the Water Gap's best-kept secrets is Millbrook Village (twelve miles north of the Kittatinny Point Visitor Center along the Old Mine Road.) The National Park Service runs this restored nineteenth-century village during the warmer months as part of its stewardship of the Water Gap. At Millbrook, employees and volunteers dress up in period costumes and demonstrate such long-lost arts as spinning, weaving, and black-smithing.

The original Millbrook Village was founded in 1832. Abraham Garris damned up Van Campen's Brook to provide water power for his gristmill. People came to work at the mill, as well as provide other needed services to the farmers in the surrounding area. Before long the area had become a small, yet bustling community. At its height Millbrook had a population of approximately seventy-five, and contained a hotel, church, and various businesses. However, when a railroad line was built along the opposite side of Kittatinny Ridge, it gave rise to newer and more modern mills, and

Millbrook was doomed. It was a ghost town when the Park Service took it over and restored it to its former luster.

(Millbrook Village is primarily a summer attraction, although the community does celebrate Millbrook Days on the first weekend in October. It's best to call ahead before going to make sure that there will guides available and buildings open.)

Morristown

(Morris County)

THE name "Morristown" doesn't have the same instant day-trip identification of, say, Cape May or Atlantic City. All the same, this Morris County city, which actually feels more like a small town, has a wealth of attractions that make it an excellent choice for a family looking for a pleasant way to spend the day.

The nice thing about Morristown is its diversity; while most of the sites are history-oriented, there are so many unique parks, museums, and homes to tour that no one should really get bored.

The chief attraction is the Morristown National Historic Park. Dedicated in 1933, as a crowd of ten thousand people packed onto the lawn of the Ford mansion looked on, Morristown was the first National Historic Park in the United States. It consists of three different areas: Fort Nonsense, Jockey Hollow, and Washington's Headquarters/the Historical Museum and Library. These tell the story of how Washington's tattered and half-starved army of approximately 10,000 soldiers braved the infamous "hard winter" of 1779–80, as freedom hung in the balance. With weather conditions here rivaling, if not exceeding, those at Valley Forge, along with bad food, inadequate shelter, and primitive medical supplies, it's a miracle that only eighty-six men died at Morristown during the army encampment.

The peculiar name Fort Nonsense supposedly comes from the soldiers' amazement at being ordered to build an earthen fort on a 600-foot-high hill with no apparent military significance. This story, however, belongs in the same file as all those "Washington slept here" tales. The hill provides

28 *The house in which James P. Allaire lived when he was at the Howell Works. (Photo by Pat King-Roberts)*

an excellent view of the surrounding countryside, particularly of New York City to the east. Clearly, Washington established the outpost to make sure that the British wouldn't sneak up on him, especially from New York, which they occupied while the Continentals were at Morristown. Today nothing remains of the outpost, but a climb up the hill is worth it, particularly on a clear day, when you can see the twin towers of the World Trade Center shimmering in the distance.

Jockey Hollow is where the soldiers built their drafty, cramped, barely heated wooden huts and tried to survive the howling winds and snow of the terrible winter of 1779–80. Although at the time there were 1,200 huts here, today there are just five that were built in the 1930s by the Civilian Conservation Corps. Looking at these, however, and even knowing that they're not the originals, one can't help but wonder at the fortitude of the troops who "lived" in them during a time when they were virtually without food or pay, and had nothing but their faith in the idea of a free and independent country to sustain them. Those who sometimes lose sight of the roots of American democracy can find them easily enough at Jockey Hollow. The National Park Service has deliberately kept the park free of monuments and other typical military park clutter, so that visitors can experience it much as Washington's troops did.

Washington's headquarters while the army was at Morristown was in the Ford Mansion. The home was built between the years 1772–74 by Col. Jacob Ford Jr., who died there of pneumonia in 1777 while serving in the Continental Army. In December 1779, his widow Theodosia offered Washington and his staff the use of the house as their headquarters. (Martha Washington arrived there to keep George company.) They remained there until June 23 of the following year—a total of 200 days, during which time Mrs. Ford and her four children were limited (by choice) to two small rooms on the first floor. The home is somewhat sparsely furnished today because this is the way Mrs. Ford had it during Washington's tenure, since she was afraid of the house being ransacked by Colonial troops.

In the rear of the Ford house is a historical museum and library. The museum contains a vast amount of Revolutionary War period weaponry, as well as other implements such as a soldier's mess kit. (Anyone who is scared of going to the doctor today should take a gander at the primitive eighteenth-century surgeon's kit on display—now that's scary!)

29 Thomas A. Edison in his seventies. (Courtesy U.S. Department of the Interior, National Park Service, Edison National Historic Site)

By now if you've seen all this you're probably exhausted, but Morristown is just getting warmed up. Below is a list of some of the other attractions waiting for you in this big city with the small-town flavor:

☐ Historic Speedwell. Who invented the telegraph? If the first name that leaps to mind is Samuel Morse, then you're neglecting the invaluable and historically ignored contribution of New Jerseyian Alfred Vail. Suffice it to say that without Vail's assistance, there might not have been a telegraph. It was at Speedwell, on the second floor of a factory, that the telegraph was first demonstrated publicly, as Vail and Morse sent messages back and forth over two miles of wire. Indeed, the original nails on which they hung the wire are still in place on the beams. (The factory is now a national historic landmark.) Speedwell also contains over a half-dozen other buildings of historical interest.

☐ If you like flowers, shrubs, trees, and other things growing and green, then the Frelinghuysen Arboretum is for you. Sprawled over 127 acres, it is a green-thumber's delight, complete with a lilac garden, a rose garden, a crab apple collection, and a stunning variety of azaleas and rhododendrons.

□   The Morris Museum of Arts and Sciences is an exceptionally large and extremely complete museum housing exhibits on numerous subjects, including Native Americans of North America, colonial life, minerals, fossils, and art. Kids especially enjoy it here because of the Five Sense Gallery, a "please touch" type of exhibit, and a small zoo with alligators and other critters.

□   In 1852, Paul Revere's grandson Joseph Warren Revere bought a 200-acre farm in Morristown and built a huge country house that he called the Willows. Since then there have been just two other owners of the land, and the last, Caroline Rose Foster, donated it to the Morris County Park Commission before she died in 1979 at the ripe old age of 102. The county left the property as it was, a working farm of the nineteenth century. Now called Fosterfields, the farm is an eye-opening look at how our ancestors worked the soil. Everything at Fosterfields is authentic, and that makes it even more enjoyable.

DID YOU KNOW?

The Wick House, located in Jockey Hollow, was the site of one of the most amazing—albeit undocumented—stories of the Revolutionary War.

One day, twenty-one-year-old Temperance Wick was out riding her horse when she was accosted by several Continental soldiers quartered nearby. When the soldiers saw the good horse Tempe was riding, they told her that the army needed such fine animals, and that they were going to take it. But Tempe—an experienced rider—dug her heels into the horse's flanks and raced away from the men.

Arriving home just ahead of the pursuing soldiers, Tempe led the horse into the house, through the kitchen and parlor, and then into a guest bedroom. The soldiers searched the barn, the outbuildings, and all the other logical places for a horse to be, but never thought of the house. According to the

30   Edison's home, Glenmont. (Photo by author)

31   Edison at his desk in the library of his West Orange Laboratory. (Courtesy U.S. Department of the Interior, National Park Service, Edison National Historic Site) See photo on next page.

legend, Tempe kept the animal hidden in the bedroom for three weeks, until the army left Morristown. Only then did she bring the horse back to the barn (which, for the horse, must have been quite a letdown).

The Thomas H. Kean New Jersey State Aquarium/ Walt Whitman House

Camden (Camden County)
Aquarium
1 Riverside Drive
Whitman House
330 Mickle Street

WHILE it might not replace surf and turf in popularity, the combination of fish and history means fun, excitement, and education too, in Camden.

The New Jersey State Aquarium is Camden's shinning jewel, and an important symbol of that city's rebirth. Nestled along the Delaware River, the aquarium has helped bring both tourists and business attention back to Camden. Since opening in 1992, the aquarium has played host to millions of visitors, who watch and learn about the more than 4,000 fish that now call the facility home.

At the aquarium, the emphasis is on education and interaction, rather than watching fish perform cute tricks with rubber balls. Seal-feedings and talks with divers through "scuba-phones" are typical examples of the presentations there.

This doesn't mean, however, that the aquarium isn't fun. There are plenty of interactive exhibits that let kids and their parents get up close and personal with some denizens of the deep. One of the most popular are two "please touch" tanks, where you can actually feel the rough, leathery hide of a shark, a ray, and other fish. In fact, the whole second floor is like a

---

32   The reconstructed soldier's huts at the Morristown National Historic Park. (Photo by Pat King-Roberts)

---

miniature interactive science museum, where you can do everything from identifying smells to solving quizzes about ocean pollution.

The aquarium is dominated by a gigantic 760,000 gallon tank—the second-largest indoor tank in the United States next to Epcot Center— which contains more than 600 fish swimming back and forth. One of the best times to be there is when the sharks are fed.

Too often eating at a place like this is noisy, dirty, and unpleasant, but the aquarium has thought of that too. A promenade deck outside the cafeteria provides a stunning view of Philadelphia. If you like weather, take special note of the aquarium's dome; it changes color according to the current environmental conditions.

When you've had your fill of fish, try visiting the Walt Whitman House. Just down the road from the New Jersey State Aquarium on Mickle Boulevard, the house is where one of the world's greatest poets spent the last eight years of his life, from 1884 to 1892.

Despite what you've seen on television and at the movies, writing is not a particularly lucrative profession. No one proves this better than Walt Whitman, who struggled financially throughout his entire life. His poems were condemned by many in the straitlaced United States (Europe was much more understanding), and he always seemed to be living with

friends or relatives because he was losing jobs and didn't have any money. Even his landmark work, *Leaves of Grass*, was not highly thought of in the United States throughout most of the poet's lifetime.

(However, there seems to be no truth to stories that have the aged Whitman selling copies of *Leaves of Grass* and other works door-to-door to scrounge up a few bucks. Several biographers, as well as the guide at the Whitman House, have cast doubt on the tale.)

Finally, in the twilight of his life, Whitman managed to sock away enough money to buy a small house in Camden for $1750. Legend has it that the house was only worth $900, but the poet was in the midst of a heated argument with his brother, with whom he lived, when he excused himself, walked around the corner, and bought the house in a fit of I'll-show-you temper.

Whitman was a likeable, if somewhat eccentric, figure in Camden. With his flowing white hair, long white beard, and plain attire (usually he dressed all in gray, although he sometimes wore blue), the poet stood out on the street. Although he was pleasant to those he met, nodding and smiling in response to greetings, he almost never spoke; when he did, it was in a soft and deliberate manner.

The Mickle Street house is packed with Whitman memorabilia, much of which is discussed by the guide during the tour. The reason there is so much material is that Whitman was very concerned with self-promotion (that's why he had over 150 photographs of himself taken throughout his life) and saved many items for the posterity he was certain would come. He also had a devoted group of followers who instantly swooped down on the house immediately following the poet's death and kept it, essentially, as a shrine to him.

Whitman didn't care much for the house, calling it a "shanty" in one letter. Indeed, those who first visit the poet's impressive tomb in nearby

33 The Ford Mansion (Washington's headquarters) (Photo by Pat King-Roberts)

34 The factory building at Historic Speedwell in which the telegraph was publicly demonstrated for the first time (Photo by Pat King-Roberts)

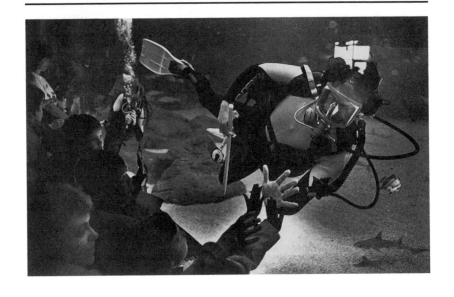

Harleigh Cemetery assume that his home will be just as imposing, and thus drive right by the tiny row home without even a sideways glance. This probably gives Whitman, looking down from poets' heaven, quite a few chuckles. (See chapter 15 for more information on Whitman and his tomb.)

For most of his tenure in the house, Whitman, crippled by illness, was cared for by Mary Davis, a sea captain's widow. Much of the furniture there is hers. As for the Good Gray Poet, there are photos, articles of clothing, personal effects, and many other items to make him come alive.

Duke Gardens

U.S. 206 South, Somerville (Somerset County)

IN 1893, James Buchanan Duke spent approximately $33,000 to buy a large tract of land in Somerville. As the years went by Duke acquired many more surrounding parcels of land without seriously straining his pocketbook. As the founder of the American Tobacco Company, one of the most powerful and successful monopolies of the late-nineteenth, early twentieth century, Duke had more than enough money to do whatever he wanted.

As it turns out, one of the things he wanted to do was create a fabulously landscaped estate in Somerville. Thus began an amazing transformation: At a cost of over ten million dollars and thousands of hours of work by landscapers, gardeners, and laborers, Duke's rolling farmland became a gorgeous garden, complete with nine manmade lakes and 200-foot high hills. For the plantings, Duke imported more than two million shrubs and trees from all over the world.

The result was what is today called the Duke Gardens. Open from October through May, the one-hour-plus tour through this pastoral collec-

35 *The front entrance of the Thomas H. Kean New Jersey State Aquarium at Camden. (Courtesy the Thomas H. Kean New Jersey State Aquarium)*

36 *A scuba diver in the 760,000-gallon tank at the aquarium. (Courtesy the Thomas H. Kean New Jersey State Aquarium)*

tion of trees, flowers, and shrubs is reminiscent of the magnificent palaces of European royalty.

Duke Gardens is actually a series of interconnected greenhouses. Each has its own specific theme and is climate-controlled to maintain the perfect temperature and humidity for the plants. Among the garden themes that you'll encounter are: Italian, Edwardian, French, Chinese, English, and desert. While it is hard to pick out a favorite from among so much beauty, it is impossible to forget the fragrant smell of orange blossoms that wafts through the air in the Indo-Persian Garden or the serenity of the Japanese Garden. You don't have to be a gardener, or even have a green thumb, to enjoy Duke Gardens.

Cape May Point

(Cape May County)

IN the later part of the nineteenth century, the Jersey Shore was still largely undeveloped, and large tracts of land were available to be molded any way one wished. Two men who took advantage of that opportunity were a pair of Philadelphia merchants, who in 1875 founded the town of Sea Grove, which we today know as Cape May Point.

Both John Wanamaker (of department store fame) and Alexander Whilldon were devout Presbyterians, who eyed the success of the Methodist Camp Meeting town of Ocean Grove on the northern New Jersey coast and decided to emulate its success for their own faith. However, like all the other Jersey Shore towns with religious roots (except, of course, Ocean Grove), Sea Grove's emphasis gradually changed from worship to frolic. Today, Cape May Point, along with Cape May Point State Park, provide a different type of day trip than what you may be used to at the Jersey Shore.

Like a chameleon, Cape May Point and Cape May Point State Park can present different appearances. To some they are merely places for outdoor recreation such as fishing, picnicking, and hiking.

But once you visit Cape May Lighthouse, you begin to realize that this is one of the Shore's special places. It is commonly accepted that this historic structure, built in 1859, is the third lighthouse at Cape May Point.

37 Gunther the gray seal gets his teeth brushed. (Photo by Alex Vagelli; Courtesy the Thomas H. Kean New Jersey State Aquarium)

The first was built in 1823 (thanks to erosion, its site is now well out to sea) and the second in the late 1840s. The current lighthouse has always been a popular place to visit (more than 1,800 people trooped up its steps in 1883). Today, a walk up to the watchroom at the top offers a spectacular view of the surrounding region.

For those who like diamonds, those who like rock hunting, and those who just like finding things, Cape May Point State Park offers its famous "Cape May Diamonds," which can be found just lying around Sunset Beach. Before launching into your Carol Channing impersonation, however, be forewarned that these diamonds are actually small pieces of clear quartz, smoothed and polished by the ocean, that gleam in the light like precious gems.

Sunset Beach is also the site of an historical oddity. Here, just a few hundred yards off the beach, are the remains of the concrete warship *Atlantus*. The ship, which is indeed made of concrete, was built by the government during World War I, when a shortage of steel threatened to put a crimp in the U.S. war machine. Although it never saw action in the war—some government genius finally realized that concrete doesn't float too well—it was being utilized as part of a scheme to bring ferry service to Cape May in 1926 when it sank like a stone. It has remained at the foot of

Sunset Beach ever since, slowly sinking into the sand (despite being designated an historic site by the state).

Another wartime artifact, this one from World War II, is also on display—of a type—at Cape May Point. Just off the beach are the remains of a bunker built in 1942, when people were frantic with worry that German submarines were going to be popping up off the coast at any minute. Although once it had a crew that vigilantly kept watch over sea and sky, the decaying hulk has been deserted for over three decades—or is it? Stories have persisted for years that the bunker is haunted, that yelling, laughing, and cursing can be heard coming from inside the long-abandoned building. Some even claim to have seen crew members standing on top of the bunker, only to have them suddenly vanish. Illusion? Tall tales? Who knows?

One thing that is for certain, however, is that Cape May Point offers what could be the best bird watching in the United States. Those knowledgeable in such things say that the area has more variety than anywhere else in North America. (As far back as 1810, pioneer American ornithologist Alexander Wilson observed that Cape May "has the greatest variety of birds.") Among the feathered friends sighted at Cape May are twenty-four species of hawks (the area averages 66,000 hawks per season), eight owls, seventeen sparrows, thirty-six warblers, and forty species of shorebirds. Other birds that are seen at Cape May Point, but hardly anywhere else in New Jersey, include black rails, purple gallinules, Eurasian green-winged teals, western kingbirds, lapland longspurs, and white-winged crossbills.

Bird watching, fishing, rock hunting, a lighthouse, hiking, even a haunting—it's hard to beat all that for a day trip.

High Point State Park

(Sussex County)

LIKE lemmings to the sea, most New Jerseyians sooner or later make a pilgrimage to High Point State Park. This, as the name suggests, is the highest point in the state—1,803 feet above sea level. When you add to

---

38 Walt Whitman circa 1872. (Courtesy Special Collections and Archives, Rutgers University Libraries)

that a 220-foot-tall obelisk that you can climb to get even higher, you can see that when people say that they're "looking down" on New Jersey from here, they mean it in the most literal sense!

The history of High Point State Park illustrates land-use planning at its finest. Because the land is tucked up in the northwest corner of New Jersey, it remained isolated and untouched for centuries. The only building of consequence in the area was the construction in 1888 of High Point Inn near the shore of Lake Marcia.

However, the land probably wouldn't have stayed that way forever had it not been for the Kuser family of Bernardsville, who bought much of the property in 1909. Fourteen years later, Col. Anthony Kuser and his wife donated ten thousand acres to the state so that the land would be preserved for wildlife protection, bird watching, and water conservation.

Thanks to the Kuser's foresight, we can today enjoy High Point State Park in all its natural splendor. The first stop for many visitors is the 220-foot-high obelisk; the Kusers provided the funds to build this monument to New Jersey's soldiers. The top provides a view of three states—New York, New Jersey, and Pennsylvania—plus such natural features as the Catskills, Poconos, and the Delaware Water Gap. From this height can also be seen Lake Marcia, New Jersey's "highest" lake at 1,600 feet above sea level.

Naturally, the main magnet of High Point State Park is its many outdoor activities. Chief among these is hiking (a word to the wise, however; the terrain is frequently uphill and rough). There are ten trails running through the park, including a section of the Appalachian Trail. Fishers can try their luck at catching trout, and large-mouth bass in season, at the lakes and streams in the park; swimming is also permitted in Lake Marcia during the summer.

Other activities include camping, boating, skiing, snowmobiling, and picnicking. The park also contains the state's first natural area, the 200-acre John Dryden Kuser Natural Area. Dedicated in 1965, the area contains a variety of plants and animals, including a stand of Atlantic white cedar, the famous wood of choice of Jersey Shore boat-builders.

Visiting High Point State Park will allow you to say, without qualification, that you've been "on top" in New Jersey.

---

39   The Walt Whitman House on Mickle Boulevard in Camden. (Photo by Pat King-Roberts)

DID YOU KNOW?

Do you need some more ideas about where to go and what to see? Here are some more suggestions for enjoyable New Jersey day trips:

- Take a winery tour. Did you know that New Jersey has a "growing" wine industry? New Jersey ranks among the top wine-producing states in the country. There are over a dozen wineries scattered throughout the state, primarily in the south and northwest. Many of them give tours, have festivals, and offer wine-tasting.
- Visit historic Clinton. You can't help but soak up beauty when walking around this charming Hunterdon County town. Look closely at the red mill with its water wheel; that scene is *de rigueur* for any self-respecting calendar about New Jersey. Throw in the Hunterdon Art Center, and the close proximity of both Spruce Run and Round Valley state parks, and you've got a day trip that could last a week!
- Go to a museum. They're not dark old things filled with dusty dinosaur bones any more. Museums today are alive with the excitement and energy of children and adults enjoying learning while having fun. A short list of interesting New Jersey museums includes the Children's Museum (Paramus), the New Jersey State Museum (Trenton), Franklin Mineral Museum (Franklin), the Aviation Hall of Fame (Teterboro Airport), and the Newark Museum (Newark).
- Visit the Jersey Shore. Although this might seem obvious, did you know that many shore attractions open early in the spring and stay open well into the autumn? And even if everything is closed tighter than a miser's wallet, one of life's incomparable joys is walking on a quiet beach or boardwalk.
- Go on a whale watching or sightseeing cruise. Can there be any better way to spend the day than cruising along the water, with the sea breeze tousling your hair and feeling your heart skip a beat as you catch sight of a whale or dolphin?

CHAPTER SIX

Celebrated Sons and Distinguished Daughters

T H E   P E O P L E in this chapter have two things in common. The first is that they're all famous; each and every one of them have, at one time, been world-renown actors in the great play of life. The second thing they share is a link with New Jersey. Some, like Dorothy Parker and Paul Robeson, were born in New Jersey, but made their mark outside the state. Others, such as Clara Barton, came here and made a significant contribution to the history and heritage of the state. Either way, they are celebrated sons and distinguished daughters of New Jersey, and their stories are now to be told.

Clara Barton.

The immediate reaction to that name is *the Red Cross*. And indeed, Barton's establishment of the famous relief agency is clearly her most important work in a lifetime filled with achievement.

Less well known, however, is that in the decade before the Civil War, Clara Barton performed another very important contribution to society in New Jersey—a contribution that saved lives as surely as did her later work with the Red Cross. The only difference is that in New Jersey, these lives were being threatened not by bullets, but by ignorance.

In the spring of 1852, Clara Barton was a thirty-year-old woman besieged by self-doubt and bouts of depression. In March of that year, she wrote in her journal that she was "badly organized to live in the world or among society," and that she had grown "weary of life at an age when other people are enjoying it most."

"I contribute to the happiness of not a single object and often to the unhappiness of many and always my own, for I am never happy," she wrote. "How long I am to or can endure such a life I do not know."

Contributing to her frequent dark moods was the fact that she was an ambitious, intelligent, resourceful woman in an age when it was virtually useless for a woman to be any of those things. Her burning desire to accomplish something helped propel her into what has been called "the first ambitious project" of her life, the establishment of a free public school in Bordentown, New Jersey.

In the autumn of 1851, possibly to alleviate her gloom, Barton journeyed to New Jersey to visit Mary Norton, a friend who taught school in nearby Hightstown. A teacher herself, Barton had taught in Massachusetts and Washington, D.C., for over a decade, but was seeking new horizons by the time she came to New Jersey. When after a few weeks Barton became restless and wanted to leave, Norton begged her to teach winter school—a feat never before undertaken by a woman—in Hightstown. Eagerly accepting, Barton taught a class of forty farm boys for several months.

What bothered her about the job, however, was that her students came only from families who could afford to pay for the privilege of education; in essence, the school was a private one, although the term was not then in vogue. The children of those who could not afford school were simply left to their own devices, because they were not considered worthy of education.

Although the New Jersey legislature had passed a bill designed to spread public schools throughout the state, widespread opposition to the measure had made it a paper law without hope of enforcement. This bothered Barton, who longed for the true public education system she had encountered in Massachusetts.

While at Hightstown, Barton heard about the deplorable state of education in nearby Bordentown; gangs of boys, it was said, were lolling about the streets with nothing to do. Going there, she found the rumors to be true: "I found them [the boys] on all sides of me. Every street corner had little knots of them idle, listless, as if to say, what shall one do, when one has nothing to do?"

Talking to the boys, Barton found that they, far from being gleeful at escaping the classroom, were actually unhappy about it. "Lady, there is no

40 Clara Barton during her days as a school teacher. (Courtesy American Red Cross)

school for us," said a fourteen year old. "We would be glad to go if there was one."

With her reforming spirit thus stoked, she marched up to Peter Suydam, chairman of the local school board, and demanded to know why there wasn't a free public school in Bordentown.

Calling the boys "renegades," Suydam explained politely to the tiny but determined Barton that they were more fit for the penitentiary than school. "They wouldn't go to school if they had a chance," he said, adding that a female schoolteacher could do nothing with them.

Suydam's words were like a red flag waved in front of a bull. Barton offered to open a school for them and to teach without pay, as long as the school board backed her efforts.

Suydam had more objections: The boys' parents would never send their kids to a "pauper school"; the entire town would be up in arms at the idea; and, the ladies who taught private schools in the town would be Barton's enemies.

But Suydam had reckoned without the persistence of the New England woman. Eventually, she won him over. On July 1, 1852, the school board issued her a teacher's certificate and established a small, shabby school-house for her. Notices a foot square "advertising" the school were posted throughout the town.

On the first morning of school, Barton, with "a few books and a desk outfit," walked to the building. There she found six boys, ranging in age from six to fourteen, sitting on the rail fence waiting for her. With a confident smile she led them into the long-abandoned building.

"I recall at this day," she later wrote, "the combination of odors that greeted the olfactories. The old musty smell of a long shut untidy house, the pungent flavor of freshly cut southern pitch pine, and the bitter soot of the long iron stove pipe rusting for years."

She and her six charges devoted the morning to cleaning the school-room. In the afternoon Barton led her students on a geographical trip around the world, so that by the end of the day, "We were travelers and really knew more about the world and its ways than we ever had before in our lives."

When she arrived at school the next morning Barton got a shock; her class of six had more than doubled in size, to sixteen. By that afternoon it had become twenty, and by the end of the week forty boys were in attendance. On the Monday morning of her second full week fifty-five boys jammed into the little schoolhouse, forcing Barton to give up her desk and chair. In the third week a breakthrough occurred when girls began showing up as well. The larger boys squeezed smaller ones beside them to make room for the new arrivals.

---

41 The Clara Barton schoolhouse today in Bordentown. (Photo by Pat King-Roberts)

As classes continued to grow, Barton recruited several assistants and expanded her "classroom" into a hallway above a tailor's shop. Many people began taking their children out of the private schools and sending them to Barton.

Barton enjoyed living in Bordentown. She loved taking long walks through the woods, with the "silver flow of the Delaware [River] below [the] rocky bluffs." She also enjoyed tramping through Point Breeze, the former estate of Napoleon Bonaparte's elder brother Joseph. Although Joseph had been gone from Bordentown for twenty years, the grounds were much as he had left them. Barton considered the "miles of shrubs and flowers, its walks, its rests, the ripple of brooks, and the unceasing song of birds—the repose of nature—a home fit for a King."

Barton's roommate for much of her time in Bordentown was Frances Childs, who Barton had recruited to become her first assistant teacher. The two teachers got along famously.

"She said to me once," Childs wrote, "that of all the qualities she possessed, that for which she felt most thankful was her sense of humor. She said it helped her over many hard places."

Yet even at the height of her triumph, Barton was haunted by doubt. At a time when most people embraced a career for life, Barton continued to smolder with new ideas and attitudes. "Had ever one poor girl so many strange wild thoughts, and no one to listen or share one of them or ever realize that my head contains an idea beyond the present foolish moment," she wrote.

One thing she did not have to worry about was the success of her school. By the end of the first year, enrollment was a building-bulging 600 students, and the town had to build a new $4,000 schoolhouse. This might have been the thing to keep Barton in Bordentown, and history would have been very different indeed. However, along with the new building, the school board created the position of principal. Then, in a scenario all too familiar today, the school board gave the job to a man, despite Barton's overwhelming qualifications.

Grievously disappointed, Barton tried to continue teaching. But after a few months, a persecution campaign organized by her new boss and her own mental anguish caused Barton to suffer from a severe case of laryngitis. Citing this as the reason, she resigned her position.

"I could bear the ingratitude, but not the pettiness and jealousy of this principal," she later wrote.

Early in February 1854, Barton left for Washington, D.C., where the clouds of civil war were already gathering. Although she couldn't know it at the time, Barton's teaching career was over. Ahead lay the Red Cross.

In later years Clara Barton would be credited with starting the first public school in New Jersey. While this may or may not be true—there seem to have been some small steps toward public education in a few large cities in the state—there is no doubt that the success of Barton's school, and the notoriety it received, set the wheels of New Jersey public education firmly in motion. No longer could elitists claim that education should be just for those who could afford it. Clara Barton had shattered the lies and the excuses, and in so doing opened the school door for *all* children in New Jersey.

Who was the first president of the United States?

If you're like 99.99 percent of the people in New Jersey (as well as the rest of the country), your answer is "George Washington." That would be a good answer, too—except that it's wrong.

In actuality, the first president of the United States was Elias Boudinot of New Jersey.

However, don't begin throwing out your vast collection of Washington's Birthday decorations; the Father of Our Country is still the first president of the United States as we know it. It's actually just some historical hair-splitting not significant enough to change all the textbooks, that designates Boudinot as the first president. Still, it's appropriate that Elias Boudinot is denied his rightful place in history, for no other figure from this era of independence is so important, and yet so obscure, as this eminent New Jerseyian.

Elias Boudinot was born on May 2, 1740, in Philadelphia. Around 1750 Boudinot's father, a silversmith, moved first to Rocky Hill and then to Princeton, in order to be closer to a copper mine in which he held an interest. Thus New Jersey became young Elias's home; it would remain so for the rest of his life.

Although he wanted to be a minister, because of his family's feeble financial state young Boudinot had to choose a career that did not require college, and so became a lawyer (and isn't that a switch!). After marriage to Hannah Stockton in 1765, it seemed as if Boudinot was ready to follow a familiar path in colonial times: establish a career, marry, have children, and work at becoming prosperous.

But big changes were in store for everyone in the colonies, including Boudinot. Perhaps he should have seen it coming when his nine-year-old daughter, Susan, during tea at the home of Royal Governor William Franklin (son of Benjamin) of New Jersey, walked to the window and deliberately dumped the drink onto some nearby bushes.

Shortly thereafter, a group of colonists protesting the high tax on tea reenacted Susan's action on a larger scale by throwing chests of tea into Boston Harbor. The Boston Tea Party set the colonies on a collision course with Great Britain that finally erupted into war at Lexington and Concord in April 1775. Although at first Boudinot hoped for reconciliation with the mother country, by early 1777 he was firmly on the side of independence. Soon he would be in the midst of the revolution he had once opposed.

Boudinot plunged headfirst into the conflict in April 1777, when George Washington asked him to become the commissary general of prisoners for the Continental Army. Although Washington's letter arrived on April Fool's Day, the job was no joke; the commissary general was responsible for taking care of British prisoners of war, arranging prisoner transfers, making sure that American prisoners were being treated right, and a variety of other delicate tasks. Although constantly hampered by a lack of funds with which to buy American prisoners food, clothing, and other necessities, Boudinot greatly improved conditions for the captive Continentals. A compassionate man, Boudinot could not bear to see or hear of Americans suffering and so, many times, when money was tight, he used his own. Boudinot wound up spending $45,000 of his own funds to buy supplies and other items for the Continental prisoners.

Boudinot worked as the commissary general of prisoners for over a year. Upon resigning the often-frustrating post in May of 1778, he served as a New Jersey delegate to the Continental Congress. Following the completion of his term, he returned home and tried to pick up the pieces of his family and professional life, which had largely been ignored during his time in public service.

For three years Boudinot remained a private citizen. He obviously worked overtime at building up the family fortune, for within a few years he had large land holdings in New Jersey, Ohio, Pennsylvania, North Carolina, and New York. Then, in July 1781, the nation came calling again; the New Jersey legislature elected him to the Congress to fill an unexpired term. Somewhat reluctantly, Boudinot went back into public life.

By the summer of 1781, the assistance of the French had helped swing the war pendulum in favor of the United States. When Washington trapped Cornwallis at Yorktown in October of that same year, everyone thought that the war was over and that a peace treaty with Great Britain

42 *Elias Boudinot in later years. (Courtesy the American Bible Society)*

was imminent. The war was over, all right—but peace remained as elusive as ever.

Meanwhile, Boudinot continued to be reelected to Congress by the New Jersey legislature. Although a patriot, his vast land holdings made him favor the aristocracy and all the privileges that went with being a member of that class. This got him into several spirited scraps with a young Virginian named James Madison, a vociferous champion of the common man.

At this point the former colonies were operating under the Articles of Confederation, the forerunner to the Constitution. This document elevated the states to supreme sovereignty over the union; so much so, in fact, that the country was referred to as the "united States," the queer capitalization being used to distinguish the superiority of each individual member over the union of the whole.

The Articles of Confederation did not provide for a president of the nation as we know the office today; the closest thing was the president of Congress. It had been the practice to rotate the office yearly among the states, and when the new session of Congress opened in November 1782, New Jersey had yet to contribute a president. Thus it didn't take too many people by surprise when Boudinot was tapped for the post. Apparently, however, the election threw Boudinot's plans into disarray, as he indicated in a November 4 letter to his wife:

> The things of this World are as uncertain as the Wind. . . . This moment I have accepted the President's chair of Congress, not without a trembling hand. . . . The confusion of my affairs and the total derangement of all my Plans and indeed the great loss & Expense that must ensue to me in my circumstances with the difficulties that will necessarily devolve on you, have not been unthought of by me. . . . But these reflections even are now in vain . . . the ways of Providence are in the great Deep.

Some of those difficulties became quickly apparent to Hannah, when Boudinot followed with another letter two days later that basically told her to pack up everything, scrape together every cent she could, wind up his affairs, and get to Philadelphia without delay. Such were the woes of the patriot's wife!

Boudinot's presidency came at a critical time for the young republic. Although the Yorktown victory had ended the fighting, negotiations with Great Britain had not yet produced a peace treaty. Not only did Boudinot have to continually monitor the negotiations, he also had to deal with several crises that revealed how weak the Articles of Confederation were as a governmental framework. One flaw was that nothing compelled the states to participate in Congress, and several times Boudinot had to beg states (Delaware, Maryland, and Georgia were prime offenders) to send delegates to Philadelphia so that the government could function.

Another problem was that there was no revenue-raising mechanism in place, and the government was always down to its last dollar. This brought the country to the brink of anarchy when several hundred soldiers demanding back pay marched on Philadelphia and surrounded the building where Congress was meeting. Finances were so bleak that when peace negotiations with England faltered and it looked as if the war might be renewed, Congress had to tell Washington he couldn't plan any military activities because the government couldn't afford it.

However, it wasn't all bad for the man from New Jersey. On September 3, 1783, came the event that the entire nation had been waiting for, and the occasion that made Boudinot the answer to the trivia question: "Who was the first president of the United States?" On that date, Great Britain signed the Treaty of Paris, formally ending the state of war between the two countries. Before this, the states had technically still been colonies; this document formally recognized, for the first time anywhere, their existence as a free and sovereign nation. Since the treaty was signed during Boudinot's term as president of Congress, Elias Boudinot became the first president of the new nation of the United States of America.

Another happy occasion during Boudinot's term was the issuance of the first national Thanksgiving Day Proclamation. Although the document was drafted by a congressional committee, the language is very reminiscent of Boudinot, and it would not be surprising to someday discover that he had a hand in the writing.

As the end of his term as president drew near, Boudinot requested that he be allowed to return to his home in Elizabeth as a private citizen, and not be reelected to the Congress. This wish was granted, and once more Boudinot picked up the pieces of his life.

But the United States simply could not afford to let a man of Boudinot's talents go. Subsequently he served six more years in Congress, and ten years as director of the fledgling United States Mint. After retiring to Burlington in 1805, in a magnificent home at the corner of Broad and Talbot streets, he returned to his first love, religion, and helped to found the American Bible Society in 1816.

Elias Boudinot died on October 24, 1821, at age eighty-one, and was buried in Burlington next to his wife, who had died thirteen years earlier. A true giant of the tumultuous era of independence, he has been overshadowed by the greatness of contemporaries such as Washington, Hamilton, and Jefferson. Yet even if the memories have faded, the result of Boudinot's many years of public service live on in the great monument to liberty and freedom that he helped to create called the United States of America.

DID YOU KNOW?

When the army demanded back pay and accosted the Congress in Philadelphia, it made many members fearful that the city was unsafe. Boudinot adjourned the body and reconvened it in Princeton, thereby making the college town the official capital of the United States. At first Congress met at the home of Col. George Morgan; subsequent meetings were held in Nassau Hall on the college campus. The sudden notoriety turned the sleepy little village upside down. The formerly quiet streets were suddenly filled with the hustle and bustle of clattering carriages, people constantly coming and going, and merchants hawking all manner of goods and services at all hours of the day and night. It was a distinctive time for the little town—especially when men such as George Washington, John Paul Jones, and Thomas Jefferson could be seen walking the streets—but also a riotous one.

Fame is like cancer; it tends to feed upon itself until it kills its host. Such was the case with New Jersey–born and bred Dorothy Parker, one of the leading writers of the early twentieth century, who was devoured by fame as well as her own self-doubt as she desperately searched for meaning in a world that frequently didn't make sense.

Dorothy Parker was born in West End, New Jersey, then a separate community in Monmouth County but now part of Long Branch. Her parents were Henry and Eliza Rothschild, who packed up the family every June and brought them to the Jersey Shore to escape the heat and sooty summer air of New York City.

The Rothschilds loved the shore. With Eliza pregnant in the summer of 1893, the Rothschilds were particularly looking forward to relaxing in the Cedar Avenue home they had rented before the new baby arrived in November. At the shore they frolicked in the surf, attended nightly band concerts, and strolled past the huge, glittering Long Branch casinos, where thousands of dollars were won or lost on a single nod of the head.

The vacation came to an abrupt halt on August 22, when Eliza went into labor. Shortly thereafter, she gave birth to her fourth child, two months premature. Years later, displaying the wit that would make her famous, Dorothy Parker described her birth as "the last time I was early for anything."

The shore had always meant happiness for the Rothschild family, and so they continued to go there each summer after Parker's birth. Possibly Henry was hoping that the salt air would invigorate his wife, who grew frailer and more tired with each passing year after Parker's birth. In July 1898, after a short illness, Eliza died in the Cedar Avenue home. Parker's father promptly went out and found another mother for his children, a spinster schoolteacher named Eleanor Lewis. Naturally, all the children hated her, as children are wont to do with the "replacement." When Eleanor suddenly died also, in 1903, of a cerebral hemorrhage, the double deaths cemented a permanent fascination with death in young Dorothy. (They also made her wary of mothers. A loving mother never appeared in any of her short stories.)

In the spring of 1906 her father enrolled Parker in Miss Dana's School for Young Ladies on South Street in Morristown, New Jersey. There is conflicting evidence on whether or not she enjoyed her tenure there, with the school's emphasis on preparing a young lady to be a good wife and mother. Parker stayed at the school until she graduated in 1910, shortly before it went bankrupt (because of yet another death in Parker's life—the founder of the school, Elizabeth Dana).

Parker had always shown an affinity for writing short verse. Her letters home from the Dana School to her father were filled with clever sayings and rhymes, such as the following:

> Dear Papa,
> This morning I received your "pome,"
> How did you do it all alone?
> When you come down on Sunday, Pa,
> No, nothing rhymes except cigar.

In 1913, when Parker was twenty years old, her father died. Without money, and no family relations to fall back on, she drifted for a while. However, she was still writing light verse, and in 1915 this helped land her a job at *Vogue* magazine in New York. Around the same time she met and fell in love with stockbroker Edwin Pond Parker II. The couple was married in June 1917. Although long after the marriage had ended, she would crack that she married Parker because he had a "nice, clean name" (she hated the name Rothschild because it was so Jewish), in the beginning the two of them did indeed care for each other.

Nineteen-seventeen was also the year that Parker moved to *Vanity Fair* magazine and began her meteoric rise to fame. Uncertain what to do with her at first, editor Frank Crowninshield eventually made her the drama critic. This was the perfect forum for Parker's acidic wit and ability to write short, snappy sentences that cut like a stiletto. And cut she did—early and often. She dismissed one play with the comment that it provided an excellent atmosphere in which to do knitting: "If you don't knit, bring a book," she added. For another show she refused to print the names of cast and crew because she was "not going to tell on them." In one of her most memorable columns, she ignored the play completely, and instead reviewed the overwrought performance of the woman sitting next to her, who had lost a glove.

At the same time that she was performing hatchet jobs on Broadway productions, she became friendly with two other *Vanity Fair* writers, Robert Benchley and Robert Sherwood, who were just like her: witty, sarcastic, and self-deprecating. The three became inseparable, and began lunching at the Algonquin Hotel. The hotel was becoming a meeting place for other literary lights of the Roaring Twenties, including Alexander Woollcott, Harold Ross, and Franklin P. Adams. Like schoolchildren playing hooky the group would sit at a long table in the Algonquin for hours at a time during work hours, laughing, eating, drinking, and cutting up anyone and anything that struck their fancy. Thus was born the legendary "Round Table at the Algonquin."

Of the entire group, Parker was the cleverest. Quips, cracks, and jibes rolled off her tongue like rainwater off a roof; even her friends were afraid of her withering comments. Many of her bon mots were picked up and run in the New York newspapers, and it wasn't long before she was being hailed as "America's Wittiest Woman." Once a person gets a reputation like that, it gains its own berserk momentum, as Parker soon found out. Like Yogi Berra, Parker didn't say half the things attributed to her, but it didn't matter; before she was twenty-seven years old, Dorothy Parker was a superstar. It would prove to be a hard label to live up to.

In 1927 Parker moved to *The New Yorker* as the magazine's leading book critic. For the next few years, using the nom de plume Constant Reader, she unleashed her scathing wit on books ranging from novels to cookbooks. However, she was also working on her own writing; between 1926 and 1933 she produced three poetry volumes and two books of short stories. All were critical and commercial successes and further cemented her reputation as a literary whiz kid.

But lurking just beneath Parker's surface were uncontrollable demons. Her preoccupation with death, coupled with an utter lack of self-worth and a constant search for the unattainable ideal of true love, turned her into an alcoholic before she was thirty. (Her Round Table friends helped; most were alcoholics as well.) Haunted by feelings of inadequacy, Parker tried to kill herself four times between 1923 and 1932; these failed attempts led her to even harsher conclusions about herself, and drove her into a bottomless pit of depression from which she never escaped.

Despair ruled Parker's life. "What fresh hell is this?" she would exclaim when the doorbell rang, expecting as always to find nothing but pain and trouble awaiting her on the other side of the doorway. When her ever-present bottle of Scotch failed to numb her pain, Parker turned to Veronal, a sodium barbital-style sedative. Although a prescription was needed to obtain Veronal in New York, none was required in New Jersey. Parker went on a drugstore binge in Newark, buying Veronal as well as emery boards, talcum powder, and other things in order not to arouse suspicion.

The themes of hopelessness, despair, death, and suicide permeated virtually all of Parker's work, painting a vivid portrait of a mind in torment. Typical of her sparse, world-weary style is the poem "Resume." In eight chillingly mater-of-fact lines, Parker lists the problems with all the various methods of suicide, such as the awful smell of gas, and the cramps that a drug overdose can cause. "You might as well live" she decides sardonically in the last line. (The phrase is a direct quote from Robert Benchley, who made the comment to her in the hospital after her first suicide attempt.)

Sadly, although much of Parker's work is filled with that type of edge-of-the-cliff intensity, her literary legacy is scarce almost to the point of being nonexistent. She was always careless, even disdainful, of deadlines, and editors never knew if a piece from her would *ever* arrive, never mind by the deadline. "It is a high forceps delivery every time we manage to get a piece out of her," commented one of her editors in frustration. Another thought that she detested writing, and so avoided it whenever she could.

Eventually, Parker solved her problem with writing and deadlines by ceasing to write. In 1934 she and her second husband, an actor named Alan Campbell, moved to Hollywood to begin a career as a screenwriting team. This decision effectively killed Parker's creativity. Like countless other writers before and since, she was chewed up and spit out by the Hollywood formula of always having someone else rewriting what you've just written. As her work was revised, edited, changed, and discarded, Parker became even more bitter and discouraged, possibly because she knew that she was bastardizing her talents for the sake of drawing a hefty salary and being able to drink and live in style. From 1934 to the end of her life, Parker produced just eleven more short stories and little other work of consequence.

After Campbell's death in 1963, Parker returned to New York City. There, alone as always, with only a dog and alcohol for company, she died on June 7, 1967.

In her later years, Parker had told a friend, "Don't feel badly when I die. I've been dead for a long time." There was more truth in that statement than anyone knew. Dorothy Parker had died the moment she laid down her pen in the early 1930s and stopped writing her incredible short stories and poems. The rest of her life was just a long, slow ride to the mortuary. Sadly, it seems as if she was more aware of this than anybody.

Here are some of the most famous lines from "America's Wittiest Woman":

☐ "If all the girls in attendance [at the Yale prom] were laid end to end, I wouldn't be surprised."

☐ When *The New Yorker* was struggling to survive in its early years, publisher Harold Ross asked Dorothy why she hadn't come in to write her article. Her response: "Somebody was using the pencil."

☐ During one of her hospital stays, Parker pressed the button marked NURSE: "This should ensure us at least forty-five minutes undisturbed privacy."

☐ After she had an abortion: "Serves me bloody right for putting all my eggs into one bastard."

☐ "Men seldom makes passes at girls who wear glasses."

☐ Upon looking at an apartment to live in: "This is much too big. All I need is room enough to lay a hat and a few friends."

☐ Upon being asked where all the people at a party had come from: "When it's all over, they crawl back into the woodwork."

☐ "I require only three things of a man. He must be handsome, ruthless, and stupid."

☐ After hearing that a female friend had injured herself in London: "She must have hurt herself sliding down a barrister."

Like Dorothy Parker, Paul Robeson was a keen observer of the world around him. Unlike Parker, however, the internationally renowned African-American singer, actor, and social activist used the spoken word rather than the written to tell people exactly what he thought of that world. The tragedy of Paul Robeson was that he lived in a time when it was dangerous to speak your mind.

Paul Leroy Robeson was born in Princeton on April 9, 1898. His father was the Reverend William Drew Robeson, a slave in North Carolina until age fifteen when he escaped to the North via the Underground Railroad. Maria Louisa Bustill Robeson, Paul's mother, burned to death when he was six years old when hot coals from the household stove fell onto her dress and ignited it.

A few months after his wife's death, Reverend Robeson moved the family first to Westfield and then Somerville. Despite being one of only two black children in Somerville High School, young Paul graduated with honors.

In 1915 the seventeen-year-old Robeson entered Rutgers University, only the third black student ever to attend the school. Having starred in football at Somerville, Robeson wanted to play on the Rutgers team almost as much as the coach, George Foster Sanford, wanted the big, strapping athlete to play. But this was not a time of racial tolerance. At the first scrimmage, as Robeson later recalled: "One boy slugged me in the face and smashed my nose . . . and then, as I was down, flat on my back, another boy got me with his knee . . . dislocating my right shoulder."

These injuries kept him in bed for ten days. But Paul Robeson was no quitter, as his teammates soon found out. On his first practice back he made tackle after tackle on defense, despite receiving an inordinate amount of punishment from the other players. The crowning blow came when a player stepped on Robeson's outstretched hand and ripped off his fingernails. In a rage, on the next play Robeson shredded the interference, grabbed the ball carrier, and hoisted him over his head. At that moment Sanford yelled out, "Robey, you're on the varsity."

It was one of the best decisions Sanford ever made. Robeson starred in football for Rutgers, twice being named a Walter Camp All-American. He also won letters in baseball, basketball, and track. No slouch in the classroom either, he won Phi Beta Kappa honors, and was chosen class valedictorian.

After graduating from Rutgers, Robeson enrolled in Columbia University Law School and settled down to study for what he assumed would be a career as an attorney. But fate had other plans. He began to be drawn toward the theater, appearing in productions like the Harlem YMCA's presentation *Simon the Cyrenian*. Although he continued to pursue his law degree, the acting itch grew steadily worse. In the summer of 1922 he had a featured role in the play *Voodoo*, which subsequently toured London.

Upon his return to the United States Robeson completed his studies at Columbia and in 1923 received his law degree. "At this time," he remembered, "I was an aspiring lawyer. . . . Theatre and concerts were furthest from my mind." After working for several months at a prestigious law firm in New York City, however, he quit when a white secretary wouldn't take dictation from him. But the law's loss was the theater's gain. Eugene O'Neill, whom Robeson had met before, offered him the lead role in *All God's Chillun Got Wings*, and an actor was born. (O'Neill called Robeson "a young fellow with considerable experience, wonderful presence and voice, full of ambition and a damn fine man personally.")

Robeson's work in *Wings* got him the lead in another O'Neill play, *The Emperor Jones*. While the play wasn't a great success, it led to another defining moment in the young man's life. One scene required him to exit while whistling; unable to whistle, Robeson reached back to his roots as a boy in his father's church and sang a spiritual instead. The majesty of his deep bass voice was instantly electrifying. Everyone knew that it was something special indeed.

Robeson couldn't have picked a better time to become an entertainer. This was the era of the legendary Harlem Renaissance, when black performers like Josephine Baker, Eubie Blake, and Claude McKay fostered a growing recognition of African-American artists. Black actors, actresses, and singers were in demand on Broadway and in Hollywood to play real roles, not the demeaning, feet-shuffling clowns of years past. Young, talented, and handsome, Paul Robeson was every casting director's dream.

Robeson became known as much for his singing as his acting. One critic wrote that his was a voice in which "deep bells ring." His concert tours both at home and abroad were tremendously successful. Singing mainly spirituals, Robeson poured his heart and soul into each verse, leaving both he and his audience emotionally drained at the conclusion. His performance as Joe in *Show Boat* (both the play and film), in which he sang Jerome Kern's *Ol' Man River*, still stands as an entertainment milestone.

Yet something else was happening to Paul Robeson during these years of his growth and maturity as an artist. Always conscious of prejudice—he and his wife, Eslanda, had moved to London in the 1920s to escape the poisonous racial atmosphere in the United States—Robeson began to link the sufferings of blacks with those of other oppressed peoples around the world. Now, instead of singing at opulent concert halls, he began giving concerts in small auditoriums at inexpensive prices so that the less-affluent could attend. Expanding his repertoire to include folk music from other countries (which won him a broad international following), he announced that he would not sing any music that he couldn't feel in his soul.

In December 1934, Robeson went to the Soviet Union to meet filmmaker Sergei Eisenstein. Unaware of his popularity in that country, he was stunned when thousands of Russians roared their approval of "Pavel Robesona." He was also pleasantly surprised by Soviet society. Racial toler-

43 Paul Robeson early in his career. (Courtesy Special Collections and Archives, Rutgers University Libraries) ance was taught in the schools, and Russia's numerous ethnic groups were being encouraged to get along. After the bitterness and hatred he had experienced in the United States, Robeson found this atmosphere unbelievably refreshing. "I feel like a human being for the first time since I grew up," he told Eisenstein. "Here I am not a Negro but a human being. . . . Here, for the first time in my life, I walk in full dignity."

This trip began a fascination with Russian life and the Soviet Union for Robeson, an appeal that went so far that he even enrolled his son Paul Jr. in a Russian school in 1936. It was far more the lack of racial prejudice than any infatuation with communism that led Robeson down this path, and in the 1930s he was not alone. Many people, both in the United States

and abroad, were drawn to the Soviet Union because of the country's reputation as a champion of the oppressed.

Things changed quickly, however, once World War II ended. As Stalin inexorably drew the Iron Curtain around Europe, the Soviet Union changed from wartime ally to enemy. Anyone who had ever said anything complimentary about Russia was considered a traitor. The House Un-American Activities Committee bred an attitude of paranoia and suspicion throughout the country by grilling supposed "communists" and "fellow travelers." It didn't take a genius to know that Robeson's extremely vocal support of Russia in the past was going to come back to haunt him.

The persecution began innocently enough, with a few concerts being canceled. Then the press began to pepper Robeson with questions like "Are you a communist?" Robeson was hauled before the California Legislative Committee on Un-American Activities, where he was asked if he was or had been a member of the Communist party—a charge he angrily denied. Then, in August 1949, a howling mob attacked people leaving a Robeson concert in Peekskill, New York. While the police who were supposed to provide protection stood idly by, dozens of innocent people were beaten by anti-Robeson thugs. When an "investigation" ordered by New York Governor Thomas E. Dewey failed to blame the police or the rioters for the incident, Dewey redirected it to find out whether the concert was "part of the Communist strategy to foment racial and religious hatreds."

Harassment of Robeson steadily increased. The FBI kept him under constant surveillance and work became almost nonexistent, thanks to an entertainment-industry boycott. (Robeson's annual income at one point shrunk to $6,000.) Former friends now crossed the street to avoid him. In August 1950, the State Department canceled his passport, a move that one newspaper said would "be acclaimed by every firm-minded American." Throughout it all, Robeson remained defiant. "I will not retreat," he said. "Not even one thousandth part of one inch."

In June 1956, came the confrontation everyone was waiting for: Robeson was called before the House Un-American Activities Committee. Those hoping for a public crucifixion, however, were disappointed. Instead of cow-towing, like most other witnesses, Robeson repeatedly attacked the committee, questioning their integrity and denouncing them for the witch-hunt mentality they had fostered. "You are the nonpatriots,

44 Paul Robeson as Othello, with Uta Hagen. (Courtesy Special Collections and Archives, Rutgers University Libraries)

and you are the un-Americans and you ought to be ashamed of yourselves," Robeson charged, in his memorable bass voice.

As the 1950s ebbed, so did the anticommunist zeal; Americans began to pull their heads out of the sand and realize what they'd done to many innocent people who had merely expressed a different point of view. For Paul Robeson, however, the regrets came too late. The years of struggle and anguish had taken their toll on his once-powerful body. Beginning in 1958, his health began to fail. In December 1963, besieged by illness, he retired from public life.

After Eslanda died in 1965, the frail Robeson went to live with his sister Marion in Philadelphia, where he died on January 23, 1976. Death had finally done what years of persecution could not—still Paul Robeson's powerful voice.

Robeson's death was reported on page one of the *New York Times*, which devoted a long introspective story to his life. "The tragedy of Paul Robeson, like that of Othello, was stark; virtue and misjudgment were sharply juxtaposed," editorialized the newspaper. "Yet Paul Robeson, like Othello on his deathbed, could honestly say, 'I have done the state some service, and they know 't.'"

DID YOU KNOW?

Known for his lightning-like quickness on the football field, Robeson made perhaps his best play during a scrimmage in the autumn of 1918. After making an acrobatic grab of a pass, wide receiver Jim Burke tumbled fifty feet down an embankment and fell into a canal. Robeson, in full football gear, raced down the bank, dove into the water, and pulled Burke to shore, almost certainly saving his life.

This chapter has already told the story of Elias Boudinot, an important figure in the fight for independence whose story has been obscured by the greatness of his fellow revolutionaries. But there's obscure, and then there's *forgotten;* a case in point is Garrett A. Hobart, New Jersey's only vice-president of the United States.

In fairness, Hobart was a capable man and not the embarrassment that some vice-presidents become. However, the vice-presidency is, by its very nature, an obscure office; if people's lives depended upon naming ten vice-presidents of the United States, we'd have a sparsely populated country. Hobart's misfortune was to be a colorless man in an invisible office.

Garrett Augustus Hobart was born on June 3, 1844, in Long Branch. The son of Addison Willard Hobart and the former Sophia Vanderveer, Hobart graduated from Rutgers in 1863 and embarked upon a highly successful law career. After marrying Jennie Tuttle in 1869, Hobart entered New Jersey politics. He was elected to both the State Assembly and the Senate, serving as the speaker and president, respectively, of each body. In his only try for higher office, he lost a race for the United States Senate.

But it is not as a national political figure that Hobart made his mark in the Republican party. He was a money man, plain and simple, good at spending his own funds and getting others to part with theirs. Hobart practically oozed cash; he was the chairman of the board of directors of a mind-boggling sixty corporations and owned banks, railroads, and even a water company.

As chairman of the New Jersey Republican Committee from 1880 through 1891, Hobart had ample opportunity to make friends with the party's king-makers, especially party chairman Mark Hanna. In 1896 Hanna got his fellow Ohioan, a pleasant, tepid man named William McKinley, the Republican presidential nomination. Hobart was able to secure the second spot on the ticket, thanks to his money, his efforts on behalf of Republicans throughout the country, and his relationship with Hanna. In the election, a national economic recession helped sweep the Republicans into the White House.

Hobart, despite a fear of public speaking (and doesn't that sound like a little slice of heaven!), was a remarkably effective vice-president. As a man used to operating behind the scenes he knew how to get things done, and Hobart became a successful liaison between the White House and the Senate. Hobart also frequently opened his home to lawmakers, and the gracious hospitality of both he and his wife—cigars and liquor were always in season at the Hobarts'—helped the administration maintain cordial relations with Congress, which made for an easy ride for McKinley.

Hobart played a crucial role on the major issue of the day, which was war with Spain over the supposed mistreatment of Cubans. McKinley was something of a dove, but Hobart was an outspoken hawk; it is possible that the vice-president's intransigence on the matter might have swayed McKinley to the war side. (When the president signed the declaration of war with Spain, he used Hobart's pen.) After the brief conflict ended with the United States victorious, the Senate was deadlocked over whether to keep the Philippine Islands or give them their independence. Hobart cast the tie-breaking vote in favor of making the country a U.S. possession.

Unfortunately, Hobart's timing was all wrong. In 1898 he began having respiratory problems, which worsened until on November 21, 1899, he died in Paterson. Two years later, McKinley, after being reelected in 1900, was assassinated. His successor was vice-president Theodore Roosevelt, who almost certainly would not have been on the ticket had Hobart lived.

Another distinguished New Jerseyan that you've probably never heard of is William F. Allen of South Orange, even though you have him to thank whenever you want to know the time.

No, Allen didn't invent clocks or even the concept of time. He did, however, devise the system of time zones used across the United States today.

Today time is an integral part of our lives. Businesses and people swear by it, and, thanks to digital clocks on everything from fax machines to microwave ovens, it is never difficult to find out precisely what time it is. However, just over a century ago things were completely different. In the largely agrarian economy of the nineteenth century, time mattered little. People lived by the sun, the seasons, and the almanac; clocks were largely superfluous.

This casual reliance on natural forces to keep time gave rise to what was called "local" time. Local time was whatever it happened to be in your particular town or area; what time it was somewhere else was insignificant, since the time in New Jersey hardly mattered for farmers in Ohio. Thus, there were over seventy different local time zones throughout the United States, virtually none of which agreed with the other.

While this was fine for most people, it drove the railroads crazy. A train traveler could quickly find his or her watch (set to local time) hopelessly wrong, and not have a clue when he or she would arrive at their destination. Even worse was the havoc that the numerous time zones wrecked on railroad schedules: When a person arrived in Columbus, Ohio at 1:30 P.M. New York local time, were they too late, too early, or right on time to catch the train leaving at 1:30 Columbus local time?

45 Garrett A. Hobart. (Courtesy Special Collections and Archives, Rutgers University Libraries)

Beginning in the early 1870s, the railroads made several attempts to come up with a standardized time system, but to no avail. In 1882 they dumped the problem into Allen's lap.

William Frederick Allen was born on October 9, 1846, in Bordentown, New Jersey. His father, Joseph, an engineer, was killed during the Civil War. After completing his education at the Bordentown Model School and the Protestant Episcopal Academy in Philadelphia, Allen got a job in 1862 with the Camden & Amboy Railroad as a surveyor and engineer.

Ten years later Allen joined the staff of a publication called the *Official Guide of the Railways and Steam Navigation Lines of the United States and Canada*. (Imagine asking for that by name at a newsstand!) This was merely a collection of all the various timetables then used for trains and ships. The next year Allen, an intense man with a close-cropped beard and mustache, became the guide's editor, and so became intimately familiar with the mass confusion generated by the various time zones. Thus, in 1875, he was the logical choice to be named secretary of the General Time Convention/Southern Railway Time Convention, which met periodically to try and solve the vexing problem of time.

By 1882, however, the conventions had gotten nowhere; time was still a mess. Scientists and businesses favored establishing a standardized time system, but hesitated to tamper with such a cherished American tradition as local time. ("If you derange the habits of a people too much they will have none of it," warned a foe of standardized time.) However, Allen doggedly continued working on the problem, evaluating various time standardization schemes and soliciting opinions as to how best to accomplish the objective. Impressed by his work, in 1882 the convention asked him to develop a time standardization proposal for their meeting in April 1883.

What the New Jerseyian devised was a model of simplicity and common sense. Borrowing the idea of four time zones from the theorists, he made the divisions across the country—the same ones used today—conform more to existing railroad lines, rather than the strict by-meridian designs of the scientists. (This is why the time zones today bend and bulge in spots, rather than divide the country with razor-straight lines.) This gave his plan the benefit of practicality over theory. He also paid close attention to state boundaries, trying whenever possible to keep whole states within a single time zone—again, a crucial distinction between his scheme and previous ones, which usually sliced states right down the middle. This made the time zones easier for people, who would be losing local time as a result, to accept. Once the convention accepted his plan, Allen began lobbying various influential people in cities across the country to accept the new time system.

While today it would take an act of Congress to do something so monumental as merge dozens of different time zones into just four, at this time the railroads were the main economic power in the United States. The Iron Horse usually did what it wanted. So the railroads, with great public fanfare, unilaterally implemented standard time in the United States on Sunday, November 18, 1883. This day would forever be known as the "Day of Two Noons," because, at 12:28 P.M., all railroad line clocks were turned back to twelve noon to signal the beginning of standard time. Faced with either being totally out of step with the railroads or conforming, the rest of the country began adopting standard time.

However, conformity didn't come without a fight. This was especially true where standard time and local time differed by more than a few minutes. "Let us keep our own noon," wailed the *Boston Evening Transcript*, and the *Louisville Courier-Journal* called the concept "a compulsory lie, a monstrous fraud," and "a swindle." Some cities, like Detroit and Cleveland, simply ignored the whole thing and remained on local time. Congress thought about mandating standard time, then, faced with local opposition, decided to do nothing. (It wouldn't be until 1918 that the present system became federal law.)

Even with all the grumbling, Allen could justifiably claim that his new system "now governs the daily and hourly actions of at least fifty million people." The implementation of standard time not only meant new ways of living and working, but also influenced how people thought and acted toward each other; suddenly, being "on time" was important and punctuality became a way of judging people. The man from New Jersey had profoundly changed the United States forever.

The last "distinguished daughter" in this chapter is unique in several ways. First of all, she's the only person who wasn't born in the United States. Secondly, while she was well known during her lifetime, her national fame came later, as the result of an epic poem. Yet her story is too important to ignore. That's why the final entry in this chapter is the tale of brave, resourceful, and determined Elizabeth Haddon Estaugh, who came to the New World all by herself and wound up founding a town that still bears her name—Haddonfield.

Elizabeth Haddon was born in 1680 in the County of Surrey, Great Britain. She and her younger sister, Sarah, were the only two of seven children born to John and Elizabeth Haddon who survived infancy. Young Elizabeth grew to be a smart, lively, and serious child.

The Haddons were Quakers, a persecuted religious sect at that time in England. One of the Haddons' frequent visitors was fellow Quaker William Penn, who regaled the family with his tales of the New World. Young Elizabeth listened raptly to Penn's stories about the woods, the Indians, the animals, and the way he and others were literally carving a new and tolerant society out of the wilderness.

In 1698 John Haddon bought several thousand acres of land in western New Jersey. It seems clear that he intended to move his family there, yet for some reason he never did. Elizabeth, however, had never forgotten Penn's stories of this exciting region. In the manner of teenagers since time immemorial, she pestered her parents to let her go to America to oversee the family's land holdings. Finally, in the manner of parents since time immemorial, they gave in; in the spring of 1701, Elizabeth Haddon, accompanied by two servants and a document giving her the power to "look after and occupy" her father's lands, set sail from England.

Landing at Philadelphia in June 1701, Elizabeth quickly set out for her family's land. On the way, she saw that all Penn had said was true: compared to the built-up, bustling community of homes and shops that she had come from, New Jersey was a primordial wilderness. What few houses existed were separated by miles of dense woods, from which either friend or foe could pop out at any moment. Roads were virtually nonexistent, as were stores and businesses. If you couldn't make it yourself, you couldn't have it. It was a rough, raw, and untamed land, and quite possibly, dangerous for a young woman on her own.

Elizabeth Haddon, however, couldn't have been happier. Here was a place totally different than the noisy and dirty city she had come from; here was a place where the scent of wild roses perfumed the air, where deer and rabbits hopped freely about, and where the only sound was the rustle of leaves in the wind. She moved into a small house built by John Willis, who had surveyed the Haddon lands, called it "Haddonfield" (it was two miles outside the boundaries of modern Haddonfield), and immediately began expanding it.

Elizabeth's house was on Cooper's Creek, which served as a main transportation artery in the absence of roads. As one of the few signs of civilization in the area, the home received frequent visits by travelers looking for a hot meal and a dry place to sleep. In this they were not disappointed; all were welcomed to Haddonfield.

Of particular importance in those days was Elizabeth's medical skills. A salve she made was called "the sovereignest thing on earth," and her ability to bandage wounds were a godsend in an area where proper medical services were nonexistent. The Native Americans in the area also depended on

Haddon for medicine, much of which she made from herbs she grew. In gratitude for her kindness, they shared with her some of their medical secrets and local cures. Haddon sent medicine to other parts of New Jersey and Pennsylvania, and it was said that never a day went by without a need for her medical knowledge.

In 1702 Haddon married a Quaker minister named John Estaugh. Although her husband's religious work kept him on the road frequently, Haddon was far from idle. She received numerous visitors, her medical skills were always in demand, she was clerk of the Women's Meeting, and she handled her father's business affairs with intelligence and skill.

In 1713 she and Estaugh built a much larger house. This became the first settlement in what is today Haddonfield. Soon a thriving community had sprung up there, with the Estaugh's house at the center of the activity.

Throughout her life Haddon remained a kind, gentle, person, as illustrated by a contemporary account of her: "Her heart and house were open to her friends, whom to entertain seemed one of her greatest pleasures; [she] was prudently cheerful, and well knowing the value of friendship was careful not to wound it herself, nor encourage others in whispering and publishing the failings, or supposed weaknesses."

In 1742 John Estaugh died. Although childless, Haddon continued her many activities for the betterment of Haddonfield, surrounded by grandnieces and grandnephews. Finally, on March 30, 1762, after a three-month illness, Haddon died at the age of eighty-two, "as one falling asleep, full of days, like unto a shock of corn fully ripe." On her memorial plaque was etched a fitting tribute: "A woman remarkable for resolution, Prudence, Charity."

For the brave Quaker woman, the adventure was over.

DID YOU KNOW?

There are many stories told about Elizabeth Haddon's life in the New World. However, the most famous one concerns her forthrightness. In fact, the tale so impressed Henry Wadsworth Longfellow that he wove part of it into his epic poem "Tales of a Wayside Inn."

Before she was married, Haddon was among a group of Quakers, including John Estaugh, who were traveling by horseback to Salem. At one point, Haddon slowed her horse because the saddle needed adjustment. As the rest of the party rode ahead, Estaugh came to her assistance. Haddon seized the opportunity to tell Estaugh that she thought he had been chosen by God to be her life's partner. In his poem, Longfellow had her say: "I will no longer conceal what is laid upon me to tell thee, I have received from the Lord a charge to love thee, John Estaugh."

Since women generally didn't speak until spoken to during this era, Haddon's bold talk about love and marriage must have sent the shy Estaugh's head reeling. But to his credit, the young minister listened, then told her that while he found Haddon pleasant in many ways, he had had no similar directions from God.

The two, however, did indeed get married, and according to all accounts, it was a pleasurable union indeed. "I'll venture to say, few if any, in a married state, ever lived in sweeter harmony than we did," Haddon would later write. Fortunately for John Estaugh, Elizabeth Haddon had spoken before being spoken to.

CHAPTER SEVEN

Great
Storms

AH, WEATHER! Is there anything more fascinating in life—or more frightening?

Just like the little girl with the curl, when the weather is good, it is very good, offering us gorgeous sunshine, bright blue skies, and refreshing breezes. But when it is bad, weather—in the form of howling blizzards, ferocious hurricanes, raging nor'easters, and the like—can be very bad indeed.

Due to its geographic location nearly halfway between the equator and the North Pole, and also because it is a coastal state, New Jersey enjoys (or suffers from, depending upon your perspective) a broad diversity of weather. Hurricanes, nor'easters, heat waves, cold snaps, blizzards, ice storms, tornadoes—we get them all here. And, although we all like nice weather, it is the storms that get our attention, these awesome examples of Nature's fury that make us realize that there are some things that will always be beyond the control of humanity.

"500 Girls Wanted."

No, that isn't a plea from some overzealous Don Juan that was snuck into this book by mistake. It's the beginning of a story about the most fearsome snow storm ever to strike New Jersey: the legendary Great Blizzard of 1888. Rarely has a storm caused such an impression that its memory remains over a century later, but such is the legacy of the Blizzard of '88.

(Incidentally, that "500 Girls" line was written on a sign, along with a second line, "To Eat Snow," displayed outside a Newark business practically buried by the big storm. No one knows if the request was fulfilled.)

People expect a noted Arctic explorer to know about snow. So, when Adolphus W. Greely, famous polar investigator and head of the United States War Department's Signal Service, predicted fair weather for the mid-Atlantic states for the first few days of the week beginning on Sunday, March 11, 1888, people tended to accept the forecast. In fact, there was no reason to doubt it: The winter of 1888 had been the region's mildest in seventeen years. With the middle of March rapidly approaching, spring was just days away. Everyone's thoughts were on flowers blooming, trees budding, and the return of warm weather—anything but snow.

However, on that fateful March 11, a rather innocent-looking low pressure trough centered near Augusta, Georgia, was about to make a liar out of Greely. During the day, the trough was blocked from its normal course up the East Coast by a large dome of high pressure, which stalled the storm east of Cape May by the morning of Monday, March 12. At the same time, extremely cold winds from Canada were drawn into the storm, where they mixed with warm southerly winds and picked up plenty of Atlantic moisture. The result was a blizzard of epic proportions, a storm so powerful that meteorologists consider it a 500-year event because it can occur only once in a half a millennium.

The storm began innocently enough; a cold, chilly rain fell throughout most of New Jersey on March 11. During the night, the temperature plummeted, and the rain changed to snow. Even more ominously, the wind steadily picked up until, as one Egg Harbor City observer recalled, "[it] blew with the force of a hurricane at intervals, doing considerable damage to property."

The Great Blizzard of 1888 had arrived. It would not leave until Wednesday, March 14—three days destined to go down into New Jersey weather history.

Although virtually the entire state received snow, the southern counties might be excused for saying, "What blizzard?" Cape May County reported ten inches of snow—a lot, certainly, but not in line with "the greatest storm ever" reputation of the blizzard—and Atlantic City recorded a mere seven inches of the white stuff.

It was the central and northern portions of New Jersey that got hammered. Snowfall totals in some towns and counties more than doubled

---

46 Snowdrifts as high as people were common throughout New Jersey cities after the Great Blizzard of 1888. (Courtesy Special Collections and Archives, Rutgers University Libraries)

those in South Jersey: Toms River, 24 inches; New Brunswick, 24 inches; Rahway, 25 inches; Warren County, 24 inches; Morris County, 20 inches; Union County, 25 inches. (These, in turn, were more than doubled by the totals of some towns in eastern New York State: Saratoga, 50 inches, Albany, 47 inches, and Troy, 55 inches.)

The storm hit suddenly. The Toms River newspaper *New Jersey Courier* reported that the temperature dropped thirty degrees in forty-eight hours, from 44 degrees Fahrenheit to 14. In Newton, the thermometer plunged from above freezing to a bone-chilling one degree above zero in approximately thirty hours.

The arrival of the storm was something terrifying to behold. The *New Jersey Courier* of March 14, 1888, reported the blizzard's beginnings: "On Sunday afternoon a rain storm from the southeast, accompanied by high winds, set in, and continued without intermission until about two or half past two o'clock on Monday morning, when the wind, increasing to a gale, shifted to the northwest. The first blast of the storm, after the shift of the wind, was terrific, and most of our residents were aroused by the rocking of their houses upon their foundations. With the wind came snow, flying, swirling, drifting before the blast, and by seven o'clock fully one foot of snow had fallen, which, however, was piled up in drifts some of which attained the height of five or six feet."

The paper also described the effects of the storm: "Fences were obliterated, doors and windows shut in, and business was entirely suspended. All communication with the outside world was cut off, no mails have arrived at the time of writing, and the telegraph wires beyond the station at Long Branch are down. Attempts were made on Monday [the 12th] to get two trains through, but neither succeeded." Noted the paper, in an obvious understatement: "We are snowed up."

The big cities didn't fare much better. Trenton was cut off from the outside world for sixty hours. Trains stopped running on Monday, and didn't begin operating again until Thursday. Every hotel in the city was jammed to capacity with stranded rail passengers; many travelers sought refuge in private homes.

A more serious consequence of the paralyzed transportation system was that no food could be brought into the capital city. Many grocery stores ran out of everything and had no way to get more. On top of that, work simply ceased in the city, so that even if there would have been food, many people didn't have money to buy it. "No money and no work and depleted provisions have undoubtedly made a thousand people in this city suffer terribly," said *The New York Times* of March 15.

In Newark things weren't much better. All the telegraph and telephone wires were either down or crossed and just a single train was able to struggle out of the city on March 12. Despite the post office's "rain, snow," pledge, just one small mail pouch from nearby Elizabeth made it into the city. Businessman desperate to get to New York City offered sleigh drivers up to $100 to take them to the Hudson River. This was a futile gesture, however, since most streets were clogged with waist-high drifts.

The threat of famine also stalked the Newark streets. As the *Newark Evening News* of March 14, 1888 reported: "Unless the railroads are cleaned and trains are running by Friday many Newarkers will go hungry for nearly every kind of food, except that made with flour." The storm had hit on Monday, the usual stocking-up day for city butcher shops, cutting off the supply of fresh meat into the city as completely as if a spigot had been twisted shut. Poultry dealers and fish sellers were in the same snow-filled boat. Coffee, sugar, eggs, and milk were also in short supply.

Even the dead were indisposed by the storm. Bodies stacked up in funeral homes, with no prospect of being buried soon. People who died at home were simply left where they were.

Jersey City was even cut off from the neighboring suburbs. According to *The New York Times* of March 12, 1888, "It was worth a man's life to venture from Bergen Heights across these meadows to the city." Calls for ambulances went unanswered, as did cries for milk by hungry infants; dozens of milk delivery wagons were abandoned on the streets by their drivers. Although schools tried to open, they soon realized their folly and closed. Unfortunately, some people didn't get the message. One plucky child tried to reach school but was overcome by the blizzard and collapsed into a snow bank, where she lay helpless until fortunately rescued by a passerby. ("It took a long time to thaw her out and prepare her for the rest of her homeward journey," said the *Times*.) A policeman named Longe, going above and beyond the call of duty, carried three schoolteachers from the No. 12 school home on his back!

Sadly, not all of the snow stories were so cheerful. At noon on Monday the 12th, the Singer factory in Elizabeth decided to close, and send the 1,800 employees (out of 3,200) who had struggled through the storm back home. Many women refused to brave the blizzard a second time, but most men decided to risk the quarter-mile walk to the railway station. The men left the factory in groups of twenty, hoping that there was strength in numbers. But nothing could fight the awesome power of Nature, as one man recalled:

> We meant to keep together, but the storm was so terrible that before we were halfway we were hopelessly separated. As I went on, I met other men who had gone before. Some were helpless. The face of one was a perfect glare of ice. His eyelids were frozen fast and he was groping blindly along . . . as I came up he fell into a drift. At last . . . I reached the station. Six men had been terribly frozen on the way. The hands of some of them, the ears of others and even portions of their bodies were frozen. A man named Sherwood had both of his hands frozen to the wrists. A man named Ellis was picked up out of

the snow . . . and died soon afterwards. Two other men were missing from our party. I do not doubt that they are buried in the drifts.

There were other deaths as well. A schooner cook named Beach froze to death in the rigging of his ship. A New Brunswick farmer out shoveling found the body of a woman who had collapsed on his property and quickly froze to death. In Raritan Township, Henry Henrithan left Milltown in a "somewhat intoxicated" state, and got lost in the snow. When neighbors went to his home to tell his wife, they found Mrs. Henrithan dead in bed from cold and hunger, and the children half-starved and frozen.

Even remaining indoors did not guarantee safety. The storm with winds so fierce that their icy effects were felt some 600 miles away in Bermuda sought out people wherever they were, as this account by Laura Gwinnup of Blairstown (Warren County) shows: "We cannot keep warm in the room, and nearly freeze when we come in the kitchen, the snow blowes in the doors so that we have to shovel it out in large quantities."

In Camden there was a different problem. Between the blizzard winds and low tide, the water was literally blown out of the Delaware River. Boats and ferry boats scraped bottom and could not carry either cargo or passengers into port on either side. The water level dropped so low that Camden's water pumps would not work, and the city was gripped by a severe water shortage.

The winds also wreaked havoc in many other New Jersey communities. Winds of ninety miles an hour and more at Sandy Hook piled snow drifts up to fifteen feet high all across the peninsula. In Burlington the winds crushed the sturdy Burlington Thread Mill as if it were made of paper mache, not brick, and in Cape May, the howling gale destroyed numerous oceanfront homes.

Faced with devastation, some businesses tried to cope with humor. Several merchants offered 1,000 pounds of free snow with every $1 purchased. Outside a Newark saloon, a sign proclaimed: "Any man who relates any snow reminiscences here will be compelled to treat the house."

Undoubtedly there were many snow tales being told during those days. One of the most remarkable was that of Samuel Decker of Newark. After visiting Midvale (five miles from Pompton Junction) on Sunday the 11th, he arose on the following morning to find a thick curtain of white outside, and no prospect of returning home. Finally, after waiting two days with no letup in the storm's fury, his patience gave out. Borrowing a pair of boots, he set out on foot for Pompton Junction, despite the unanimous opinion of everyone in the house he was leaving that the next time they would see him would be in a coffin. Although he had to fight his way through snowdrifts up to his armpits, Decker arrived at Pompton Junction only to find that there hadn't been a train there for days. Incredibly, he decided to plunge on to Paterson, a "mere" fifteen miles away. Even more incredibly, he made it, despite not eating anything for eighteen hours and only taking one five-minute break during the entire trip.

This type of story, however, was few and far between. More often, the tales were of incredible hardship, frozen extremities, lack of food, and countless other problems caused by the Great Blizzard. People were exhausted from dealing with the snow and the mess it made of everyone's lives. "Winter has 'lingered' in the lap of Spring. It should now March on," sighed the *Newark Evening News* on March 14.

Finally, after hammering the state for three straight days, the storm moved out to sea. On Thursday, March 15, people ventured out of their homes, some for the first time in days, and looked at what the storm had wrought. What they found would go down in history, and still be talked about in mythic terms, over a century later.

(Just to prove that this was indeed a phenomenal weather event, the storm intensified as it roared across the Atlantic. On March 19 it slammed into Berlin, whipping the city with heavy snow and high winds. The floods brought by the storm wiped out nearly three dozen Hungarian villages.)

?

DID YOU KNOW?

One of the major casualities of the Great Blizzard of 1888 was the reputation of a poet named John Whitaker Watson, who had had the misfortune of writing a popular ode called "Beautiful Snow" just a few years before. A Connecticut newspaper offered a five-cent reward for Watson's arrest and conviction, and a group of citizens in Hartford hung the beleaguered poet in effigy. In New Jersey, when a man stood up among a group of stranded train passengers and offered to recite "Beautiful Snow" as a means of entertainment, a collection was quickly taken up to buy his silence.

Of all the types of storms that strike New Jersey, none is more vicious or deadly than a major hurricane. To be struck by one of these Atlantic behemoths is like being attacked by a mindless monster with unlimited destructive power; just when you think it can't get any worse it does. The memories of a major hurricane linger long after the storm itself has gone—such as in the case of the Great Atlantic Hurricane (the naming of hurricanes was still nine years in the future) of 1944.

The storm formed on September 9, 600 miles east-northeast of Puerto Rico and quickly grew in strength and intensity. Just four days later, the *Philadelphia Inquirer* warned of "a great hurricane fraught with peril for life and property . . . bearing down on the North Carolina coast."

The storm banged into North Carolina early in the morning on September 14, and then set its sights on New Jersey. As it barreled toward the state, the barometric pressure plummeted to 27.97 inches and the winds increased to 134 miles per hour, with gusts to 150. Clearly, this was going to be a storm that New Jerseyans would long remember.

Being furthest south, Cape May was the first to feel the storm's fury. Wind and rain from the storm had been lashing the entire coast for several days, almost like a boxer softening up his opponent with jabs before landing a haymaker. In the late afternoon of September 14, with hurricane-force winds (over 75 miles per hour) buffeting the town and tides surging to nearly ten feet above normal, the haymaker was swung at Cape May.

Sometime before five o'clock that afternoon, a wave described as a "40 foot [high] tidal wave" crashed into the town. The towering wall of water demolished Cape May's boardwalk, destroyed Convention Hall (musical instruments from the building were found scattered about the area), and splintered two piers (Hunt and Pennyland). Roads were not only washed out, but buried by tons of sand and debris. Three hundred families had to be evacuated.

Thus began a swath of unprecedented devastation along the Jersey Shore. Ocean City suffered a fate similar to that of Cape May: The boardwalk was devastated, the roof blew off the Breakers Hotel, and the mast of the *Sindia*, which had been jutting out of the beach as an Ocean City landmark for over forty years, was snapped off at the sand line.

However, as always when weather is at its most violent, the strange and unpredictable happened. In their book *Great Storms of the Jersey Shore*, Larry Savadove and Margaret Thomas Buchholz recounted an amusing incident in Ocean City in which a family had to flee their home just as they were sitting down to dinner. Later, the table leaf, with dishes of meat, peas, and potatoes lined up neatly, was seen floating down the street.

47   The Asbury Park Fishing Pier in the aftermath of the Hurricane of 1944. (Courtesy Special Collections and Archives, Rutgers University Libraries)

Atlantic City also bore the storm's fury. The Grand Dowager of the Jersey Shore suffered extensive property damage, including the loss of the entire Boardwalk near the Absecon Inlet. The storm cut the world-famous Heinz Pier pier in half, sending great chunks careening down city streets. On Madison Avenue, eight teenage boys maneuvered a forty-foot section of Boardwalk down the street, like Huck Finn poling a raft down the Mississippi. Countless homes and businesses were flooded by sea water. Structures were tossed around like pieces on a Monopoly board. Convention Hall, the Armory, and the railroad station were packed with dazed evacuees, who were stunned by the storm's sudden fury. That night Coast Guardsmen patrolled the devastated city, making it seem more like a bombed-out city from the current world war than the sun and fun capital of the Jersey Shore.

Long Beach Island because of its precarious position dangling off the coast is always a ripe target for storms, and the Hurricane of 1944 was no exception. Besides the normal damage caused by the wind and tides, a mammoth wave—some say it was thirty feet high—inundated the southern part of the island. The inexorable wall of water knocked houses from their moorings and set them floating on what had been solid ground but was now turned into a lake by Nature's ire. The buildings that stayed put lost walls, roofs, and whatever else the storm could pry off. Huddled in their homes as the water rose around them, people watched once-solid

structures and mountains of debris go floating by on the street as if they were dried leaves caught in an autumn breeze.

Pictures of the southern part of Long Beach Island in the storm's aftermath show such utter devastation it's hard to believe that the area wasn't the victim of a massive explosion. Buildings were not merely damaged, but annihilated; little remained of many except for piles of wood and brick. In Harvey Cedars alone, so many homes were either destroyed or severely damaged that it was deemed impossible to tell where the structures had once stood.

The northern part of the coast was attacked with the same viciousness. Officials in shore towns in Ocean and Monmouth counties also reported a giant wave—some said it was fifty feet high—that crashed into the shoreline, destroying whatever was in its path. Piers, boardwalks, homes, and businesses were strewn about like toys thrown by an angry child. The boardwalks that were wrecked read like a road map of shore towns: Bay Head, Point Pleasant, Belmar, Ocean Grove, Asbury Park, and Long Branch.

Of course, the rest of New Jersey didn't escape the hurricane's wrath. The northeastern part of the state suffered the most rainfall, with Rahway and Elizabeth reporting over eleven inches. Rahway was also the single-day rainfall champ, with six inches falling on September 13th. Trees, their soil already softened by the rain preceding the hurricane, were uprooted by the thousands, littering roadways, yards, and train tracks throughout the state. Included among these were orchard trees; 700,000 bushels of apples were blown from trees by the storm, which helped contribute to agriculture losses totaling $3.5 million.

Overall property damage was estimated at $25 million. Nearly 700 buildings were destroyed, and over 3,600 damaged. The storm took eight lives, all in shore communities.

The day after the hurricane the air was as still as death. People ventured out of their homes, looked at the devastation, and just shook their heads. In just a matter of hours their lives had been turned inside out, uprooted like many of the trees lying scattered about. These memories would linger long indeed.

Nor'easters are storms unique to the small portion of the United States that New Jersey inhabits. To someone from Kansas, a nor'easter is an icy wind that comes roaring down from Canada and acts like a super air conditioner, plunging the entire region into the deep-freeze. But to a New

Jerseyan, the word "nor'easter" means much more than that—as it did during those fateful March days in 1962, when the most memorable of all nor'easters arrived.

March 5, 1962, was just another Monday in New Jersey. At the Algonquin Theatre in Manasquan (Monmouth County), Jerry Lewis's latest film, *The Errand Boy*, was playing. Whitewall tires were selling for $35.54 a pair, and twenty-seven pieces of furniture cost a mere $329. The New York Yankees were beginning preparations to win—yawn—yet another world championship. For entertainment, people enjoyed watching the life and death struggles of an intense TV doctor named Ben Casey. On the international scene, President John F. Kennedy struggled with escalating cold war tensions.

The weather forecast for that day was "cloudy, chance of snow, mixed with rain developing," not much of a herald for the arrival of the greatest nor'easter of them all.

Actually, the Great Nor'easter was two storms: one had come steaming over the middle portion of the country, spreading snow and cold in its wake, while the other had formed off the Georgia coast. The two joined forces in the east, then began heading north up the Atlantic seaboard.

The timing couldn't have been worse. The storm arrived during spring tide, which is when the sun and moon are aligned with the earth and tides are higher than normal. To make matters worse, at the same time a strong high pressure system stalled over Newfoundland, blocking the storm's path. New Jersey was in the bull's-eye of the storm's wrath.

All this was unknown, however, on March 5. The weather was bad—a steady east wind along with driving rain combined to make it a miserable day—but nothing out of the ordinary.

By the next morning, however, it was becoming obvious that this was no ordinary storm. Damage reports were trickling in from some shore communities: the Loveland Town Bridge had collapsed in Point Pleasant; Ocean Grove's boardwalk was damaged; there was flooding in Sea Bright, Atlantic Highlands, Bradley Beach, Long Beach Island, Ocean City, Sea Isle City, and numerous other towns; and, perhaps most surprisingly, the storm hadn't abated. If anything, it was increasing in intensity.

Tuesday, March 6, was D-Day—"Destruction Day"—for many shore towns. That morning, police on Long Beach Island discovered that the ocean had broken through the protective barrier of sand dunes at Holgate; seawater was racing across the street and joining Barnegat Bay on the other side of the island. Alarmed authorities began evacuating Holgate. But the pain had just begun for Long Beach Island.

Up and down the shore, things got bad quickly on that fateful Tuesday. Bulkheads, such as the one that protected Sea Isle City, held under the fearful onslaught of the pounding waves. Unfortunately, the waves were so high that the water simply flowed over the bulkheads as if they weren't there. The water swept into the streets of Sea Isle City, quickly submerging streets and rushing into basements. The Fean Hotel, the Madeline Theater, the Excursion House, the Amusement Center, and other businesses in Sea Isle City were washed away by the waves. Virtually all of the town's 1,200 residents had to be evacuated.

Everybody waited for the wind to swing around that day, to come from the west, and not the east, so that it would stop pushing great mountains of ocean water in front of it. What no one knew was that the storm, locked firmly in place by the blocking high, had created a 1,000-mile fetch (an area where ocean waves are generated by wind) far out in the ocean. As the wind roared down this incredibly long fetch, it piled up more and more water in front of it, until by the time the waves arrived at the shoreline they were as big as three-story buildings.

Shakespeare called it "the hungry ocean," and this storm was proving how voracious the sea's appetite could be. Wildwood, Absecon Island, and Ocean City became actual islands as seawater cut their mainland links. Brigantine lost practically all of its "protective" sand dunes. Forty-foot-high sand dunes on Island Beach were either moved or destroyed, changing in a geological blink the island's topography.

The hungry sea ate more than sand. In Asbury Park, sections of the boardwalk were buried under tons of wind-whipped sand. Boardwalks just vanished in Bay Head, Seaside Heights, Long Branch, Sea Girt, Sea Isle City, Atlantic City, Cape May, and numerous other shore communities. Structures were flattened as if they'd been made of cardboard.

People kept waiting and waiting for the wind to weaken, for the waves to diminish, for the terrible storm to finally leave. For two and one-half days, and five consecutive high tides, the relentless nor'easter battered the shore. Low tide ceased to exist; it was high tide, higher tide, highest tide.

While much of the shore got rain or sleet from the storm—and even the rainfall totals weren't much, averaging just about two inches at Atlantic City—the interior sections of the state got snow. This was bad news for a Boston cab driver, who had decided that he had had enough of winter that year. Without bothering to inform his superiors he turned his hack south for Florida and was happily motoring through New Jersey when the storm forced him to a halt in New Brunswick. There he was intercepted by the state police, who interrupted his trip long enough to escort him to the Middlesex County Jail.

Although the entire state, and particularly the shore, was hard hit by the storm, the hands-down winner of the "most devastated" award was Long Beach Island. The eighteen-mile barrier island was breached by the ocean and bay in five places. The worse was at Seventy-ninth Street in Harvey Cedars, where a channel over sixty feet wide and fifteen feet deep was established where once there had been roads, sand, and homes. Nearly 50 percent of the town's ratables were lost.

The rest of the island fared little better. By the time Wednesday, March 7, dawned, the storm had destroyed the sand dunes, beaches, and whatever else the island had been counting on for protection. This left buildings at the ocean's mercy, and the raging surf delivered the knockout blow. Houses were ripped from their moorings and sent careening into the swirling waters. The island six miles at sea was nearly put out to sea permanently: overall it lost 270 homes, with 180 more suffering severe damage.

Finally, on Thursday, the storm began to weaken. Gradually during the day the wind and rain slacked off, and the tides did not surge in with the violence of past days. Friday dawned clear and breezy; Nature had simply wore itself out.

---

48 After the December 1992 nor'easter, all that was left of some boardwalks were their supports. The boardwalk itself was ripped apart and blown away by the storm. (Photo by author)

Slowly, like a KO'd fighter down for the count, the state began shaking out the cobwebs and climbing to its feet. Along the shore, however, it was a different story. A week after the storm, a newspaper story about Harvey Cedars said: "Nobody lives in Harvey Cedars anymore. There are no roads. There is no drinking water. Wreckage is everywhere and where there is no wreckage there is just sand. . . . The houses are everywhere, in no order, sometimes piled two or three together. Around them crushed and mangled cars and trucks lie half buried."

The week after the Great Nor'easter began just like the previous week. The Algonquin was showing *Second Time Around*; an "automatic" dryer was selling for $99, and Ben Casey was again battling death. It *seemed* like just another week—but for thousands of Jersey Shore residents, it would never be the same again.

Perhaps the only good thing about the 1962 nor'easter was that it was over. The state would not see its like again. It was, those in the know assured weather-weary New Jerseyians, the "storm of the century."

Three decades later, in what must be the quickest 100 years ever recorded, the "storm of the century" returned.

Thursday, December 10, 1992, began as just another chilly, late-autumn day in New Jersey. There was just two weeks until Christmas, and most people were far more worried about shopping and making other holiday preparations than they were about the weather.

Little did they know, however, that surging toward them up the eastern seaboard was yet another storm that would send meteorologists and weather historians diving for the record book.

As is the case many times when titanic storms smash into New Jersey, what happened with this storm was that a strong high-pressure center in northern Maine blocked the storm's progress up the eastern seaboard. Stalled just off the Virginia coast, the storm grew rapidly in strength and fury. This was particularly true of the winds, which exploded into hurricane force because of the great difference in air pressure between the two strong weather systems.

The storm smashed into New Jersey like a runaway locomotive. Winds of ninety miles per hour and higher were clocked in several communities. The rain came down in blinding, wind-driven sheets that made driving impossible and walking almost suicidal. As much as four inches of rain fell in twenty-four hours in several locations along the coast. The flooding was so deep in Sayreville that rescue workers didn't even know where they were until they saw the tops of streets signs poking up from the water. Inland, northern and western New Jersey had snow to go along with the shrieking wind—a foot or more in some places. In Sussex County, road crews would no sooner plow a highway than the wind would push the snow right back onto it again, sometimes in drifts up to two feet deep.

As always in a nor'easter, the Jersey Shore had the worst of it, with some likening it to the hurricane of 1944. Those who laughed at that comparison had only to look at the tidal surge measured at Ventnor Pier in Absecon: nine feet, two inches—exactly the height reached by the mighty 1944 hurricane. Others pointed to marks on their homes or businesses made by flood waters from the March 1962 nor'easter, and how the water from this storm crested those marks by nearly a foot.

Although this storm occurred in the 1990s, in an age of computers, fax machines, and other devices that supposedly provide instant communication with anywhere in the outside world, it quickly swept people back into the 1890s. Many communities were isolated, without electricity (Jersey Central Power and Light had the largest number of outages in their history) or telephone service, getting by on candlelight, wood-burning fires, and dry food just as their ancestors would have done 100 years ago. Train service up and down the shore halted on December 11 and didn't resume for several days. Major roads, such as the Garden State Parkway and Route 35, were also closed by the combination of wind and water. The causeway and bridge leading from Long Beach Island was also closed.

Structures along the shore were devastated by the storm's mighty one-two wallop of waves and winds. Boardwalks seemed to suffer particularly hard; sections of the wooden walkways in Point Pleasant, Ocean Grove, Seaside Heights, Long Branch, and dozens of other towns were wrecked. Bradley Beach officials reported their boardwalk 98 percent destroyed. In Manasquan, a fifty-year-old asphalt walkway that had survived numerous storms and hurricanes was torn up and flung around the beach.

Particularly hard hit was Belmar; the wind literally ripped up the boards as if they had been fastened with velcro instead of nails. All that remained for hundreds of feet were the boardwalk supports, sticking up out of the sand like ghostly fingers pointing skyward as if to identify the culprit. In Spring Lake, it was much the same. One couple reported part of the boardwalk in their driveway, and part of it on their front lawn.

The storm also swept away hundreds of tons of sand from already-depleted beaches. Some of it was blown onto roadways, where bulldozers were later able to push it back on the beach. Much of it, however, was merely swept into the ocean. In Mantoloking, the sand-starved beaches revealed an eerie sight: the long-buried bodies of twelve cars entombed in the sand after the March 1962 nor'easter as protection against future storms. The storm had uncovered the rusting wrecks, as if to establish its kinship with the legendary nor'easter of thirty years ago.

What the wind and waves didn't destroy the flood tides did. Peak tidal surges were among the highest ever recorded for the Jersey Shore. Water pushed into the back bays—the tide was reported as high as eleven feet above mean low water in some bays—had nowhere else to go but onto streets, and from there into basements and cellars. Thousands of people were evacuated from dozens of towns, including communities such as Point Pleasant Beach, that normally don't get flooded out.

Lending a surrealistic air to the entire storm scene was the presence of Christmas items among the wreckage. The tides rose so fast that many people had to literally flee for their lives, and there was no time to try and rescue packages, ornaments, and other signs of the season. Thus it was not uncommon to see gaily wrapped gifts, plastic Santa Clauses, and brightly colored strings of lights floating along the streets.

After several days the storm finally, begrudgingly, moved away, the tides returned to normal, and life resumed—although at a much more subdued pace—at the Jersey Shore and elsewhere in the state. But in the aftermath, having suffered through two "storms of the century" in thirty years, some

shore residents and officials were talking about the unthinkable: not re-building in certain places that storms repeatedly struck.

(Not that there is anything new in this debate. On September 15, 1944, the *Asbury Park Evening Press*, in editorializing on the devastating hurricane that had just ripped the shore apart, said: "The prospect of replacing expensive boardwalks and other beachfront structures every decade or less and depending upon the whims of nature to spare or wreck them can no longer be followed. It is vital that hereafter the possibility, and even probability, of devastating storms be taken into account before capital is invested along the beachfront.")

For now, the debate continues: Should we continually rebuild and re-plenish structures and beaches that are repeatedly destroyed by storms, or is this just the equivalent of Sisyphus forever trying to roll his boulder up that hill? One thing is certain: As far as "storms of the century" go, Nature has its own way of counting the years—and it's impossible to know when the bill for the next 100 years might come due.

Of course, there have been many other storms that have wrecked havoc in New Jersey.

One of the worst was the Hurricane of 1821, which remains the only hurricane to have its eye pass over the state. This storm came boiling up out of the Atlantic in early September, and struck the state hard on the afternoon of the 3rd. As the *Sussex Register* reported: "A very severe gale of wind from the S.E. accompanied with heavy rain, visited this place last Monday afternoon . . . prostrating the fences to the ground, uprooting and twisting from their trunks the largest trees, and leveling the corn and buckwheat with the earth." Another casualty of this storm was a unique area of Long Beach Island called Great Swamp. Located where the northern portion of Surf City is today, Great Swamp was a freshwater oasis of animals and tall cedar trees nestled within the sand and salt of Long Beach Island. The hurricane's winds knocked down the trees, and the waves poured salt water into the region, turning Great Swamp into a marshland. Today Surf City is built on the bones of Great Swamp.

49   A destroyed section of the Point Pleasant boardwalk in the aftermath of the December 1992 nor'easter. (Photo by author)

Since New Jersey gets hammered with hurricanes and nor'easters, it's only fair that there's other weather activity that we miss out on. Tornadoes, as a rule, don't occur in the state very often; when they do, they usually last just a few minutes, rather than the much longer time that the devastating Midwestern twisters spend on the ground. The state, however, has had its share of tornadoes: on June 19, 1835, one struck New Brunswick, killing five people on its seventeen-mile rampage. Fifty years later, a twister ricocheted back and forth across the Delaware River from Camden to Philadelphia, killing six people and causing $500,000 in damages. Possibly the worst tornado in recent memory was the one that struck at Seabrook, Cumberland County, in 1975, causing $10 million worth of damage.

Ironically, the Great Blizzard of 1888 did not produce the most snow ever in the state. That distinction goes to the February blizzard of 1899, which dumped almost inconceivable amounts of snow throughout New Jersey. Accumulations of two feet were considered puny; Warren County, with 30 inches of the white stuff, Mercer with 34, and Gloucester with 36 were far more the norm. The winner of the rather dubious honor for most snow went to Ocean and Burlington counties, each of which had 40 inches of snow.

Ice storms tend to be regional events, hitting a particular area or county rather than an entire state. However, in late February 1902, the most severe ice storm on record blanketed much of the state with sleet and ice. Telegraph, electric, and telephone lines from north to south were knocked down by the sheer weight of the ice, which also disrupted railroad traffic. As might be expected, trees took the heaviest hit. A weather observer in Somerville reported "so many of our beautiful shade trees with their top branches broken off by the heavy sleet." Another observer in Rancocas wrote that the storm "broke trees down with the weight of the ice—such devastation has never been seen here before. The town looked as though a tornado had struck it. Pine forests suffered great damage."

Although lightning strikes can occasionally be deadly, they mainly strike trees and cause damage to buildings. But on Saturday, July 10, 1926, a single lightning bolt caused over $70 million worth of damage in New Jersey. A bolt from a summer thunderstorm struck a building containing explosives at the United States Naval Ammunition Depot at Lake Denmark in Rockaway Township (Morris County). The strike caused the building to explode, which led to a series of chain-reaction explosions at other magazines on the compound. Each explosion brought a new wave of debris hurtling into the air, flames leaping skyward, and shells and other explosives whistling to earth where they, too, exploded. The next day, the *New York Times* described the area as "charred and smoking. Not a blade of grass nor a green shrub remains. Trees are stripped of branches. The ground is pitted with craters."

DID YOU KNOW?

- New Jersey's coldest morning occurred on January 5, 1904, when the temperature at the New Jersey Weather Service's River Vale location (Bergen County) dropped to a bone-chilling − 34 degrees Fahrenheit. (This is also the record low temperature for New Jersey.) Not to be outdone, Layton in Sussex County checked in with − 31 degrees F. The temperature dipped below zero throughout the entire state with the exception of Cape May City, where it was a balmy 0 degrees F.

50   The boardwalk at Ocean Grove after the December 1992 nor'easter. (Photo by author)

- The hottest days in New Jersey were July 9 and 10, 1936, when the temperature was at least 100 degrees Fahrenheit everywhere in the state except at Atlantic City, where "cooling" sea breezes kept the mercury to 94 degrees. The hottest reading ever recorded in the state was on July 10, 1936, at Runyon in Middlesex County: an egg-frying 110 degrees Fahrenheit.

- New Jersey's weather played a critical role in United States independence. A storm on Christmas night, 1776, helped keep the Hessians who were occupying Trenton indoors and enabled Washington and his small force to approach the town almost unawares and capture it after a brief fight. This victory revived the flagging morale of the Continental troops and helped keep Washington's largely volunteer army together.

Subsequently, Washington's army suffered through the brutal winter of 1779–80 at Morristown. This was the famous "Hard Winter," when the Delaware River was frozen for an incredible seventy-five days (December 21, 1779–March 4, 1780), and Philadelphia recorded just one day in January when the temperature went above freezing. A thermometer in New York City during January reportedly registered a reading of −16 degrees Fahrenheit; by mid-month every principal port from Maine to North Carolina had frozen over. Washington and his troops endured this terrible weather at Morristown while living in makeshift log cabins. In February, a Continental soldier at Morristown wrote that the "ink freezes in my pen, while I am sitting close to the fire."

 # Ghosts, Tall Tales, and Legends

D E E P in the Pinelands, in a room lit only by the flickering glow of a candle, a pregnant woman struggled to give birth.

Outside, a fearsome thunderstorm had suddenly boiled up. The night sky, so peaceful just minutes ago, was now the scene of a heavenly sound and light show of massive proportion; thunder exploded in the darkness like bomb blasts, while lightning ripped jagged holes across the black curtain of night.

In the small home, a group of elderly women who were assisting their pregnant neighbor looked at one another uneasily. Several pulled their shawls tighter around their bony shoulders; something was not right. They could *feel* it.

In unison, they turned to the small bed, where the woman was tossing and turning in agony as the birthing time approached. There were rumors that she was involved with sorcery and witchcraft; some even whispered that she had been in league with the Prince of Darkness himself. In the warmth and security of their own homes, the women had dismissed these stories as nonsense. Now, with the storm raging outside, and the candlelight casting eerie shadows on the walls, the women felt the cold hand of fear touch their hearts. What if they hadn't been just stories after all?

All at once, the moment to bring life into this world arrived. Forgetting their fears, the women quickly and efficiently attended to their neighbor. Shortly, a healthy baby boy was delivered. The women wrapped him in a homemade blanket and handed him to the anxious mother, who smiled wanly. The women smiled too; all that talk about witchcraft had been just that—talk. Everything was fine.

That's when the baby began to change.

First its human features melted away, as if they were made of wax that had suddenly become white-hot. Then the fat, chubby body stretched out like a rubber band, until it looked more serpentine than human. From its feet sprang horse's hoofs; from its shoulders sprouted bat wings. With a terrible sound of cracking bone, the face stretched and grew until it became a horse's elongated snout.

As the women and the birth mother watched in stunned disbelief, the thing that had once been a human child but was now something else entirely rose up on its two back legs until its horrible head grazed the ceiling. It snarled at the frightened women; smoke came from its nostrils. With a fierce cry, the creature began whipping its heavy, forked tail about the room, beating the women—including the mother—mercilessly. Finally, with a guttural sound, the beast flew up the chimney and out into the darkness, its great wings sounding like thunder in the suddenly still night.

So was born the Jersey Devil, the unlucky thirteenth son of Mother Leeds.

Unquestionably the state's most famous legend, the Jersey Devil is also New Jersey's most popular folk tale. Ever since his—or, more properly, its—birth in 1735, the devil has been embraced by each succeeding generation, which adds its own special twist to the tale so that the story changes just as rapidly as its audience. Each new version of the story adds another chapter to the life of this strange and fascinating creature.

Some say he was born as described above, a normal baby doomed to become a monster by his mother's interest in the black arts. Others say that Mother Leeds, already burdened with twelve children, was driven to despair when she found herself pregnant for the thirteenth time. "I hope this time it's a devil," she shouted angrily, forgetting the old axiom to be careful what you wish for, it might come true.

Whatever the circumstances of his birth, the devil flew off that night to begin a life tormenting the residents of the Pinelands. Everything from crop failures to droughts and fish kills have been blamed on this infamous beast.

Although everyone in the Pinelands knew about the Jersey Devil (Walter Edge, two-time New Jersey governor and United States Senator, said that when he was a boy in Atlantic County, he and his friends were "threatened with the Jersey Devil, morning, noon, and night"), the creature was just a regional phenomena until one amazing week in 1909. Then, clearly making a bid for larger fame, the devil swept out of the Pinelands during the week of January 16–23 and instituted a reign of terror unparalleled throughout western New Jersey. From Camden to Trenton, the devil rode on wagons, attacked animals, killed chickens, tried to break into homes, and terrorized citizens in numerous cities. Not only did hundreds of people see the creature, but the incidents were reported in newspapers throughout the state. Suddenly everyone knew the Jersey Devil.

After that spree, however, the devil became shy once again, and retreated deep into the forest, where it has largely remained to this day. It still makes occasional forays, however, like the one in 1966 in which a poultry farm near the Mullica River was attacked by something that went on a savage rampage, killing over two dozen ducks, geese, cats, and dogs—including a ninety-pound German shepherd.

In recent years, civilization has nibbled at the corners of the Pinelands, and it's the opinion of some that the Jersey Devil is dead, killed by the encroachment of concrete and asphalt. This, however, seems like a premature obituary. The wily creature has been considered dead before (most notably in 1925, when its "carcass" was put on display by a Gloucester County man who supposedly shot the beast), but has always turned up again. It seems like it would take a lot more than urbanization to kill so cunning a creature.

Today, every time the wind blows hard in the Pinelands, and there's a

51 The Jersey Devil. (Interpretive drawing by William A. Herbert, Jr.)

crash in the underbrush, it's blamed on the Jersey Devil. Oh yes, we say with a grin and a wink, that's him, that old devil. Then we hurry on our way, particularly if night is coming on, and the shadows are getting longer, and mysterious sounds are creeping closer to us with each dying gasp of the sun.

For who knows what really lurks deep in the strange, uncharted region of pine forests and cedar water of the Pinelands? Here, where the wind moans through the trees, where distant lights flicker and vanish without warning, and where the wet, swampy ground sometimes seems to reach out and grab at your feet, there are clearly things best left unknown—and unseen. One of these could well be the Jersey Devil.

DID YOU KNOW?

It's awfully hard to kill the Jersey Devil. The creature has been reported dead, only to turn up again, more times than Elvis! Vivid proof of this came in the early nineteenth century. Naval hero Stephen Decatur paid a visit to the Hanover Iron Works to make sure that the cannonballs being made were the right size and shape for fighting the Barbary Pirates. While lining up a shot on the firing range, Decatur saw the Devil flying right across the target area. With cool precision, Decatur sent a shot right through the beast. The Devil, however, ignored the wound, and continued on its way.

What does the Jersey Devil look like? Although descriptions and portraits often vary, there are a few elements that have remained consistent in the legend. See if you can guess which body part most commonly describes the Jersey Devil:

1 Body of a (kangaroo, horse, chicken)
2 Head of a (rat, zebra, dog)
3 Face of a (bat, snake, horse)

52   Is this the house where evil was born? According to local legend, this is the Shourds house, circa 1950, in Leeds Point, where the Jersey Devil first greeted the world. (The house is no longer standing.) (Courtesy Special Collections and Archives, Rutgers University Libraries)

4. Wings of a (dove, duck, bat)
5. Feet of a (donkey, wildebeest, pig)
Answers: 1, kangaroo; 2, dog; 3, horse; 4, bat; 5, pig.

Of course, the Jersey Devil isn't the only legend to emerge from the Pinelands. This vast, mysterious wilderness has many more tales to tell, tales like that of "Fiddlin'" Sammy Giberson.

Sammy was born in Burlington County in September 1808, and if he wasn't playing a fiddle at the moment of his birth he almost certainly picked one up the instant the doctor smacked his bare bottom. By the time he was a man, no one in the Pinelands could make the cat-gut sing like Sammy.

One night, after partaking of the local refreshment at a New Gretna inn, Sammy began proclaiming his fiddling excellence. "I could even beat the devil in a showdown," he boasted.

A gasp went up from the audience. It wasn't wise to challenge Old Scratch like that.

Later that night, Sammy headed home. Suddenly the moon scurried behind some clouds and the air turned sharply colder. Sammy looked up and saw a stranger barring his way.

"I hear you think you can beat me dancing and fiddling," said the stranger ominously. When Sammy asked who he was speaking to, the stranger drew himself up to his full height.

"The devil," he snarled. "Now start playing."

Sammy knew that he would have to play like he'd never played before. Pulling out his fiddle, he began playing for all he was worth, and the devil began dancing. For hours the contest continued; first Sammy played, then the devil. Each was the equal of the other.

Finally, with dawn approaching, the devil admitted that Sammy was indeed a superb fiddler. Suitably impressed, Satan promised to teach Sammy some tunes that no mortal had ever played before.

The devil must have kept his word, for from this point on Sammy Giberson became the most amazing fiddle player the world had ever seen. He

GHOSTS AND LEGENDS

173

could play just as well lying on the ground as he could standing up, and the music he played was like nothing ever heard by human ears. When people asked where he had learned these tunes, Sammy just smiled.

Soon it was whispered that Sammy disappeared into the deep woods with his fiddle on certain nights. Before long the sound of two instruments would come floating through the pine trees, strange, haunting music that was not of this earth. The residents called them devil duets.

Finally, death claimed Sammy Giberson. His fiddle was locked in its black box and placed on a shelf. That, however, did not silence it. People swore that they could hear music coming from the box—the same mysterious music that Sammy used to play. Eventually the fiddle vanished.

There are those, however, who claim that the fiddle didn't just disappear; they say that Sammy reached out from the grave and took it himself. The proof, they confide, can be heard late at night: If you listen closely, you can still hear the sound of Sammy's music, floating through the trees from the deepest, darkest part of the forest.

The white stag of Shamong is another classic Pinelands tale. It seems that one stormy night many years ago, a stage coach was lurching along on the rutted roads, trying desperately to reach the warmth and security of the Quaker Bridge Hotel. Frantically the driver whipped his team of horses, as the thunder crashed above him, and the rain came down in stinging bolts from the angry heavens. Desperate to reach shelter, he was overjoyed when he suddenly saw a light in the distance, which he knew came from the hotel. With a triumphant cry he urged his team on.

All at once, from out of nowhere, a great white stag suddenly appeared in the road directly in front of the stage. With a shouted oath the coachman reined in his horses. As he got down to investigate this strange phenomenon, the creature vanished as dramatically as it had appeared. His

53   F. A. Fralinger (far right) *points out to state troopers and Game Warden Wesley Gibbs the strange, devil-like tracks that he found at Whitesbog in 1952. A prankster was later found to have made the prints. (Courtesy Special Collections and Archives, Rutgers University Libraries)*

curiosity piqued, the driver walked down the soggy roadway a bit, to see if he could find any evidence of the stag.

Suddenly the coachman's eyes grew wide. Up ahead, camouflaged by the driving rain until he was right on top of it, was a bridge across a raging river—or what was left of a bridge. The storm and the rushing water had torn it apart, and if the coachman had continued to push his horses forward the entire stage would have plunged into the river. Since then, white stags have been considered a good luck symbol in the Pinelands.

Legends. Tall tales. Are they wholly imagined or is there some shred of truth at their center? Are they merely fabrications, or are they the stuff of cold, hard fact? Before you answer, consider the strange case of Peggy Clevenger of the Pinelands.

Put simply, Peggy Clevenger was a witch. Not a black-clad, hook-nosed, broom-flying Halloween witch, but a real witch, the type that knew how to make natural forces do her bidding.

Everyone in the Pinelands knew what Peggy was. Usually they gave her a wide berth, but sometimes that wasn't possible. This was the case when a man thought that Peggy had bewitched him. Declaring that he was going to kill her, he drew Peggy's picture, then cut up some silver coins and loaded them into his shotgun. Unfortunately, his aim was off, because when he fired he hit Peggy's hand in the picture. The next day Peggy was seen with a badly mangled hand. She said her dog did it, but everyone knew better.

"The old devil," grumbled the shooter. "If I'd only got her heart instead of her hand, I'd fixed her."

Peggy had the ability to turn herself into a rabbit. Once a few boys were out with their hunting dog when a rabbit was spotted. The boys and dog all gave chase and seemed to have the rabbit cornered until it jumped into the window of Peggy's house. In the twinkling of an eye Peggy was at the exact same window, glaring out at them. Both boys and dog turned tail and ran.

Supposedly, Peggy kept a hotel called the Half-Way Place, which was so named because it was halfway to the Jersey Shore from the Pinelands. Considering the whispers about Peggy, and what went on in that hotel, it's a fairly safe bet that few people ever signed the guest register of the Half-Way Place.

Among the many stories told about Peggy was that she kept a large cache of gold hidden in her house. This supposed fortune proved to be her undoing.

One night, a fire roared through Peggy Clevenger's house. With the first light of dawn, rescuers poking through the still-smoldering ashes found Peggy's body—with her head cut off. Plainly, no fire had done that. It was murder, pure and simple, and suspicion immediately fell on Peggy's daughter and son-in-law, who had been seen at her home the night of the fire. Despite a lack of evidence, this was the accepted version of Peggy's death for several years. Then a Pinelands man got terribly sick, and it seemed obvious that he was going to die, but he didn't, despite getting sicker and sicker. People began saying that he couldn't die, because he was harboring a terrible secret that needed to be told before he could be released.

Finally, after months of suffering, the man gave in to the inevitable: He admitted that he had killed Peggy for her gold—which he never found—and set the fire to cover his tracks. No sooner had he confessed than he closed his eyes for the final time.

Whatever happened to Peggy Clevenger's gold? Did someone else find it, or is it still out in the forest, lying under a bed of pine needles, waiting to be discovered? Is it possible, as the locals say, that Peggy's headless body is still searching for it, wandering through the Pinelands on its eternal quest? Is anyone brave enough to find out?

Ghosts are one of the most terrifying of all supernatural phenomena. The idea that some restless souls continue to walk the earth after their death sends a chill down the spine of even the bravest mortal. New Jersey has its share of these strolling spirits.

On May 6, 1937, the dirigible *Hindenburg* exploded while trying to land at Lakehurst in Ocean County. The disaster, which was reported around the world, spelled the end of lighter-than-air transport. Since ghosts are often associated with tragedy, perhaps it's only logical that the ghost of an airman has been reported in Lakehurst. The ghost haunts Hangar Number One at the Naval Air Station; several officers have reported seeing the spectral figure, which vanishes when approached. Is this spirit someone involved in the *Hindenburg* disaster, or is it the ghost of a former soldier who was once stationed at Lakehurst and was killed in a war? No one knows—and the ghost isn't telling.

Ghosts sometimes turn up in the strangest places. In Union County, the ghost of Hannah Caldwell, a woman killed by a stray bullet during the

Revolutionary War, reportedly haunts the Union County Courthouse in Elizabeth. Railroad tracks throughout the state are where you'll find the Hooker Man (also called the Long Valley Ghost). According to legend, this one-armed apparition was struck by a train while walking on the tracks in life and is still taking his strolls—although in a different reality. In Branchbrook Park, on the border of Newark and Belleville, a spectral figure in white has been seen floating near a tree where a fatal car crash occurred that killed a honeymooning couple.

Then there's the phantom of Parkway Exit 82.

As if it's not difficult enough to drive the Garden State Parkway, with its ubiquitous toll booths, there have been reports of ghostly activity near Exit 82 in the Toms River area. Supposedly, on nights when the fog is thick, a very tall person suddenly runs out onto the roadway and frantically waves motorists down, as if he desperately needs help. When the drivers slow down, however, the figure disappears. Supposedly, this stretch of the Parkway has been the scene of an unusual number of accidents. Could some of these be the result of the Phantom of Exit 82? No one knows, but think twice when driving along that stretch, especially on foggy nights.

Another eerie ghost story concerns a place called the Water's Edge Cafe in Jefferson Township (Morris County). Built originally by Alfred T. Ringling of circus fame, the structure became a restaurant in the 1940s. The first ghostly sightings were reported in the 1960s. The British owner of the building repeatedly saw a shadowy figure on the stairs and in one of the rooms. The ghost was described as having dark hair and hateful eyes. When questioned, the spirit identified itself as Armon Hirsuit, but a search of local history books turned up no record of that name.

Soon the restaurant began showing symptoms commonly associated with a haunting, including sudden cold spots in rooms and objects moving with no apparent cause. Other ghosts popped up: One was a woman in a powder-blue Victorian dress, who told a psychic that she was the eatery's caretaker; another was a male ghost with dark hair, who was wearing a suit with a wide collar.

Who were these ghosts in life? What was their connection to the building that still attracts them today, long after their death? This type of information can hold the key to understanding hauntings, but the answers are often difficult to obtain. It's rare to not only know who a ghost is, but why he or she remains in a certain place. However, precisely such a case has occurred in Basking Ridge.

Bill Baily's dream had always been to build a large house that could be used as an artist's colony, but he died unexpectedly in 1931, before the house was finished. His wife, Sarah, however, kept the dream alive, and in 1936 the large, rambling structure was finally completed. Given Bill's love for the house, it probably shouldn't be too surprising that his ghost began appearing throughout it. His wife remained in the house until 1941, when it was turned into a boy's school. Bill wasn't heard from much until the mid-1970s, when a couple bought the home. Before you could say "Boo," windows starting opening and closing, the television began channel-surfing on its own, and strange noises came from all over the house. The topper came in 1986, when during a test for paranormal existence Bill himself suddenly appeared at the front door.

Ironically, that episode seemed to help both sides. The couple learned to get along with Bill, and he apparently decided to leave them alone. However, Bill remained very protective of the house he loved, even to the point of closing the windows when it rained. (Now that's the kind of ghost we should all have!)

Another New Jersey house that seems to have more than just mortal occupants is an old Victorian structure in Midland Park. Although more than one ghost has been reported there, the spirit that everyone seems to see is that of a small, yellow and white cat. This feline phantasm stays mainly in a third-floor bedroom, where even those who don't see it often find a warm spot on the bed, and a small, round indentation on a comforter or blanket.

From early in the twentieth century comes a ghostly New Jersey tale identified only as occurring somewhere across from the South Branch River. There, in a place known as the haunted meadow, was often seen "a man riding on a rig without horses or shafts to it, just as if he sat perched about four feet above the bare axle, on which the two wheels turned almost like lightning." From the wheels of this ghostly wagon came blue light, which sparked out continuously as the vehicle careened around the dark meadow at high speeds. Some said it was the ghost of a man called Joseph Pittenger; others claim that the meadow was simply haunted. As proof, they cited the fact that cows placed there at night to graze would go wild, stampeding in all directions as if the demons of hell were after them.

In 1964 the pioneering folklorist Father Henry Charlton Beck related a story of the haunted church of St. Boniface in Jersey City. According to Beck, who was quoting a nineteenth-century magazine article, the house of worship was infected by a cacophony of hideous sounds: "At one instant the house would seem still as a tomb, and then suddenly a burst of wild voices would seem to issue simultaneously from all parts of the building, reverberating along the aisles in fierce laughter, and dying away only to give place to a second succession of shrieks more ghastly and unusual than the first."

The ghost apparently caused quite a stir in Jersey City. Crowds of people searched for the spirit, who was spotted on the church steeple by a young girl. She described the ghost as "gigantic in appearance, with eyes hollow and fiery, like marsh lights, and wearing a long flowing robe which resembled a cloud, so vapory and mistlike was its texture."

A poltergeist (a mischievous spirit) was supposedly the cause of some mysterious events at a New Egypt (Ocean County) farm. After a slow start in which it amused itself by moving kitchen utensils and hairbrushes around, the spirit got warmed up and began hurtling deadly objects through the air, including a hail of spice jars. Terrified, the family called in psychic investigators from Brookdale Community College. They managed to get rid of the cranky ghost—but not before one of the investigators was nearly killed when a forty-five pound tinker's anvil inexplicably launched itself at his head, just barely missing him.

Although many people dismiss ghosts as figments of over-active imaginations, new stories of inexplicable phenomena are constantly coming to light. In 1994 it was revealed that Courtroom 1 in Toms River (Ocean County) was being plagued by a number of strange occurrences: door knobs jiggling by themselves, motion detectors tripped inside empty rooms, lights turning on and off, and spectral figures being spotted like a middle-aged man neatly dressed in a shirt and tie and a tear-shaped figure that looked like white smoke. Another possible haunting has recently been reported at Hudson County Community College in West New York. Employees at the former convent report hearing strange sounds and voices, and one caught a glimpse of a female ghost in a black dress carrying books.

Another thing to consider is this: If indeed there are no such thing as ghosts, then why are there nearly 100 cases of homes in New Jersey where no other explanation except supernatural activity has been found for unexplained occurrences?

Perhaps we're laughing off the reality of ghosts too quickly.

Those who lived around Lake Hopatcong in Morris County certainly weren't laughing two hundred years ago. That's when a strange beast that reportedly lived in the lake was scaring local inhabitants half to death.

According to the story, the creature was so large that next to it an ox seemed like a fawn. The beast had a horse's head, an elephant's body, and sported a huge set of antlers. Sometimes its great head would suddenly burst from the water with a violent splash, rising up like the periscope of some horrible submarine.

What happened to this gigantic creature? No one knows for sure. The Lenape Indians told the early settlers of Boone Town (Boonton) that the beast drowned while crossing the lake on thin ice. Its carcass, they said, was at the bottom of the lake. When the settlers rowed out to the spot the Indians had described, they could see, on the bottom, a huge skull with antlers extending ten feet in length.

Legends are very much a part of the cultural heritage of the Ramapo Mountain People, who live in and around the towns of Mahwah and Ringwood. One of the most well-known is about the Jack o' Lantern.

According to the story, the Jack o' Lantern is a mysterious light that suddenly appears in the woods at night. However, if you go toward the light it vanishes, only to reappear somewhere else. The more you follow the light the more it darts from place to place. Soon you are hopelessly lost.

Another Ramapo legend concerns a magic barrel full of gold that rolls down a mountain every night at midnight. If a person can stop the barrel before it disappears into an old well, they are entitled to all the gold it contains. However, there's always a catch in the world of the damned: If someone is successful in stopping the magic barrel, then monsters and snakes will suddenly appear, forcing the person to flee for dear life. Supposedly the magic barrel is still at it, merrily rolling down the mountain every midnight and waiting for someone to figure out how to claim it.

The Screech Woman is a particularly eerie Ramapo tale. Her name comes from the hair-raising scream that she emits at night—a scream that races through the mountains like the clarion call of death, chilling everyone who hears it.

Like the Pinelands, the Ramapo Mountains are a strange and mysterious place. Who knows what inhabits these hills, especially late at night, when the mortal world is asleep and things unseen emerge to spend a few hours on earth? Could there be such a thing as a magic barrel, a screech woman, and/or the mysterious lights of the Jack o' Lantern? Who can answer these questions for certain?

What gives us pause, in these increasingly uncertain times, is the fact that the more science and technology teaches us about our world, the less we seem to know. For example, what has caused the plague of misery to descend on many of the people who worked on the Route 55 extension in Deptford (Gloucester County)? Reports say that the New Jersey Department of Transportation was warned not to build this road, because it went over a sacred Indian burial ground. The warning was ignored, the road was built, and now many of the workers have had their lives tragically altered by heart attacks, car accidents, miscarriages, and other misfortunes that have befallen family and friends.

Much of this chapter so far has dealt with the eerie, the unexpected, and the frightening. Let's shift gears now and end this chapter on a happier note, with some unusual and humorous stories about New Jersey.

Millville singer and storyteller Jim Albertson has a veritable Santa's bag of stories about the Garden State, some of which he relates on his audio recording "Down Jersey—Songs and Stories of Southern New Jersey" (Smithsonian Folkways, 416 Hungerford Drive, #320, Rockville, Md., 20850).

Have you ever been lost in a boat? If so, then Albertson's tale of the "South Jersey Boat Compass" is just for you. The back bays and rivers of South Jersey can be difficult to navigate, especially during fog. That's when a South Jersey boat compass comes in handy. To use one, stand in front of the boat with a basket of New Jersey tomatoes, and every few minutes drop a tomato into the water. When you don't hear a splash, turn hard.

Many of Albertson's tales follow classic storytelling themes that can be found in legends throughout the United States. Two of these concern a legendary New Jersey trapper named Charlie Balderston.

One day, Charlie was out in the woods when he discovered two bear cubs in the bottom of a dead tree. He decided to remove the cubs, but no sooner had he gotten inside the tree when the sunlight was blotted out from above. Looking up, Charlie saw that the mother bear was shimmying down the inside of the tree as well. Thinking quickly, Charlie pulled out his knife, grabbed the bear's tail, and jabbed. The mother bear, getting the point, shot out of the tree like a rocket, enabling Charlie—without the cubs—to get away safely.

Another Charlie Balderston story is the day of the Great Hunt. While out hunting one day, Charlie saw six wild turkeys perched in a tree. With one shot Charlie split the branch that the turkeys were on; the birds' feet slipped into the crack, and the branch snapped shut. He cut off the branch and was heading home with a fine day's catch when he looked up and saw a flock of ducks coming toward him from the north, and a flock of geese heading away from him toward the south. Then, just to make things really interesting, he saw two rabid foxes approaching him, hungrily eyeing the turkeys.

Charlie was in a quandary: Should he shoot the ducks and/or the geese and take his chances with the foxes? Or should he deal with the hungry and dangerous foxes, and let the birds get away?

Charlie was pondering the situation when he suddenly slipped on a wet rock. His gun flew out of his hands and struck the rock, which caused the weapon to fire: The bullet hit another rock and split in two, dispatching both foxes. Meanwhile, the barrel of the gun flew into the air one way and hit some geese, while the stock went the other way and struck some ducks. The force of the gun going off knocked Charlie backwards, into a creek; when he came up, he was holding a beaver in one hand, an otter in the other, and his pants were so stuffed with fish that a button popped off his trousers and shot the rapids.

Yet another New Jersey folk tale that follows classic lines concerns a family named Boyd, who raised hogs that they turned into sausage and sold. One of the boys in the family had invented a sausage machine that was a sheer wonder; all you had to do was put the hog into it at one end, turn the crank, and out popped the sausage at the other end, all neatly packaged and ready for market.

The Boyds had a prize hog, a fine, strapping animal that they knew would bring a good price at the market. One day, they put the hog into the machine, turned the crank, and shortly were driving to the county fair with a truck crammed with sausage. At the fair they immediately sold a five-pound package of sausage to a woman, and they thought that it was going to be a good day. Unfortunately, at that moment the heavens opened up, and rain drenched the fair. Realizing that they were not going to do any more business that day, the Boyds loaded their sausage back onto their truck and returned home.

Once there, however, the family was faced with a problem: What were they going to do with all the sausage? There was too much to put into the freezer, and it would certainly spoil before the next time came to bring it to market. Then, someone had an idea; they put the sausage into the sausage-making machine at the other end, and turned the crank backwards. Sure enough, out of the other end popped the prize hog.

Now this may seem like just a tall story, but the proof, as they say, is in the pudding (or in this case, the sausage): At the Boyd farm it was always easy to identify the prize hog—it was the one with the five-pound hole in his leg from where the woman had bought the first package of sausage.

By definition, legends are folk tales told about real people, such as those about Davy Crockett. Charlie Balderston was real and so, quite probably, was the Boyd family. Nobody, however, was the equal of Woodbury (Gloucester County) native Jonas Cattel.

Jonas was a mailman, and a darn good one. In a journey documented in *Ripley's Believe It or Not*, he once delivered, on foot, a letter from Woodbury to Cape May. He also fought for the United States against the British in the Revolutionary War. His main claim to fame, however, came as a result of a fishing trip.

One day, while fishing in the Cohansey River with two friends, Jonas noticed the dorsal fin of a shark approaching the boat. Attempting to curb the fish's appetite for people, Jonas and his friends threw everything overboard they could think of: flour, sugar, lemons, wood, oars, and even tools. Nothing satisfied the creature; it continued to circle the boat, and those on board could hear the dinner bell sounding in the shark's brain.

Then, one of the other men remembered that the name Jonas is a derivative of Jonah, as in the famous Bible story of Jonah and the whale. Feeling that what was good enough for the Bible was good enough for them, the two fishermen tossed poor Jonas overboard, where he was instantly swallowed in one gulp by the shark. This, however, also failed to mollify the shark. It continued to circle the boat.

With nothing left to do, the two remaining fishermen doffed cowboy hats that they found in the boat, lassoed the shark, put a saddle on it, and rode the big fish up the Cohansey to Bridgeton.

The sight of two men riding a shark caused quite a stir in Bridgeton. The shark was hoisted out of the water and hung upside down from a telephone pole, where it began to smell worse than hot tar on a summer's day. It was decided to cut the shark up into cooking-size portions. A fisherman took out his knife and cut the shark open straight down the middle. No sooner had he done so than out jumped Jonas Cattel.

Jonas had always been an industrious person, and he proved it by showing that he had not been idle inside the shark. He had collected all the tools and the wood that the shark had swallowed and built a refreshment stand, which he proceeded to haul out of the fish. From that stand Jonas sold apple pie and lemonade to the tourists who had come to Bridgeton to see the giant shark, netting himself a pretty penny in the bargain.

The devil, you say? Don't say that too loud in New Jersey. You never know who—or what—is going to respond.

 *Historical Happenings*

A S O N E of the original thirteen states, New Jersey has seen a lot of history come its way. Indeed, even when it was a colony New Jersey was making history, such as when it established the first Indian reservation in 1758.

In a state with so much history to its credit, it's difficult to point to a few examples as the definitive moments in its past. The events in this chapter, therefore, have been chosen not only because of their historical significance, but also because of their unusual nature. It's safe to say that the people you're about to meet—among them an egoistical radio performer, a sullen general, and a brave young woman—and the events they've participated in or caused to happen are all unique, interesting, and have had consequences that went far beyond the boundaries of this state.

The news coming from the radio on the night of October 30, 1938, was anything but good for the United States.

At home, the Great Depression still had its icy grip firmly around the nation's throat, despite the best attempts of President Franklin D. Roosevelt to break it. Abroad, a shrill-voiced German named Adolf Hitler was making increasingly belligerent speeches that seemed to many like a prelude to war. It was an uneasy time.

But as people settled around their radio on that Sunday evening, one day before Halloween, they had no inkling of the drama that was about to unfold—a drama that would soon make them, as well as a part of New Jersey called Grovers Mill, part of American folklore.

That night, most people tuned into Edgar Bergen's popular "Chase and Sanborn Hour." The ventriloquist and his wise-cracking wooden sidekick, Charlie McCarthy, commanded a vast 35 percent of the radio audience. A mere 3.6 percent of the listeners tuned to a competing program on the CBS radio network called "The Mercury Theatre on the Air."

The Mercury Theatre was the brainchild of Orson Welles, the twenty-three-year-old "boy genius" of Broadway. But his reputation had not helped his ratings, and the prospects didn't look good for the show about to be broadcast: a reworked version of H. G. Wells' famous 1897 story *War of the Worlds*, a tale of Martians invading the earth.

There were problems with *War of the Worlds* from the beginning. The novel took place in turn-of-the-century England, and its leisurely style reflected that era. Welles knew that if the story was to be successful on American radio, it would have to be juiced up, modernized, and moved to the United States. Thus, except for the central idea, the entire novel was scrapped and an entirely new script was written—in a typewriter-torching time of six days.

(The author of this script has been a source of controversy for years. Many people credit Howard Koch, a young playwright who had just begun writing for the Mercury Theatre. In his 1970 book about the show, *The Panic Broadcast*, Koch does nothing to discredit this notion. However, until the day he died Welles adamantly claimed that he and other Mercury members did "as much of the writing . . . as the writers themselves." He was particularly incensed at Princeton University psychologist Hadley Cantril, who wrote a psychological profile of the broadcast in 1940 called *Invasion from Mars*. After going round-and-round with Cantril about authorship, Welles fired off this blistering telegram: "Howard Koch did not write *The War of the Worlds*. Any statement to this effect is untrue and immeasurably detrimental to me.")

The script that caused all the controversy replaced H. G. Wells' prose with a series of terse news bulletins, in which the alien invasion was presented to listeners as if it was actually happening at that moment. Not only did the bulletins make the story immediate and believable—this was when radio broadcasts were routinely interrupted by special bulletins bringing the latest bad news from Europe—but they also confused the listener's sense of time. Having frantic bulletin after frantic bulletin piling up made it plausible that events that should have taken hours were happening within minutes.

---

54 This monument stands at the lake in Grovers Mill near where the Martians supposedly landed. (Photo by Pat King-Roberts)

How was Grovers Mill selected to become so famous? According to Koch, it was pure coincidence. While driving in New Jersey on Route 9 the day before beginning work on the script, he realized that he needed a starting point for his invasion, so he stopped at a gas station and asked for a map. He could have been given a map of any state in the union, but since he was in New Jersey, the attendant displayed his state pride by handing him a map of the Garden State.

"Back in New York starting to work," Koch wrote, "I spread out the map, closed my eyes and put down the pencil point. It happened to fall on Grovers Mill."

For the next six days, the script was written, rewritten, rehearsed, and polished—tasks that normally took weeks, not days. Koch called those six days a "nightmare."

So, when the Mercury Theatre took to the air on that fateful October 30, the chance that it would be a historic broadcast was most unlikely. Consider: Welles tinkered with the script right up until air time; members of the Mercury troupe thought the show "dull"; and, just a fraction of the radio audience was tuned in.

However, as the saying goes, truth is often stranger than fiction.

As usual that Sunday night, millions of people initially opted to hear

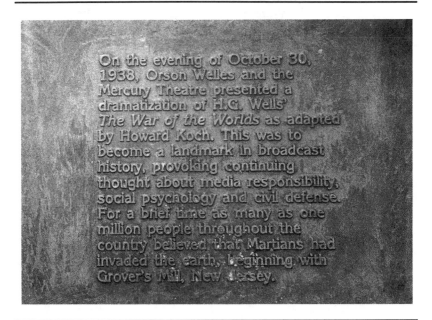

On the evening of October 30, 1938, Orson Welles and the Mercury Theatre presented a dramatization of H.G. Wells' *The War of the Worlds* as adapted by Howard Koch. This was to become a landmark in broadcast history, provoking continuing thought about media responsibility, social psychology and civil defense. For a brief time as many as one million people throughout the country believed that Martians had invaded the earth, beginning with Grover's Mill, New Jersey.

Edgar Bergen banter with Charlie McCarthy. Twelve minutes into the show, Nelson Eddy came on to sing "Neapolitan Love Song." As was common then, many listeners began flipping through the dial—what to-day's television generation calls "channel surfing"—until Bergen and McCarthy returned. About 4 million of these station wanderers stopped at the CBS radio network.

What they heard was a progressive series of frantic "news bulletins" and "eyewitness reports" about some very frightening happenings at the "Wilmuth Farm" in Grovers Mill. Having missed the show's beginning, when it was plainly stated that the program was an adaptation of "War of the Worlds," the newcomers were plunged into a maelstrom of horrifying news about the arrival of creatures from Mars. To a jittery populace thor-oughly conditioned to having ominous news bulletins break into their radio programs, and who trusted radio as a reliable source of information, there was no doubt that what they were hearing was very real.

The panic started to build. People began calling their friends, family, or neighbors, to warn them that the earth was being invaded by tentacled creatures with saliva dripping from "rimless lips." The news spread like wildfire; the American Telephone Company reported that telephone vol-ume increased 39 percent during the broadcast, and 25 percent the next hour.

Meanwhile, back in the studio, Welles and his crew blithely continued with their program, unaware of the panic they were causing. When they finally got word, an announcement was made that it was only a radio show. It was forty-two minutes after the broadcast began. It was also much too late.

By then pandemonium reigned. To their horror, the growing number of listeners had heard familiar New Jersey landmarks and place names fall to the Martian machines: Princeton, Trenton, the Pulaski Skyway, Bay-onne, and Newark—all destroyed or captured by the evil aliens. The fight at Grovers Mill between the Martians and the "State Militia" was de-scribed as "one of the most startling defeats ever suffered by an army in modern times." Out of seven thousand soldiers, just 120 were reported to have survived; the rest were "strewn over the battle area from Grovers Mill to Plainsboro, crushed and trampled to death under the metal feet of the monster, or burned to cinders by its heat-ray."

The broadcast ended with Welles, playing a Princeton astronomer,

55 The wording on the "Martian" monument. (Photo by Pat King-Roberts)

discovering that the Martians had been killed by germs that they had no biological defense against. In his playful epilogue, Welles said that the broadcast was the Mercury Theatre's Halloween version of "dressing up in a sheet and jumping out of a bush and saying Boo!" However, it's doubtful that many people heard those final words; they were too busy fleeing from the Martian invasion in one of the greatest instances of mass hysteria ever recorded.

As might be expected, the broadcast caused extreme consternation in the Trenton-Princeton area, scene of most of the "fighting." "Alarm Centers on Princeton" reported the *Newark Evening News* of October 31, 1938. "Terror and hysteria persisted well past midnight in Princeton in the wake of 'War of the Worlds' broadcast last night," began the story. Hysterical telephone callers overwhelmed Princeton police headquarters, which had just one man on duty. A dozen undergraduates at Princeton University were called home by frantic parents. A man rushed into a Kingston church screaming that the world was coming to an end, while in Dutch Neck people prayed in the streets. State police headquarters in Trenton was flooded with phone calls, and traffic was reported as "unusually heavy" at Penn's Neck and on the Brunswick turnpike (Route 1).

Other parts of the state fared no better. East Orange police headquarters received over 200 calls from frightened people who wanted to know

how to escape the Martian's poison gas. Two families from Manhattan burst into the Maplewood police station, frantically wondering how they could get home now that the Pulaski Skyway had been destroyed.

In a single block in Newark, more than twenty families rushed out of their houses with wet handkerchiefs and towels over their faces to thwart the poison gas. Panic-stricken, they began dragging furniture and other belongings out of their homes and loading them into their cars so that they could flee before the Martians arrived. It took an ambulance, three police cars, and an eight-man police emergency squad to calm them and unsnarl the traffic jam they had created.

In Orange, a movie theater was emptied by a man screaming that the world was ending, and frantic children were reported running through the streets in their pajamas. In West Orange, patrons fled in terror from a restaurant, leaving half-eaten meals—and unpaid bills.

Adding to the excitement in North Jersey was the fact that electric lights throughout Bergen County flickered from 6:15 to 6:30 P.M. This helped convince people that the invasion was real.

The Jersey Shore didn't escape the "Martian Menace" either. A man from Bradley Beach raced out of the house in his pajamas and ran down to a nearby bar where he knew his son to be. Wild-eyed, he burst into the bar and ordered his son home. A Red Bank resident was so convinced he smelled poison gas and smoke that he called the police and asked what he should do.

When all was said and done, it was left for a man who lived on the "Wilmuth" (actually Wilson) farm to have the final word on the entire affair. The Andersons were one of three tenant families living on the Wilson farm. On the night of the broadcast, Mrs. Anderson, who had been listening to the show, burst in on her husband James, who had gone to bed, and told him that Martians were reportedly all around them, dealing out death and destruction. Mr. Anderson got up and went out to the front porch, where he was greeted by bullfrogs croaking, crickets chirping, and the stars beaming down at him from a crystal-clear night sky.

"Darn fools," he snorted, and went back to bed.

Initial reaction to the broadcast was swift. The next day, newspapers ran front-page stories vilifying Welles. Soon, however, more thoughtful journalists like the *New York Tribune*'s Dorothy Thompson praised Welles

---

56 This old-fashioned water tower was supposedly mistaken in the dark for one of the Martian "machines" and fired upon during the invasion frenzy. (Photo by Pat King-Roberts)

for showing just how easy it was in the new age of mass communication to stampede a cattlelike public.

The show, she wrote, demonstrated "the incredible stupidity, lack of nerve and ignorance of thousands . . . [and] proved how easy it is to start a mass delusion."

"Mr. Welles . . . made . . . the perfect demonstration that the danger is not from Mars but from the theatrical demagogue," she added.

As for Welles himself, it has always been assumed that he never intended to cause a nationwide panic and that his apologies for doing so were sincere. However, years later, Welles admitted during a television interview that he felt at the time that radio's reputation as a voice of authority had become too great and that he thought people should question it instead of just blindly obeying.

"[I felt] it was time for someone to take the starch . . . out of some of that authority: hence my broadcast," he said. There are also indications that Welles timed the broadcast to have the news bulletins become more urgent at precisely the moment when he knew listeners were spinning their dials away from Bergen and McCarthy.

Today, we smugly assume that we're too sophisticated to fall for anything so obviously contrived as a invasion from Mars, despite the fact that one joke on late-night TV started a nationwide toilet paper shortage scare. Hopefully, if such a hoax is successful again, we won't react like some folks in Peru, who, after listening to a Spanish translation of "War of the Worlds" and finding it to be a joke, stormed the radio station, burned it to the ground, and killed several announcers.

But do we really know for sure?

In grade school children are taught that Boston's famous tea party was a prelude to the American Revolution. The events of December 16, 1773, when a party of patriots dressed as Indians dumped a load of British tea into Boston Harbor to protest Britain's taxation policies, stands as a legendary moment in our national heritage.

What's not taught, however, is that New Jersey had its own tea party, one that was just as bold and daring as the one in Massachusetts.

Today the picturesque town of Greenwich in Cumberland County lies peacefully alongside the Cohansey River. Its main street, called Greate Street, is lined with historic homes dating back over a century or more. It's the type of town where you can practically hear the birds taking a breath between songs as you walk underneath the large, leafy trees that dot the thoroughfares.

But on the evening of December 22, 1774, peace was the last thing to be found at Greenwich. That night the town was a bubbling, foaming cauldron of anger, all of it directed at the British ship *Greyhound,* and a cargo of tea that the brig had brought into Greenwich. Before the night was over, Greenwich would have its own tea party.

The series of events leading up to Greenwich's crowning moment in New Jersey history began on December 12, 1774, when the *Greyhound,* with J. Allen in command, appeared in Cohansey Creek. Since the ship was too small to have transported the tea across the Atlantic Ocean from its initial loading point at Rotterdam, Holland, it's likely that the *Greyhound* met a larger British ship somewhere (possibly the Delaware Bay) and took the tea on board at that point.

However, taking the tea on board was one thing; finding someplace to unload it was quite another. As he made his way up the Delaware River, someone probably told Allen that tea was not exactly a popular item to be bringing into the colonies right then. In October, the citizens of Annapolis, Maryland, had forced the owner of the ship *Peggy Stewart* to burn his vessel, because it contained imported goods from England, including several chests of tea. Philadelphia had turned back the *Polly* with its load of tea by refusing permission for the captain to dock. The Boston Tea Party had made tea the lightning rod for all the injustices that the colonies felt against Great Britain, and Allen was sailing into the gathering storm with an incendiary cargo on board.

Then he thought of Greenwich—and a man named Daniel Bowen.

Bowen was a known British loyalist living at a house-warehouse in Greenwich owned by John Sheppard. Allen decided to sail into Greenwich, which was then a thriving port, transfer the tea to Bowen's house, and then return for it after all the furor had died down. After all, this was Greenwich, and not a hotbed of insurrection like Philadelphia or Boston. What could happen?

Thus the *Greyhound* landed at Greenwich on December 12, and the tea was unloaded and stored in the cellar of Bowen's residence without incident. (According to the *Bridgeton Chronicle* of November 13, 1874, this building was located directly across from the town's open market square.) Allen must have mentally patted himself on the back; with a little forethought, he had defused a potentially dangerous situation.

He couldn't have been more wrong.

Allen's crew was spotted unloading the tea, and by the next day word of what was being stored at Bowen's was spreading throughout Cumberland County. The first General Congress of the colonies, which had met in Philadelphia in September 1774, had recommended that the colonies not import any British goods or merchandise, and especially tea. Yet here was the foul stuff, sitting in a Greenwich basement. This did not sit well with the county's patriots; a meeting was called for December 23 in Cohansey Bridge (now Bridgeton) to decide what to do about it.

(The exact sequence of events is somewhat ambiguous. Most accounts have Allen landing on the twelfth, and unloading the tea the same night. However, *Dunlap's Pennsylvania Packet* of January 9, 1775 states that the tea was unloaded on December 22. In view of the fact that the tea incident occurred on the twenty-second, it's likely that the correct landing date was the twelfth, which would have given the participants ample time to arrange their "party.")

Events, however, would make the meeting superfluous. In the fading light of December 22, men from Cohansey Bridge, Greenwich, Fairfield, and other towns gathered at the home of Richard Howell, four miles outside of Greenwich. From there the group, numbering about two dozen, went to the Fithian residence, where they donned "war paint" and feathers. When they emerged, there was no doubt as to their final destination: Greenwich.

It was dark by the time the group arrived in Greenwich. However, within minutes the night sky was lit up by the flames of an enormous fire burning in the market place square—a fire fueled by the chests of tea that the men had carried out from the warehouse across the street. The Greenwich Tea Party had begun.

Word quickly spread among the citizens, who rolled out of their beds and headed down to the site of the blaze. There they found the "Indians" dancing in glee around the fire, as the despised symbol of English authoritarianism went up in smoke.

Not everyone, however, could bear to part with their tea so easily. One of the raiders was a man named Henry Stacks, who also dearly loved British tea. While the fire burned, Stacks quietly collected all the precious leaves that he could and stuffed them into his pockets, coat, shoes, and wherever else they would fit. Unfortunately, he was spotted; someone stuck the name "Tea Stacks" on him, and there it remained for the rest of his life.

No sooner had the fire died out than the "Indians" vanished. The next day, Fithian wrote in his diary: "Last night the Tea was by a number of persons in disguise taken out of the House & consumed with fire. Violent

57 Dedication of Tea Burners Monument in Greenwich, September 1908. (Courtesy Cumberland County Historical Society)

& different are the words about this uncommon Manoeuvre among the Inhabitants. Some rave, some curse & condemn, some try to reason; many are glad the Tea is destroyed, but almost all disapprove the Manner of the destruction."

Almost immediately, legal machinery began to grind. The Cumberland County Committee of Safety passed resolutions condemning the act, and several attempts were made by the British judiciary to prosecute as many of the "Indians" as possible. However, these efforts came to naught; many people secretly approved of the action, (including the sheriff, Jonathan Elmer, who was the brother of one of the participants), and finding a jury that would convict was impossible.

As the years slipped by, New Jersey's patriotic tea party faded into history. Greenwich lost its status as an important port, and became the epitome of small-town America.

However, the advent of the centennial anniversary of the tea party reawakened the spirit of 1774. A huge celebration was held in Greenwich to mark the occasion. In November, 1874, the *Bridgeton Chronicle* said: "[These] patriotic sons of Cumberland County were among the first to strike the blow which gave us a name and prominence among the nations of the globe." It was, said the paper, a bold and daring act "of which the inhabitants of this county have a just reason to be proud."

GREENWICH, N. J. SEP. 30, — 08,
TEA BURNERS MONUMENT & OLD TEA HOUS

Thirty-four years later, a monument to the tea burners was dedicated on Greate Street, where it remains to this day—an everlasting memorial to the time when New Jersey freedom fighters struck a blow for liberty.

The events in Greenwich and elsewhere throughout the colonies were all leading up to one thing: the Revolutionary War. Almost four years after New Jersey's tea party, the Garden State was again the site for a critical event that helped propel the fledgling nation toward its freedom—and, in the process, produced one of the most beloved American tales of all time.

It was June, 1778. After a cool start, the month had turned blistering hot—bad news indeed for the British troops, whose wool uniforms and heavy packs, weighing up to eighty pounds, proved too much for some men as they struggled across the heat-seared New Jersey landscape. (On June 26, the English lost 200 men to the heat.) General Henry Clinton, commander of the British force of 18,000 soldiers, had abandoned his occupation of Philadelphia on June 17 and 18 to consolidate his army

with other English troops in New York City. He planned to march across New Jersey to Sandy Hook, from where his army would sail to New York. Smack in the middle of Clinton's path lay the little village (population 100) of Monmouth Courthouse, or Freehold, as it's known today.

Allowing the Americans to reoccupy Philadelphia was a great psychological boost for the colonial forces. George Washington, however, wasn't content with a moral victory. He wanted a battlefield triumph to show the mettle of his army. When he learned that the British were leaving Philadelphia, he put his own army into motion from Valley Forge. On June 24, Washington camped at Hopewell, while Clinton stopped at Allentown, twenty miles to the southeast.

Washington held a council of war to determine his army's next step. Some of his officers urged a pitched battle now, before the British got safely to New York. Others, however, agreed with the more cautious views of General Charles Lee.

Lee, a critical player in the drama that was about to unfold, has come down through history as a traitorous scoundrel, a man who tried to sell out the colonial forces once and did everything in his power to turn the Battle of Monmouth into an American disaster. Lee was a vain, egotistical, stubborn man whose motto in modern terms would be "My way or the highway." Outspoken to a fault, but a good general, Lee had fought on the side of several European powers, including England, before settling in Virginia just before the revolution began. With his political connections and military experience, he became the second-ranking officer in Washington's army.

Possibly because he had served with various spit-and-polish European armies, Lee didn't have much regard for the rag-tag colonial forces. (Nor did he think too highly of Washington—an opinion he freely shared and which undoubtedly contributed to his subsequent problems.) He favored a guerrilla war, fearing that colonial troops couldn't stand up to the British in a face-to-face battle. At Hopewell, much to the disgust of the patriotic firebrands on Washington's staff such as Alexander Hamilton, Lee reiterated his view: If the British wanted to leave New Jersey, why should the Americans do anything to slow them up?

Finally, Washington decided to attack the British, but with just a small segment of his army—a compromise that satisfied neither the warriors nor the fence-sitters. Disgusted, Hamilton wrote that the Hopewell council "would have done honor to the most honorable society of midwives, and to them only."

---

58   The Tea Burners Monument today in Greenwich. (Photo by author)

A detachment of 4,000 men under General Marquis de Lafayette was sent against the British. By the time the troops reached Englishtown on June 27 their number had swelled to 5,000. Lee was now in command, after initially turning down the assignment, then changing his mind. The plan seemed simple: attack the rear of the British Army, but don't bring on a full-scale battle.

Soon after daybreak on Sunday, June 28, Lee moved his troops forward, seeking to cut off and capture several columns of British calvary and light infantry (about 600 men) in the army's rear. Lee was so sure of victory that he turned to Lafayette and said, "My dear Marquis, I think those people are ours." He sent the same optimistic message to Washington, indicating that a quick, bloodless victory was in the offing.

By mid-day, however, as temperatures soared into the nineties, Lee's fortunes fell. Clinton, upon learning that the colonials were preparing to attack, decided to meet the assault in strength. He turned around the entire 1st Division, a force of about 9,000 men, and sent them hurrying to the rear. To his dismay, Lee found that instead of fighting several hundred British troops, he was about to battle thousands. Meanwhile, ragged battlefield communications and the unfamiliar Monmouth County terrain were causing some of Lee's troops to begin withdrawing without orders. Faced with a rapidly deteriorating situation, Lee retreated.

All this was occurring unbeknownst to Washington. After a leisurely breakfast at the Englishtown home of Dr. James English, Washington headed for the front, expecting to hear of or even witness a colonial success. Much to his surprise, however, he began encountering troops who told him that Lee was retreating, not attacking, and that the colonials seemed headed for another defeat.

Washington, at the very least astonished and more than likely furious, rode on and encountered Lee on the battlefield. What followed was one of the most controversial exchanges ever in United States military history. Kean College professor Mark Lender, in his manuscript on the Battle of Monmouth, calls the confrontation between the two generals "unique in the annals of American arms."

Galloping up to Lee, Washington reined in his horse and snapped: "I desire to know, sir, what is the reason, whence arises this disorder and confusion?"

59 Washington's legendary confrontation with Lee during the Battle of Monmouth. (Courtesy Special Collections and Archives, Rutgers University Libraries)

Lee was stunned. Expecting to be cordially greeted, and maybe even complimented on the way he had maneuvered his forces ("Flattering myself," Lee said later, that his conduct would draw "Washington's congratulations and applause"), Lee was startled by the vehemence in his commander's tone, and could stammer only "Sir—sir!" in response.

Later reports would have Washington chewing out Lee, calling him a "damned poltroon" and swearing "till the leaves shook on the trees." These, however, are colorings of the truth by those who did not like Lee in the first place and who figured that they could use a little dramatic license to give Lee the cussing they thought he so richly deserved.

After a few more remarks, Washington rode forward to take command, leaving Lee behind to lick his wounds. For Charles Lee, the war, and his career, were over.

(A few months later, a court-martial found Gen. Charles Lee guilty of not following Washington's orders to attack and of a "disorderly retreat." Lee left the army in disgrace. While his conviction might have been politically motivated by zealous patriots who detested his cautious approach, Lee's contempt of Washington also helped bring him down.)

Quickly Washington rallied his troops, and, despite his earlier admonishment about not fighting a general engagement, was soon doing exactly that. All during that blazing hot day, the colonials stood their ground against the crack British troops. That night, Clinton slipped away to Sandy Hook, leaving the Americans in control of the battlefield.

DID YOU KNOW?

Facts About the Battle of Monmouth

- The Battle of Monmouth was the longest sustained battle in history until Gettysburg, lasting from dawn until nightfall.
- Although it is commonly considered a draw (even though the British army left the field during the cover of darkness), the battle was actually a great victory for the colonial army, which, despite Gen. Charles Lee's trepidations, proved that it could stand toe-to-toe with the legendary English forces.
- Having proved that they could stand up to the British army, the battle sent confidence levels soaring among patriots, the Continental Congress, the army, and even Washington. As such, the battle can accurately be called the turning point of the Revolutionary War.
- It was the last major fight in the north between British and American forces during the war.
- It was the only battle of the war in the open field in which the main forces of both armies, and most of their commanders, participated.
- Lee died on October 2, 1782. Although his court-martial might have been politically orchestrated, there is no doubt that Lee was not very pleasant, as he proved in his will: [I do not wish to be buried] "in any church or church yard or within a mile of any Presbyterian or Anabaptist meeting house; for, since I have resided in this country, I have kept so much bad company when living, that I do not choose to continue it when dead."

It was during the battle that the second extraordinary event of the day occurred: the story of Molly Pitcher.

We have all seen images of Molly Pitcher, petticoats billowing in the breeze, determinedly loading a cannon while battle smoke wafts about her. But did this really happen, or is it just a revolutionary tall tale?

While it seems that we can (fairly) safely say that the event did actually take place, the woman who was "Molly Pitcher," however, remains a shadowy figure.

As near as can be determined, this is what happened: Molly was bringing water to the men of General Stirling's colonial artillery brigade, which included her husband, who were waging a fierce duel with their British counterparts. This was hard, sweaty work, and some men were overcome by the blistering heat and passed out at their posts. When her husband went down from the heat (not, as popularly believed, from being shot), Molly jumped in and took his place.

As stirring as this story is, however, it didn't immediately become part of American folklore. In fact, it wasn't until the American centennial in 1876—nearly a century later—that "Molly Pitcher" sprang to life. As the United States prepared to celebrate its one-hundredth birthday, a teacher in Williamsport, Pennsylvania, named Wesley Miles remembered how an old woman named Molly McCauly had taken care of him as a young boy in Carlisle, Pennsylvania, when his mother was ill, and how she had related stories about loading the cannon at Monmouth. Miles thought it would be proper to honor this patriotic woman, who was lying in an unmarked grave in Carlisle.

To get the ball rolling, he wrote a letter to the *Carlisle Herald* extolling Molly's deeds at Monmouth. This initiated a fund-raising campaign, which culminated in the dedication of a monument to Molly in Carlisle on July 4, 1876. The inscription read, in part: "Mollie Mc Cauly, Renowned in History as Mollie Pitcher, The Heroine of Monmouth."

The effects of Miles' letter were destined to reverberate throughout American history. The publicity surrounding the monument unleashed Molly Pitcher fever across the United States. Suddenly everyone wanted to know more about this previously forgotten woman, who had risked life and limb for the cause of liberty. Thus began the glorification of what had been a simple story: Molly's husband wasn't overcome by heat, he was wounded (in some versions, even killed); Molly wasn't an ordinary-looking soldier's wife, but a doe-eyed goddess; Molly didn't merely load the cannon, she recited patriotic platitudes as she let each cannon ball fly; and so on.

Today, the story has assumed such mythical proportions that it's hard to find the truth behind all the patriotic ardor. Thanks to the diary of Joseph Plumb Martin, a colonial who fought at Monmouth, and a few other eyewitness accounts, it's reasonably certain that a woman did bring water to Stirling's parched soldiers, and did actually help fire a cannon. Martin, in fact, related an interesting story about Molly:

While in the act of reaching for a cartridge and having one of her feet as far before the other as she could step, a cannon shot from the enemy passed directly between her legs without doing any other damage than carrying away all the lower part of her petticoat. Looking at it with apparent unconcern, she observed that it was lucky it did not pass a little higher, for in that case it might have carried away something else, and continued her occupation.

Who was this brave, cool-headed woman? Most historians and writers have identified her as Mary Hays, wife of John Casper Hays of Carlisle. However, as Samuel Stelle Smith points out in his excellent essay "The Search for Molly Pitcher," John Casper Hays does not appear on any military records of the period. Far more likely, says Smith, is that Molly was the wife of William Hays, a Carlisle barber who records show did indeed enlist in the colonial army on May 10, 1777, as a gunner in Colonel Thomas Proctor's Pennsylvania artillery regiment. Thanks to legal documents, we know that he had a wife named Mary. (Unfortunately, there is no reliable evidence that her maiden name was Ludwig, as is so often stated.)

As was common then, young Mary (she was about twenty-four at the Battle of Monmouth) followed her husband into the army, rather than remain home alone. Those acquainted with her said that she smoked, chewed tobacco, and swore with the best of them—certainly a far cry from the sweet, innocent beauty so often pictured!

After the war, Mary and William returned to Carlisle (even more reason to doubt that Molly's husband was killed at Monmouth!), where William died in 1787. In 1793, Mary married John McCauly, who died in 1813. Molly Pitcher–Mary McCauly passed her remaining years alone, working odd jobs in Carlisle and telling people about her battlefield heroics. One person described her as of average height, muscular, strong, heavy-set, kind, and "a very busy talker." The heroine of Monmouth died in 1833, at age seventy-nine.

This is all we really know about the legendary Molly Pitcher. Even the existence of a well from which she drew water for the soldiers has been called into question; new findings at Monmouth Battlefield State Park indicate that the Spotswood Middle Brook was the likely source of her water.

However, the fact that we know almost nothing about this brave woman shouldn't overshadow what she did on that hot June day in 1778, when American independence was on the line. Disregarding her own safety, Molly jumped into the midst of a fierce battle, not for personal gain or glory but because her young country needed her. That type of spirit is the reason the United States exists today.

DID YOU KNOW?

Was "Molly Pitcher" really two women?

This is the interesting hypothesis offered by Henry Charlton Beck in his book *Fare to Midlands*. Beck, the father of New Jersey folklore, told the story of a man who was convinced that history had confused two women: The "real" Molly Pitcher, Mary Hays, and another woman named Margaret Cochran. According to Beck, Cochran also followed her husband, who was an artillery gunner, into the army. When her husband was seriously wounded at

---

60 Molly Pitcher loading the cannon during the Battle of Monmouth. (Courtesy National Archives War & Conflict #37)

the Battle of Fort Washington in November 1776, she took over his cannon and continued firing it until she too was hit by enemy fire. Her husband died of his wounds, and Margaret was taken prisoner by the British. Eventually she was paroled, but her wounds never healed, and she became completely disabled. Because of her role in the battle, she became known as Captain Molly, but her later years were filled with pain and loneliness, and she eventually turned to prostitution. She died of gangrene around 1800.

The existence of Margaret Cochran, and her heroics at Fort Washington, are confirmed by a 1779 United States Congressional resolution, which voted Margaret Cochran Corbin (her married name) a pension because she "was wounded and disabled in the attack on Fort Washington, whilst she heroically filled the post of her husband who was killed by her side serving a piece of artillery."

Has history confused and merged Margaret Cochran and Mary Hays into one "Molly Pitcher"? It would explain some of the wild disparaties in the Molly Pitcher story, including that her husband was wounded in the battle, that Molly became a prostitute in later years, and that she became known as "Captain Molly" because of her battlefield heroics.

However, as Mark Lender points out, there could even have been more than one Molly Pitcher at Monmouth. Since the American army allowed wives to travel with their husbands, it wasn't that unusual to see women on or near battlefields. It's very possible that Mary Hays was not the only woman on the battlefield at Monmouth, just the one who has received all the glory.

Will we ever know the truth? The search for Molly Pitcher continues.

It was two A.M. on July 30, 1916. All around the huge munitions storage site called Black Tom Island in Jersey City, just across from the Statue of Liberty, everything was quiet.

It would not remain that way for long.

"At 2:08 [A.M.]," said *The New York Times* of July 31, 1916,

> a million people, maybe five millions, were awakened by an explosion that shook the houses along the marshy Jersey shores, rattled the skyscrapers on the rock foundations of Manhattan, threw people from their beds miles away and sent terror broadcast, swept into nothingness $5,000,000 worth of ammunition, and started fires and bred another explosion that did damage estimated at $20,000,000 more.

The *Times* likened this tremendous roar, which was heard as far south as Maryland, to "the discharge of a giant cannon." However, it was far more than that: It was a dagger thrown at the heart of America by foreign agents—a dagger thrown with unerring accuracy that struck one of New Jersey's most populous cities. Neither the state, nor the nation, would ever be the same again.

Before 1870, Black Tom was nothing but a barren, windswept rock jutting out of New York Harbor. Then the Central Railroad of New Jersey purchased the site as a storage area and enlarged it, turning it from an island into a 25-acre promontory. It still, however, retained its curious shape, described as looking like "a monster's head and neck."

By 1916, as World War I raged in Europe, Black Tom was a bustling warehouse site owned by the National Dock and Storage Company. The island had become the principal storage and overseas shipping location for tons of munitions and explosive powders made in the Northeast and Midwest. Seventy-five percent of all munitions and armaments sent from the United States to Europe left from the greater New York–New Jersey area, and most of this came from Black Tom.

Despite the United States' official neutrality policy in this stage of the war, most of the munitions that left Black Tom went to the Allied powers of Great Britain, Russia, and France. No mere policy could stop the nation's sympathies, which were clearly with the Allies and against Imperial Germany. Indeed, to many of the immigrants who had only recently escaped to America from Europe and now worked at Black Tom, the island was a symbol: Each crate of munitions loaded was another blow against the evil Kaiser.

The Kaiser, however, was aware of this, thanks to Germany's well-organized intelligence network. A blow at this facility would both hurt Germany's enemies and show the United States that its phony neutrality had its price. Black Tom was marked for destruction.

Many of those who emigrated to the United States were processed at Ellis Island, just a mile away from Black Tom, and settled in Jersey City, Hoboken, Bayonne, Hackensack, and other nearby New Jersey waterfront towns. For them, Sunday, July 30, was a day off, a brief break in the grueling six-day work week. Many people probably went to sleep that night thinking about what they would do with their free day: go to church, walk in the park, or just sit at home and relax.

Those dreams were rudely interrupted at 2:08 in the morning, when the first titanic blast from Black Tom rocked the entire metropolitan area.

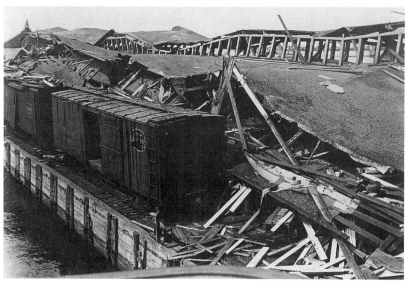

Thousands of skyscraper windows were shattered by the force of the shock wave, sending daggers of glass hurtling down to streets below. Just across the water, both the Statue of Liberty and buildings on Ellis Island were hit by chunks of flying shrapnel. The entire harbor lit up, as if a massive Independence Day celebration was taking place.

"A great pillar of flame . . . lit up the sky with a red glare," reported the *Times*.

After the initial explosion came a series of smaller ones. "Car after car and barge after barge of high explosives ignited," the *Times* said. "Some burned rapidly and some burned slowly, but all burned furiously."

Thousands of people rushed out of their homes and poked their heads out of (probably broken) windows to see what had happened. It was utter pandemonium.

"Men, women, and children left their homes in their nightclothing," said the *Times*. "Many declared they had been thrown out of bed by the force of the concussion." (This caused a death: Arthur Tosson, a ten-week-old boy who lived on Central Avenue in Jersey City, was thrown from his crib by the force of the explosion and killed.)

The force of the explosion was so great that the Reagan family of Deal, forty miles away from the blast, were nearly thrown from their beds by its power. Ten miles further south, guests of the New Monmouth Hotel in Spring Lake were awakened by the concussions.

Incredibly, fireman who had been on Black Tom at the time of the explosion, and who were battling a fire initially thought to have caused the blast, were not killed. "Firemen, blackened by smoke and their clothing torn to tatters, came staggering out of the smoke, but they were too dazed to tell what had happened," said the *Times*.

As explosions continued to bombard the harbor, frantic evacuation efforts began for those on nearby Ellis and Bedloe's (now Liberty) islands. Dodging shrapnel (and occasionally being struck by it), boats removed twenty-five family members of Statue of Liberty staffers to Governor's Island.

---

61 The widespread destruction at Black Tom Island following the explosion. (Courtesy National Archives)

---

62 The debris of the Lehigh Valley pier after the Black Tom explosion. (Courtesy National Archives)

On Ellis, the scene was much worse. Immigrants who thought they had finally escaped the horrors of the Great War now suddenly found themselves apparently right back in it. Under a shower of shrapnel, and illuminated by the fiery red glow from Black Tom, 353 frightened people from the Great Hall were loaded onto the ferry Ellis Island and conveyed to the Battery in New York City. There, four policemen were stationed to make sure no one tried to disembark.

The immigrants were not the only ones frightened. The six A.M. mass at the Mission of Our Lady of the Rosary church in Jersey City was packed to the rafters. "I can assure you," Father A. J. Grogan told a questioner, "there were many praying on their knees who had not been inside a place of worship for a long time."

Finally the explosions on Black Tom stopped, and investigators were able to ascertain the damage. The next day's (July 31) *New York Times* told the chilling story:

> Thirteen warehouses of the National Storage Company were destroyed. There remained no vestige of those nearest the base of the explosion. Not a brick to mark where they had stood—only black holes in the ground and blackened ends of broken piers pointing like death fingers through the debris-littered surface of the harbor. Where on Saturday stood huge brick warehouses there remain only giant mounds of blazing and smoking ruin, while all about them are the wreckages of barges and railway rolling stock and other debris.

Ellis Island looked like it had been attacked by enemy planes. Every window in the Great Hall and the hospital were shattered, the hospital's roof had caved in, holes pock-marked building walls, and the lawn and walkways were covered with glass, wood cinders, and other debris.

Jersey City was also hard hit. Damage to City Hall alone came to $25,000; virtually every window and glass door in the building was broken, and the ceilings in the courtroom and the Assembly Chamber were destroyed. The beautiful stained-glass windows of St. Patrick's Church were ruined, as were windows in scores of churches, businesses, and homes.

Glass, in fact, was the biggest casualty in the Black Tom explosion. Plate glass damage in Jersey City was estimated at $50,000, and $35,000 in Hoboken; similar losses in Manhattan and Brooklyn totaled $300,000. The entire damage total was $20 million, which didn't count the estimated $5 million in lost munitions.

Before the flames died down investigations were launched to find the cause of the explosion. Initial speculation was that sparks from freight cars had caused a fire on a barge, which had spread to the munitions warehouses. Incredibly, with a war raging in Europe and Black Tom's critical importance to the Allies, no one seemed to suspect sabotage.

"On one point the various investigating bodies agree," reported *The New York Times* of July 31, 1916, "and that is that the fire and subsequent explosions cannot be charged to the account of alien plotters against the neutrality of the United States."

It would take over two decades to find out different. Finally, after years of investigations, charges, countercharges, dead-end leads, and false hopes, Germany in 1939 was found by an international commission to be responsible for the Black Tom explosion. As near as could be determined, three German agents snuck onto Black Tom around midnight and set small fires in some of the boxcars containing dynamite. They also placed explosives with time fuses there. These were the cause of the initial explosion at 2:08 A.M.; the highly incendiary cargo of munitions on the piers and in the warehouses did the rest once the fire reached them.

The Black Tom explosion was part of an aggressive campaign of sabotage waged by Imperial Germany against the United States in the three years (1914–1917) leading up to America's entry into the war. The campaign was successful because people mistakenly believed the United States could hide behind its oceans and watch the affairs of the world from a distance. Thus, security at Black Tom, as well as other sensitive sites, was incredibly lax. The explosion, however, brought the war to the nation's doorstep and changed the way Americans felt about their safety. In that sense, the Black Tom affair was the beginning of our sense of vulnerability to the world's problems—a feeling that remains very much with us today.

Today Liberty State Park stands on the site of Black Tom. With its flags snapping in the breeze and its lush greenery, few visitors to the park suspect that they are standing on the site where an explosion unequaled in power in a major metropolitan area occurred—an explosion whose echoes still reverberate throughout the United States today.

DID YOU KNOW?

- In January 1929, while American investigators were closing in on Germany's role in the Black Tom explosion, the German government produced a report that blamed—in all seriousness—the entire thing on New Jersey's infamous mosquitos! The report claimed that a night-watchman had started a fire on Black Tom that night to "drive away the mosquitos. . . . It [Black Tom] was about the worst place in Jersey, on account of the swamps there." Even though the report was quickly dis-

WHERE THEY BREED

counted, New York newspapers had a field day laying more blame at the feet—or on the wings—of New Jersey's mosquitos.

▪ Black Tom was not the only New Jersey munitions site struck by Germany. On January 11, 1917, the Canadian Car and Foundry Company plant in Kingsland, which was making artillery shells, was burned to the ground in an explosion and fire reminiscent of Black Tom. For hours artillery shells rained down on Kingsland and nearby Rutherford; losses were estimated at $17 million. Again, however, no one initially considered sabotage as a motive.

In the mood for a little history? The past comes alive in the nearly 100 sites of historical interest scattered throughout New Jersey:

Acorn Hall, Morristown (Morris County)
Allaire State Park, Farmingdale (Monmouth County)
American Labor Museum/Botto House, Haledon (Passaic County)
Atlantic City Boardwalk, Atlantic City (Atlantic County)
Barclay Farmstead, Cherry Hill (Camden County)
Barnegat Heritage Center, Barnegat (Ocean County)
Barnegat Light Historic Society and Museum, Barnegat Light (Ocean County)
Barnegat Lighthouse State Park, Barnegat Light (Ocean County)
Batsto Historic Village, Hammonton (Atlantic County)
Belcher-Ogden Mansion, Elizabeth (Union County)
Boxwood Hall, Elizabeth (Union County)
Bridgeton Historic District, Bridgeton (Cumberland County)
Burlington Historic District, Burlington (Burlington County)
Camden County Historical Society/Pomona Hall, Camden (Camden County)
Campbell-Christie House, River Edge (Bergen County)
Cape May County Historical Society, Cape May Court House (Cape May County)

---

63   This cartoon, published in the Evening Telegram *in 1917, illustrates how some cartoonists felt that lax security was encouraging German espionage. (Courtesy Library of Congress)*

Cathedral of the Sacred Heart, Newark (Essex County)
Cold Spring Village, Cape May (Cape May County)
Cornelius Low House/Middlesex County Museum, Piscataway (Middlesex County)
Craftsman Farms, Morris Plains (Morris County)
Delaware and Raritan Canal State Park
Dey Mansion, Wayne (Passaic County)
Drake House Museum, Plainfield (Union County)
Drumthwacket, Princeton (Mercer County)
East Jersey Olde Towne, Piscataway (Middlesex County)
Edison National Historic Site, West Orange (Essex County)
Fort Hancock Gateway National Recreation Area, Sandy Hook Unit, Highlands (Monmouth County)
Fort Lee Historic Park, Fort Lee (Bergen County)
Fosterfields, Morristown (Morris County)
Garlis Center, Branchville (Sussex County)
Garretson Farm, Fair Lawn (Bergen County)
Great Falls/National Historic Landmark District, Paterson (Passaic County)
Greenwich/Cumberland County Historical Society, Greenwich (Cumberland County)
Grover Cleveland Birthplace, Caldwell (Essex County)
Guggenheim Memorial Library, West Long Branch (Monmouth County)
Hamilton House Museum, Clifton (Passaic County)
Hermitage, Ho-Ho-Kus (Bergen County)
Historic Burlington County Prison Museum, Mount Holly (Burlington County)
Historic Speedwell, Morristown (Morris County)
Hope Historic District, Hope (Warren County)

---

64 Very close to this peaceful, flag-draped vista of modern-day Liberty State Park was the site of the Black Tom explosion. (Photo by Pat King-Roberts)

---

65 Ruins of the Canadian Car and Foundry Company munitions plant at Kingsland. (Courtesy National Archives)

Howell Living Farm, Hopewell (Mercer County)

Indian King Tavern Museum, Haddonfield (Camden County)

Kuser Farm Park, Hamilton Township (Mercer County)

Leaming's Run Gardens and Colonial Farm, Swainton (Cape May County)

Lenape Indian Village, Stanhope (Sussex County)

Liberty State Park, Jersey City (Hudson County)

Longstreet Farm, Holmdel (Monmouth County)

Lucy the Elephant, Margate City (Atlantic County)

Macculloch Hall Historical Museum, Morristown (Morris County)

Meadows Foundation, Somerset (Somerset County)

Mid-Atlantic Center for the Arts, Cape May (Cape May County)

Miller-Cory House Museum, Westfield (Union County)

Monmouth Battlefield, Freehold (Monmouth County)

Monmouth County Historical Association, Freehold (Monmouth County)

Montclair Historic Society/Israel Crane House Museum, Montclair (Essex County)

Morris County Historical Society/Acorn Hall, Morristown (Morris County)

Morristown National Historical Park, Morristown (Morris County)

Morven, Princeton (Mercer County)

Mountain Lakes Historic Designation, Mountain Lakes (Morris County)

Ocean County Historical Museum, Toms River (Ocean County)

Ocean Grove Historical Society, Ocean Grove (Monmouth County)

Old Barracks Museum, Trenton (Mercer County)

Old Dutch Parsonage/Wallace House, Somerville (Somerset County)

Old Monroe Stone School House, Hamburg (Sussex County)

Oxford Furnace, Oxford (Warren County)

Picatinny Arsenal, Jefferson (Gloucester County)

Princeton Historical Society, Princeton (Mercer County)

Red Bank Battlefield, National Park (Monmouth County)

Ringwood Manor, Ringwood (Passaic County)

Salem County Historical Society, Salem (Salem County)

Smithville Mansion, Mount Holly (Burlington County)

Towne of Historic Smithville, Smithville (Atlantic County)

Somers Mansion, Somers Point (Atlantic County)

State House, Trenton (Mercer County)

Stueben House, River Edge (Bergen County)

Sussex County Historical Society, Newton (Sussex County)

Trent House, Trenton (Mercer County)

Twin Lights of Navesink, Highlands (Monmouth County)
Walt Whitman House, Camden (Camden County)
Washington Crossing State Park, Titusville (Mercer County)
Waterloo Village, Stanhope (Sussex County)
Wheaton Village, Millville (Cumberland County)
Whitesbog Village, Browns Mills (Burlington County)
Woodrow Wilson Hall, West Long Branch (Monmouth County)

CHAPTER TEN

A Town Treasury

T O W N S are like people; each has its own personality, shaped and molded by experiences. Most people keep their personality bottled up inside them, so that when you pass someone on the street you don't know whether they're happy or sad, quiet or loud, outgoing or shy. On the other hand, a town's personality is always on display. A deserted street lined with abandoned factories and shuttered buildings reveals the sadness of prosperity gone bust, while streets full of shops, businesses, and people bustling to and fro means vibrance and vitality.

Each town in this chapter has its own individual personality, shaped by events and marked by the actions of its citizens. As you read these stories, you might be surprised to discover that they are very similar to where you live.

It remains today, as it has since its founding back in 1869, an oasis of quiet and solitude along the Jersey Shore amidst the often frenetic atmosphere of other coastal towns. This, however, is entirely within character, for it's a town that prides itself on retaining the relaxed, unhurried atmosphere of

66 Thornley Chapel is typical of the Victorian-style architecture throughout much of Ocean Grove. (Photo by Pat King-Roberts)

the nineteenth century even as the twentieth century ends in a blur of quicksilver technology. In a world of fax machines and information super-highways, this town is like a letter from an old friend: warm, cozy, and personal, something to be cherished and experienced again and again. It's "God's Square Mile" along the Jersey Shore—the town of Ocean Grove.

The story of Ocean Grove begins with the curious fact that if it wasn't for the dreaded New Jersey mosquito, there wouldn't be a town of Ocean Grove! (At least, not where it's presently located.)

In July 1867, the Rev. William B. Osborn, a Methodist minister, at-tended the first national camp-meeting for the promotion of holiness in Vineland, New Jersey. During that time, Osborn and the Rev. J. R. An-drews of Vineland spoke about the need for a permanent camp-meeting town. Both agreed that it should be by the sea, so that rest and salvation could go hand-in-hand.

Osborn and Andrews enthusiastically explored the New Jersey coast, which then consisted of nothing but scrub pines, sand dunes, and bramble bushes, with a few towns (Cape May, Long Branch, and Squan, now Manasquan) tucked in between.

Finally, a site called Seven Mile Beach (now Avalon and Stone Harbor) was selected, and Osborn and Andrews went to Philadelphia to purchase the land from the owners. Before the deal was finalized, however, An-drews suddenly remembered something; turning to Osborn, he said, "There is one thing we have forgotten."

"What is that?" the minister replied.

"The mosquitoes," said Andrews. "We don't want to buy the mosqui-toes."

Osborn looked at his friend. "That's so," he said, and just like that, the deal was canceled.

Thus the search began again, but this time with the proviso that no (or at least as few as possible) mosquitoes come with the property. As might be expected, this was a hard condition to fulfill in New Jersey, and the search lagged.

In February 1868, Osborn came upon an extremely foreboding spot: Towering above the beach were sand dunes that gradually sloped to the west until they reached the turnpike, which was nothing more than a nar-row, rutted, one-lane dirt path running from Long Branch to Squan. Growing out of the dunes were thick clusters of briers, stumpy pine trees, and a veritable forest of bushes, within which lived rabbits, birds, and an assortment of other creatures. The area was surrounded by thick woods and several small lakes.

Most people would have taken one look at this inhospitable wilderness and walked away. Osborn, however, saw something else here, something that he thought could be the answer to his long search. Struggling through the brush, he made his way down to the site of present-day Founders Park; there, despite a thick covering of snow on the ground, Osborn knelt and prayed.

Even with God's help, however, it took several more visits before Osborn was convinced that the sand-choked, tree-filled stretch of coastline should be the site of a permanent camp-meeting town. Finally, after coming back to the spot one final time in the summer, Osborn decided that his search had ended. Indeed, without icy winds, bitter cold, and snow to contend with, there was much to like about the area: The ground was high, the lakes seemed pleasant, and the tall trees afforded abundant shade. Surprisingly enough, there were also no mosquitoes. (A map a few years later prepared by Dr. John B. Smith, the state entomologist, shows the entire coastline filled with mosquitoes except Ocean Grove.) Deciding to call the new town Ocean Grove (where the first part comes from is obvious, while "grove" referred to the vast number of trees), Osborn hurried back home to begin the preparations that would make his dream a reality.

So it was that in the summer of 1869, a hardy band of nineteen people (seven ministers, plus four faithful followers and their families) arrived at the chosen site. One wonders what thoughts must have been going through their heads as they gazed upon the desolation that greeted them. In her book, *In the Beginning, God*, Mrs. W. B. Osborn described the pioneers' arrival: "When we first entered, where now our gates are, the driver stood in front of his carriage and lifted the limbs, so as to crowd our conveyance through the brush and drooping branches of the trees. The heavens were black, the grass wet, and the sands half-knee deep."

Any gloom, however, was quickly dispelled by the Reverend Osborn. Alighting from his carriage, he led the small band on a tour, extolling the virtues and beauty of the area. Before long the group had pitched their tents and begun the arduous job of carving a town out of the wilderness. The first camp meeting was held by candlelight in one of these tents on the evening of July 31, 1869.

In March 1870, the New Jersey legislature granted Ocean Grove a charter. The Ocean Grove Camp Meeting Association began selling lots in their new seaside community. According to Mrs. Osborn, the first buyer was James A. Bradley, who subsequently went on to found Asbury Park.

Despite occasional doubts about what the Camp Meeting Association was trying to do, Osborn never lost his burning faith in its mission, nor his unshakable belief that the Jersey Shore was the place in which to do it. At one point, Osborn tried to get the Rev. Joel Croft to buy a lot in Ocean Grove.

"What have you there?" asked Croft.

"Sand and the ocean," Osborn replied, "but in twenty years there will be a continuous city from Long Branch to Cape May." He could not have been more right.

In all, 373 lots were sold. By then, the first permanent building in the town, housing a book store, post office, and business office of the association, had been erected.

Much hard work was expended to transform the inhospitable terrain into a region in which people would want to live. The first annual report of the Camp Meeting Association lists these labors, most of which were supervised by the apparently indefatigable Osborn: forty thousand trees trimmed, thousands of trees cut down, thousands of loads of sand removed, the entire area brushed and cleared of debris, and roads cut, graded, and graveled.

In fact, James A. Bradley was so impressed with Osborn's ability that he asked him to become the superintendent of Asbury Park, and offered to supply the capital and share the profits with him. Osborn, however, refused. "I founded Ocean Grove for the glory of God," he told his friend, "but I am not in the money-making business."

By 1876, the little community that had begun with nineteen people in tents was on its way to becoming one of most popular spots on the Jersey Shore. The railroad was bringing an estimated 50,000 people to the town, which netted the train company $47,000 in receipts for its first year of operation. The flood of visitors, however, was a mixed blessing, as the president of the Camp Meeting Association noted diplomatically in the seventh annual report: "Our quiet has been somewhat disturbed by the influx of excursionists, who never stay long enough to be impressed by their surroundings, and being unsettled themselves, unsettle everybody about them."

The main visitors to Ocean Grove were business and professional men and their families, who were attracted by the combination of religion and recreation in this new community by the sea. One of the activities that visitors and residents alike enjoyed was congregational singing. In 1889 a reporter for the *New York Tribune* wrote that the sound of 10,000 worshippers raising their voices in song was audible a mile away, creating "such a volume of sound that the roar of the surf sounds like the bass notes of a distant organ."

Of all the buildings in Ocean Grove, none is more famous than the Great Auditorium. This magnificent structure dominates the entire town, attracting visitors from all over.

The auditorium was built to commemorate Ocean Grove's twenty-fifth anniversary in 1894. The amount of worshippers attending services in the town was straining the existing building to capacity, and all agreed that a new auditorium seating 10,000 people would be a wonderful way for Ocean Grove to celebrate its silver anniversary.

The cost of such a structure was estimated to be $50,000, a sizeable sum. However, the citizens of Ocean Grove swiftly rose to the challenge; virtually the entire amount ($42,900) was pledged in just a single day of Sunday services.

Ground was broken for the new auditorium on December 2, 1893. Incredibly, it took just three months to build this massive structure. (Today it would take three months just to approve the plans!) The final cost was $69,112.16. The building opened on July 1, 1894, and was dedicated during August of that same year.

As the focal point of Ocean Grove, a long and illustrious list of people have appeared at the Great Auditorium throughout the years, including: Enrico Caruso, John Philip Sousa, Billy Sunday, Billy Graham, Duke Ellington, Will Rogers, Pearl Bailey, Booker T. Washington, Helen Keller, and Dr. Norman Vincent Peale.

Numerous United States presidents have chosen the Great Auditorium as a forum for unveiling important policy pronouncements. William McKinley used it to announce his imperialistic policy toward the Philippines in 1899. In 1911, as the clouds of war thickened over Europe, President William Howard Taft mounted the great stage and urged that arbitration, rather than violence, be used to settle international disputes.

But of all the many dignitaries who have come to Ocean Grove, the most poignant visit was that of Ulysses S. Grant in the summer of 1884. The former president had been severely criticized in the press for the recent failure of his Wall Street brokerage firm. Many people had lost a lot of money and blamed Grant, even though it would later be revealed that the trusting Grant had been unaware of his partner's shady dealings. By the time he returned to Ocean Grove that summer, for a reunion of army chaplains, he was no longer the hero who had saved the Union during the Civil War, but an old man sick in both body and spirit, who needed crutches to walk and had to be helped into his seat.

A preacher and former Union soldier named A. J. Palmer had been chosen to introduce Grant to the huge audience waiting to hear him speak. Palmer, far from being cool toward Grant, launched into a stirring discourse about the general's many virtues, sweeping the audience along on the power of his words. At the conclusion, Palmer looked down at the much-maligned hero and cried out: "And no combination of Wall Street sharpers shall tarnish the luster of my old commander's fame for me!"

With a roar of approval the normally restrained Ocean Grove crowd leaped to its feet. For several minutes they cheered Grant wildly, with men throwing their hats in the air and women waving handkerchiefs.

Grant finally struggled to his feet and began to speak. After a few halting words, he suddenly stopped and burst into tears. "This young man has overcome me," he cried out, and proceeded to sob uncontrollably for several minutes before an audience in which many eyes were undoubtedly wet as well. Eventually the old general took his seat, remarking that never before had he been unable to control his feelings.

It was Grant's last public appearance. One year later, he was dead.

Demonstrating its affection for a former hero who others had turned their back on was right in tune with Ocean Grove's character, for the town inevitably went its own way. This was especially true in the rules that governed community life. Fueled by the Camp Meeting Association's desire for a Christian town, there were many edicts that seem overly restrictive today. The sale of liquor was banned, and hotels and merchants were forbidden to stock either tobacco or novels (it was felt that such frivolous reading distracted from more serious reflection). On Sundays, no business could be conducted, no amusements were allowed, and no newspapers were delivered. The gates leading out from the community to the surrounding area were closed at midnight Saturday, and not reopened until midnight Sunday, blocking all traffic (except emergency vehicles).

Not everyone found this type of life appealing. In 1893, a writer for an early travel guide was amazed that so many people would willingly spend their summer vacations in "a religious autocracy, which is severe in both its positive and negative regulations."

But this view was the exception rather than the rule. Somehow, as the nation swept into a twentieth century filled with world wars, flappers, Prohibition, gangsters, suburbia, hot rods, beatniks, hippies, and riots, Ocean Grove seemed unaffected by it all. With its gingerbread-wreathed buildings, quiet boardwalk, and tree-lined walkways, the town seemed to have found a way to keep time at bay. Even the much-ridiculed Sunday traffic ban brought back memories of a quieter, simpler time, when a person could walk down the street without getting run over by a car or choking on exhaust fumes.

But nothing stays the same forever, not even Ocean Grove. In 1979 the New Jersey Supreme Court declared the town's form of government unconstitutional. Out with the government went many of the prohibitions,

67   The first fresh-water well in Ocean Grove was called Beersheba. The fountain in the middle of this ornate structure stands on the original spot of the first well. (Photo by Pat King-Roberts)

including the Sunday driving ban. Now the town is part of Neptune Township.

Yet the modern world has only intruded up to a point. Ocean Grove today still remains remarkably true to its roots: a peaceful, picturesque place, where quiet reflection, common courtesy, and good feeling are present in abundance.

DID YOU KNOW?

Great Auditorium Statistics:

Cost: $69,112
Square footage: 36,225
Highest point: 55 Feet
Seating capacity: 10,000 at first, now 6,500
The Great Auditorium Pipe Organ was built at a cost of $27,000 by Robert Hope-Jones in 1907, one of the true geniuses in organ construction. The instrument, which contains 8,000 pipes ranging from 32 feet high to smaller than a lead pencil, is considered one of the most unique and powerful organs in the United States.

DID YOU KNOW?

James A. Bradley's involvement in Ocean Grove, and subsequent founding of Asbury Park, helped bring civilization to that untamed region. In an article for the *Asbury Park Journal,* Bradley related how he, quite innocently, became an integral part of the history of the Jersey Shore:

> One afternoon in May, 1870, I was walking along Broadway, New York, and suddenly ran against our friend, David H. Brown, Esq., Treasurer of the Ocean Grove Association.

68 The magnificent Great Auditorium in Ocean Grove. (Photo by Pat King-Roberts)

"How is Ocean getting on?" [Bradley asked.]

"Very fairly," said he, "why don't you buy a lot? Those who have their names put down now have first choice."

"Well, put me down for two.'"

Later, when Bradley went to Ocean Grove, he liked what he saw, despite the opinion of his manservant, who called the place "a wilderness." During an exploratory trip of the surrounding area with Osborn, Bradley came upon the desolate spot that would someday become Asbury Park. Anxious that Ocean Grove have a friend as their immediate neighbor to the north, Bradley bought the land and began planning his own community.

Millville is primarily known today as the home of the New Jersey glass industry, and with good reason. At the industry's heyday around 1900, only Pittsburgh produced more glassware than this Cumberland County town.

The area that would someday be Millville was first visited by Europeans sometime around 1754. What they found was a wilderness of sandy soil, trees, and wild huckleberry and blackberry bushes nestled beside the Maurice River. Early European settlers never saw a river they didn't try to tame, and the Maurice was no exception. A log bridge was built across the water, and the area was christened "The Bridge." Later a sturdier bridge replaced the first one, and the name changed to "New Bridge" or "Maurice River Bridge." A few houses popped up here and there, but in no real sense was it a town.

This changed in 1795, when Joseph Buck came to New Bridge. Buck was a veteran of the Revolutionary War who had seen action in many important engagements, including the siege of Yorktown. According to some reports, he was also present when Major Andre, the British spy caught in the Benedict Arnold plot, was hung.

After returning to civilian life, Buck married Ruth Seeley and settled in

69   The inside of the Great Auditorium. (Photo by Pat King-Roberts)

Bridgeton, New Jersey. For three years (1787–1790) he served as the Cumberland County sheriff.

At some point Buck discovered New Bridge, and apparently liked what he saw, for he acquired a house on the west side of the Maurice River. By this time the region was more developed, spurred by Henry Dunker and Joseph Smith, who had arrived in the area in 1790, formed the Union Company, and built several lumber mills on a lake.

Buck agreed with the ideas of Dunker and Smith for the region. In fact, when the former Continental soldier let his imagination wander, he foresaw a vast colony of mills located along the Maurice River, with elegant manor houses uptown for the owners. In 1795 Buck decided to develop the area. Either because of Buck's plan, or because of the mills already on the lake, the town gained a new name: Millville.

Enthusiastically, Buck embarked upon his vision by buying up land in Millville and building a large house there, but time was against him. Eight short years later, in 1803, he died, with his dream unfulfilled. Less than

two dozen buildings marked the spot where Buck had imagined an industrial mecca.

Buck died before witnessing the defining moment in Millville's history, although it wasn't apparent as such when it first happened. In 1806 an Irish immigrant named James Lee opened the first glass factory in Millville along the east bank of the Maurice River. Lee was a restless man, who had previously operated a factory in Port Elizabeth called the Eagle Glass Works, and he didn't remain long in Millville either. Within a few years he sold his factory there and moved to Kensington, Pennsylvania, where he embarked on yet another glass-making venture. But although Lee's stay in Millville was short, his legacy was long.

Thanks to Nature's generosity, glass-making and Millville were a natural combination. To make glass, sand is subjected to very high temperatures and then allowed to cool; the better the quality of sand, the better the quality of glass produced. Millville was not only blessed with a huge supply of fine-grained sand with few impurities, but also with a vast supply of wood in nearby forests for the glass-making furnaces.

Lee's window-glass factory, along with an iron foundry established several years later, brought the first real progress to Millville. People came to the area to work in the factories, and this pool of workers attracted other industries. Soon Buck's vision began to be realized. Millville's population soared from a few hundred people in the early 1820s to nearly 5,000 in 1870.

If Lee's glass factory was the first defining moment in Millville's history, the second was surely the arrival in town of Dr. Theodore Corson Wheaton in 1883. Born in the South Jersey community of Tuckahoe in 1852, Wheaton had degrees in both pharmacy and medicine when he brought his family to Millville to live. The entrepreneurial Wheaton practiced medicine, and also ran a pharmacy and a general store.

In 1888, Wheaton's inquisitive mind turned to the type of glass used by physicians and pharmacists, and he decided to expand his business ventures even further by entering into the glass business. Buying into the small Shull-Goodwin Glass Company, Wheaton soon found that he was fascinated by glass-making. Believing that the industry had a strong future, he bought out the remaining partners, and by 1889 the entire one-building operation was his. From these humble beginnings rose the mighty

70   Dr. Theodore C. Wheaton, circa 1900. (Courtesy Museum of American Glass at Wheaton Village)

T. C. Wheaton Company (today Wheaton Industries), one of the leading glass manufacturers in the world.

Sparked by Wheaton, the glass industry roared forward in Millville, as well as the rest of South Jersey, and by the dawn of the twentieth century the town was famous as a glass-making center. In 1908, the Philadelphia newspaper *The North American* "celebrated" Millville's fame in a jingle:

Jersey is a funny place, mosquitoes, frogs & sand,
And half pint flasks to fit the pocket are in great demand.
So they make flasks by thousands in the pint and half pint size,
And when they get a stock on hand they change & make glass eyes.
Now Millville is the city that this jingle is about,
They have no demon rum saloons—they voted them all out.
Most every workman owns his home and buys his children shoes,
That's something that is hard to do if you "hit up" the booze!

A few years earlier, an ode of a much different sort was written to the city by a young poet named Carl Sandburg, who lived in Galesburg, Illinois. In a combination of prose and poetry simply called "Millville," Sandburg expressed his feelings about the New Jersey town: "Down in southern New Jersey, they make glass. By day and by night, the fires burn on in Millville and bid the sand let in the light."

In a subsequent paragraph, Sandburg described the town: "Millville by night would have delighted Whistler, who loved gloom and mist and wild

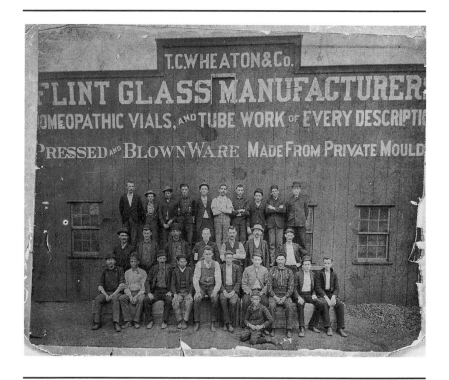

shadows. Great rafts of wood and big, brick hulks, dotted with a myriad of lights, glowing and twinkling every shade of red. Big, black flumes, shooting out smoke and sparks, bottles, bottles, bottles, of every tint and hue, from a brilliant crimson to the dull green that marks the death of sand and birth of glass."

At the height of its glory, the Millville glass industry consisted of over a dozen companies, all making glass "by day and by night." The names of many of these companies have long since slipped into history: International Glass Company, Caloris Company, Commercial Flint Glass Company, Glove Graduate Company, Nelson Creamer, Howard Davis, Kimpton Haupt, Eastern Glass, L.G. Nester, Frederick and Dimmock, Morris, Stuhl Laboratory, and Wheaton.

Glass, however, does not tell the whole story of Millville. The town is also known for another product, something that has nothing to do with factories and furnaces and everything to do with sunlight and rain: holly trees.

Millville's "holly-days" began in 1926 when Clarence Wolf, president of the Silica Sand Company, sent out packages of holly culled from local trees to the company's forty-six customers as Christmas gifts. The response was so enthusiastic that he continued doing it year after year. By the late 1930s, Wolf didn't want to rely on wild trees for the holly, so he planted an orchard of nearly 3,000 trees. By the 1950s, thanks to the tender loving care of Wolf and horticulturist Dan Fenton, the orchard contained 4,400 trees of thirty different varieties.

Because Millville holly had become so well known throughout the United States, the city commissioners proclaimed the town the Holly City of America in the 1950s, a distinction that it still retains.

Today, Wolf's holly orchard has become American Holly Products, Inc., which contains the largest American holly farm in the United States, and the custom that began as a thoughtful gesture to several dozen people has grown into a massive operation. The company ships thousands of pounds of holly around the world each year. As might be expected, holly abounds throughout Millville itself, adding grace and charm to this unique New Jersey town.

Glass-making center, industrial hub, holly city—Millville has had many identities over the years. It will be interesting to see what the future will bring.

71 Exterior of T. C. Wheaton & Co., circa 1900. (Courtesy Museum of American Glass at Wheaton Village)

DID YOU KNOW?

A former New Jersey governor and a key aide to President Franklin D. Roosevelt are two of Millville's most prominent citizens.

Although born in Medford, Edward Casper Stokes grew up in Millville after moving there with his family in 1871, when he was eleven years old. After graduating from Brown University in 1883, Stokes returned to Millville and got a job in a bank. He then began a slow but steady rise up the political ladder, serving in the state Assembly and Senate before being elected governor on the Republican ticket in 1904, defeating Charles C. Black by 51,000 votes.

Leon Henderson, on the other hand, found success not in Trenton but in Washington, D.C. Born in Millville on May 26, 1895, Henderson's childhood was spent in deep poverty. To help support his family, he quit high school and took a job in a glass factory, but a teacher talked him back into

school. He put himself through college by working odd jobs and playing semipro sports.

By 1941 Henderson was a key figure of Franklin D. Roosevelt's administration. That year he was made director of the Office of Price Administration, and charged with controlling inflation during the war years. The fact that he did so, through a series of price controls and a rationing system, was considered a minor miracle by many Washington observers. This was a highly public post, and the cigar-smoking, plain-talking Henderson made the front covers of both *Life* and *Time*. In later years, he gained fame again for bringing the nation's first federal senior citizens housing project to Millville.

In July 1778, during the Revolutionary War, four Continental army soldiers stopped for a picnic at the Passaic Falls, near a tiny village of ten houses called Acquackanonk. Later, one of the picnickers wrote about that lazy afternoon in northern New Jersey: "We composed some excellent grog, then chatted away a very cheerful half hour—then took our leave of the friendly oak—its refreshing spring—and the meek falls of the Passaic."

The men were George Washington, Alexander Hamilton, the Marquis de Lafayette, and his aide-de-camp, James McHenry (who recorded the brief respite in his diary). Although their stop at the "meek falls" that day was short, the impression it made on Hamilton was long indeed. Thirteen years later, as the first Secretary of the Treasury of the United States of America, Hamilton chose that peaceful spot as the showcase for what he hoped the young country would someday become—and in so doing founded the city of Paterson.

Born out of the clash of philosophies between two of this country's Founding Fathers, nurtured on the hum of the cotton spindle, and hardened by repeated failures that left it barely alive, few cities in the United States can claim as colorful a past as Paterson. Throughout its often-turbulent history, Paterson has attracted both speculators and innovators; it has made some people rich, and dashed the dreams of others on the rocks of failure. It has lent its name to the title of an epic poem, been the

72 Interior of T. C. Wheaton & Co., circa 1900. (Courtesy Museum of American Glass at Wheaton Village)

scene of an ugly labor strike, and built products that have changed the course of American history.

The beginning of Paterson dates to the beginning of the United States, and a duel of ideologies between Hamilton and Thomas Jefferson. To Jefferson, the future of the United States was in its farmers and the agrarian society they would create. "Cultivators of the earth are the most valuable citizens, the most independent, the most virtuous," Jefferson wrote, "and they are tied to their country, and wedded to its liberty and interests, by the most lasting bonds." Hamilton, however, dismissed an agrarian society as weak and ineffective. The only way for the United States to become strong enough to deal with the powerful nations of the world, he felt, was for it to develop a centralized government based on a robust industrial economy. He favored aligning the federal government with industry: "There is no purpose to which public money can be more beneficially applied than to the acquisition of a new and useful branch of industry," he said.

As the government's financial head, Hamilton could put the nation's money where his philosophy was. In 1791, he proposed that the federal government spend $1 million (which was then 2 percent of the national debt) to build a "national manufactory" that would, in effect, be an industrial urban complex, run by a group dubbed the Society for Establishing Useful Manufactures (SUM).

Because of the water power that would be needed to run the factories, Hamilton chose Acquackanonk as the site of this bold experiment. A surveyor had already estimated that Great Falls would be able to drive 247 waterwheels. The presence of nearby quarries, a large supply of timber (both for burning and building), and nearby deposits of bog iron ore were additional factors that helped steer Hamilton to choose the quiet village for his plan.

But Congress, already suspicious of many of Hamilton's ideas, was in no mood to agree to a scheme that would have made the federal government the country's biggest manufacturer. Undaunted, Hamilton turned to the private sector; he wrote an SUM prospectus and turned it over to New Jersey Governor William Paterson to guide through the state legislature. When he did (both the governor and some New Jersey legislators became stockholders in the new corporation, although the phrase "conflict of interest" never seems to have occurred to anyone), Hamilton named the new manufacturing community after the governor.

The governor's political skills enabled the SUM to get the sweetheart deal of the century (the eighteenth or any other, for that matter). Among the benefits that the charter granted were: exemption of SUM employees from poll taxes, general assessments, and routine military duty; a ten-year tax exemption for SUM property and buildings; the right to hold a lottery to regain projected financial losses; exclusive domain over the Passaic River; and, most significantly, the right to govern its own lands.

In May 1792, the SUM got things off and running by purchasing 700 acres in the vicinity of the Passaic Falls. Thanks to the salesmanship abilities of Hamilton's friend William Duer, the governor of the SUM, $600,000 worth of stock in the fledgling industrial empire was quickly sold. Hamilton was gratified to find foreign investors also very interested in what was happening in New Jersey. It seemed as if his vision was correct.

Then, just as quickly, disaster struck. A stock speculation scheme that Duer was masterminding unraveled, sending him to jail, causing a national financial crisis, and giving the SUM a severe black eye. Many SUM stockholders were hit hard by the economic downturn and lost interest in putting any more of their money into this great industrial experiment. Hamilton, who had initially seen himself as strictly an advisor to the SUM, leaped in with both feet to save his tottering manufacturing city. But nothing seemed to go right: French architect Pierre L'Enfant—who designed Washington, D.C.—was hired to plan the new industrial complex, but his ideas were too elaborate and expensive and he was dismissed; it was difficult recruiting local workers to staff the factories; and not enough skilled artisans were available to manage and supervise the mills.

Bleeding red ink, suffering from indifferent management, and severely undercapitalized, the SUM threw in the towel in 1796. Only two factories—a four-story stone cotton mill and a smaller building that was used for bleaching and printing—had been completed. The SUM sold off most of its machinery and whatever goods had been produced, and halted operations. Without the prospect of jobs, people deserted the area, and the population plummeted. Paterson's first great era had ended in failure.

Although down, however, Paterson was not out. Throughout its history the city has had more resurrections than the phoenix. This one began when Roswell Colt, a member of the family whose name would someday be on the gun that "won the West," and whose relationship to Samuel Colt would bring the ultimately famous gunmaker to Paterson, became governor of the SUM in 1809. Although not directly involved in manufacturing anymore, the society still owned significant land and water rights in the town, and thus stood to benefit when, slowly but surely, industries were attracted by the Passaic River waterpower that the SUM had harnessed through a series of canals (called "raceways"). Factories began popping up in Paterson, although too late for Hamilton, killed in the famous duel with Aaron Burr in 1804, to see his dream finally realized. When the War of 1812 cut off European goods to this country, there was almost no manufacturing capacity in the United States to replace them—except in Paterson.

Paterson boomed during the war years. At the start of 1815, a manufacturing census reported eleven cotton mills, a card and wire mill, a rolling mill, and a saw mill in operation, and a population of 1,500.

What the war giveth, however, the war taketh away. When hostilities with Great Britain ended in 1815, European products came flooding back into the marketplace. The British deliberately undersold U.S. manufacturers to regain their foothold with American consumers. This caused the cotton industry to collapse, which spun the country into several years of economic stagnation.

Once again Paterson hit the skids. The downfall was colorfully chronicled in an article in an 1859 edition of *Scientific American*: "The streets were again deserted; mills were locked up and stood in gloomy solitude; the spindle rusted in the socket; the wheel rotted in its pit; and the spider wove his cobwebs upon looms whose clatter drowned the workmen's song."

Reports of Paterson's death, however, were greatly exaggerated once again. The United States was changing, becoming just as acclimated to the sound of the worker's wheel and the clatter of the loom as it was to the gentle clip-clop of the plow horse; manufacturing was becoming the driving force in the U.S. economy. By 1821, the *True American* reported that Paterson contained nine mills with over 650 employees. Between 1821 and 1827 the number of spindles in Paterson cotton mills jumped from 12,600 to 23,938, while the total amount of cloth produced grew by 1 million yards. Paterson had risen again from the ashes, and this time the comeback was permanent.

Now firmly established as a manufacturing center, Paterson grew steadily throughout much of the nineteenth century. When the depression of 1837 destroyed the cotton industry, Paterson switched to machine-making and steamed forward. In the 1840s another milestone was reached when silk manufacturing began in the town. In time the silk industry would make the town internationally famous (Paterson became internationally known as "Silk City"); it would also make a very few men very rich, and breed a resentment that would lead to a cataclysmic labor strike in 1913 that would nearly destroy Paterson.

Hamilton had hoped that Paterson would become a crucible of ideas and manufacturing vitality, and in this he was correct. The town was a magnet that attracted people of vision and resourcefulness, and their achievements stamped the city as the epitome of American "can-do" ingenuity.

From Paterson came inventions that would change the world, such as Samuel Colt's revolutionary repeating revolver, and John Holland's first practical submarine. The locomotive, which transformed America, was born in Paterson in the 1830s when an English train engine arrived in town in pieces and a local carpenter named Thomas Rogers decided that he could build one just as easily. He could, and did, and by 1880 Paterson was producing 80 percent of the locomotives made in the United States. Even into the twentieth century, Paterson was still the source of epoch-making events; when Charles Lindbergh crossed the Atlantic Ocean alone in 1927, his plane, "The Spirit of St. Louis," was propelled by an engine made at the Wright Aeronautical Company in Paterson.

By the 1960s, however, Paterson was ailing. Having been born and nurtured on manufacturing, Paterson suffered the pangs of withdrawal as industry throughout the northeast heeded the siren call of cheap labor and headed overseas. The city seemed old and tired, unable to summon up its old elan; even the once-mighty Passaic Falls was a shadow of its former self, thanks to an SUM decision that diverted 75 million gallons of water a day out of its normal flow. This turned the majestic waterfall into a dripping faucet, and the Passaic River into a polluted disgrace that William Carlos Williams called "the vilest swillhole in christendom." (Williams' widow claimed that the stench of the river was so powerful that it actually peeled paint off houses.)

But Paterson had still another comeback up its sleeve. In 1976 the city's Great Falls/SUM district was designated a national historic landmark, the only industrial district in the country to receive that honor. This helped spark an interest in Paterson as a tourist destination; people began coming to see what Hamilton and others had wrought by the Great Falls. Paterson had returned from the dead yet again.

Today, although its manufacturing prominence is gone, Paterson is one of New Jersey's premier tourist attractions. Visitors come to wander through the historic district, where over fifty factories remain from the town's industrial heyday. In nearby Haledon are exhibits and sites concerning the 1913 silk strike, and the Great Falls still retain the magnetism that once wooed Alexander Hamilton. It may not be "Silk City" anymore, but Paterson remains a fascinating town.

DID YOU KNOW?

One of the greatest American writers of the twentieth century, New Jersey–born William Carlos Williams, selected Paterson as the title and general subject of his greatest work: the five-volume poem *Paterson*.

Born in Rutherford (Bergen County) on September 17, 1883, Williams earned a medical degrees from the University of Pennsylvania in 1906. He returned to Rutherford, where he practiced medicine and wrote for the rest of his life. The basic concept of *Paterson*—linking the city with modern man and, to a broader extent, American life—took Williams over fifteen years to work out. The poem's prose and poetry mixture, and the complex images and structure of the piece, proved difficult for him. "That God damned and I mean God damned poem *Paterson* has me down," he wrote in December 1943. "I am burned up to do it but don't quite know how. I write and destroy, write and destroy . . . I flounder and flunk."

Williams persevered, however; the first *Paterson* volume was published in 1946 to critical acclaim. Subsequent volumes appeared in 1948, 1949, 1951, and 1958. The poem, said one critic, is "Whitman's America, grown pathetic and tragic, brutalized by inequality, disorganized by industrial chaos, and faced with annihilation." At the time of his death, on March 4, 1963, Williams was working on a sixth volume.

Although Paterson was the country's most strike-ridden city between 1850 and 1914, no one was prepared for the consequences of the Silk Strike of 1913, which not only became one of the most devastating labor disputes in American history, but also destroyed virtually all the participants in the bargain.

The silk industry began in Paterson in 1841. By 1880 the town was preeminent in the nation's manufacture of silk and was dubbed "Silk City." However, while silk's success made the business owners rich— Catholina Lambert, one of the manufacturers, ostentatiously flaunted his wealth by building a medieval-style castle on a mountain top for his home and amassing a huge art collection within its stone walls—for most it meant nothing more than hard labor, long hours, and meager wages. Finally, on February 25, 1913, weavers walked off the job in the Docherty Mill to protest the decree that workers work four looms instead of two. Not only would this have doubled the workload, but it would eventually reduce mill jobs by half. Others quickly joined the walkout; before long 24,000 silk workers were out on the street.

The strike quickly escalated into a war between the silk owners and the Industrial Workers of the World (IWW) labor union. The workers who had begun the strike with legitimate grievances were caught in the middle; what had begun as a job action for workers' rights evolved into a grim struggle for survival between two iron-willed opponents. For month after desperate month the strike dragged on as both sides grew weaker; workers had to send their children out of town because there was no food, while mill owners were hemorrhaging money.

Finally, after five long months, unable to bear their families' hardship anymore, the ribbon workers broke with the IWW and came to an agreement with the owners. This leak in union solidarity soon became a flood, as other workers rushed to settle as well.

The strike produced no winners. Workers gained almost no concessions; the IWW lost both power and prestige; and the silk owners were greatly weakened financially. However, the biggest loser of all was Paterson. The strike saddled the town with a reputation as a seething cauldron of worker fervor, an image that frightened away other industries and helped drive the city into decline. Meanwhile, the silk industry, which had been slumping anyway, was pushed over the brink. By 1938, just 6,000 workers were left in an industry that had once employed four times that many. Paterson was "Silk City" no more.

"We are now going to settle a Town at the Falls, at a place reported . . . to be without compare to any other yet known: None equal for pleasant healthful air; Lovely Situation; second to none for Fertility."

And so it was that, in 1679, a group of recent immigrants from Great Britain to the New World, including the writer of the above words, William Emley, set off to start a town. The community that they began would be known by various names throughout its history, but we know it today as one of the most prominent towns in New Jersey history: Trenton.

When the group arrived at the "Falls," they found other English settlers already there, including Mahlon Stacy, the principal landowner in the area. Stacy had long been singing the praises of the region, writing about peaches (an unknown fruit to the English) that "hang almost like our onion" and delicious wild fruits that grew in abundance, like strawberries and cranberries.

The area that would soon be called Trenton was ideal, not only for farming, but for carving out a life. Rain was plentiful in the summer, the winters were not too harsh, and the soil was easily tilled. The surrounding forests contained a variety of hardwood trees needed for building homes and heating them. In addition, there was the broad Delaware River, which would not only provide drinking water, but could also be used to power mills. (What the early settlers would discover through trial and error, however, was that the shallow Assunpink Creek was far better for this purpose than the unreliable Delaware, where the water level always seemed to be going up or down, never reliably enough, however, to power a water-wheel.) In 1680 Stacy foreshadowed the region's future as an industrial power by building a grist mill of logs.

Initially the region had been known as the Falls or the Falls of the Delaware. When more settlers came, the name changed to the Yorkshire Tenth, because the settlers were Quakers from Yorkshire in England who had been assigned ten shares of land each. In 1714 came another, and more permanent, name change, with the arrival of William Trent. Trent was a wealthy merchant from Philadelphia who planned to develop the area. He bought Stacy's 800-acres, built a brick house near the Delaware (which still stands today), and rebuilt Stacy's wooden mill out of stone. Not surprisingly, as the dominant force in the community, Trent's name began to be associated with it, and soon the Yorkshire Tenth had become "Trent's Town," which was later shortened to Trenton.

Helped by its location along the river, which brought many travelers and settlers to the area, Trenton grew slowly but steadily throughout the first half of the eighteenth century. Although still good for agriculture, the area began to take on a more industrial flavor. Trent had expanded Stacy's single mill into a complex, and added an ironworks. In 1731 a steelworks was built by Isaac Harrow, and several tanning works were also established in Trenton.

By 1775, when war came to the colonies, Trenton, a community of about 100 buildings, laid out along seven or eight picturesque streets with the river in the background, was often described as a "pretty town." As the citizens of Trenton listened to the fiery speeches of the patriots, and heard the Declaration of Independence read from their courthouse steps, they little realized that this "pretty village" would shortly become the turning point in the Revolutionary War.

Few stories in United States history are more stirring than the tale of George Washington taking his rag-tag band of weary and dispirited soldiers across the Delaware River on a snowy, frigid Christmas night in 1776 and surprising the Hessian mercenaries who were occupying Trenton. The story has been told many times and does not need to be repeated here; suffice it to say that without the victory at Trenton, the American bid for independence might well have been snuffed out before spring arrived.

After the war was won it was time to think about the peace, and a major decision for the congressional delegates of the new country was where to locate the national capital. Several Founding Fathers, among them James Madison, pushed for the government to be centered at Trenton, which was then the geographic center of the United States. (Madison, in fact, wrote confidently that Trenton "is to become the future seat of the Federal Government.") Southern congressional delegates, however, did not agree, and so a compromise was reached: the government would be alternated between Annapolis, Maryland, and Trenton, until a permanent site could be decided upon.

This "government by pendulum," as Bordentown's Francis Hopkinson tartly called it, reached Trenton in November 1784. Unfortunately, excitement over Congress' arrival ran so high that members of the state legislature also flooded into town at the same time, anxious to see the national leaders in action. This created a severe shortage of rooms for the Congress. However, before beating a hasty retreat out of town (and whatever oversized chairs and bathtubs they had wedged themselves into for sleeping), the congressional delegation did vote $100,000 to be spent to erect federal government buildings "on the banks of either side of the Delaware." It was easy to see that they meant Trenton.

This appeared to lock it up for Trenton, but even as the citizens were celebrating forces were moving to undermine their hopes. Southerners still disliked placing the capital there, feeling that the city was too far north (in this dispute can be seen the earliest shadows of the Civil War, eighty years in the future). Then, unexpectedly, George Washington weighed in against Trenton, saying that if the federal buildings were placed on the Delaware, they would be "improperly placed for the seat of the empire."

Washington's pronouncement punctured Trenton's euphoria. The final blow came in September 1785, when Congress refused to appropriate the $100,000 approved the previous year. Sentiment in Congress for a capital along the Delaware collapsed and could not be revived. Trenton had to content itself with becoming the permanent capital of New Jersey in 1790.

Trentonians, however, shook off the disappointment and buckled down to the business of improving their town. By the mid-nineteenth century, sparked by the completion of the Delaware and Raritan Canal and its feeder canal, which enabled raw materials to easily be brought in and finished goods out, Trenton was thriving as an industrial center. Led by Peter Cooper's Iron Company (established in 1845) and the wire rope factories of John A. Roebling Sons (1848), the city became one of the predominant manufacturing regions on the East Coast. The rubber industry, iron works, and textile industry all helped fuel a population explosion of 300 percent from 1840 to 1860. In one decade alone, from 1850 to 1860, the population grew at an amazing 166 percent, from 6,461 to 17,228, as people came to Trenton in droves to claim the explosion of jobs caused by the industrial activity.

The second half of the nineteenth century featured more of the same for the city. All the industries, except leather working, grew at a phenomenal clip during the last decades of the century: the number of ironworks jumped from 23 to 40, the number of rubber factories from 2 to 13, the number of food processing plants from 8 to 23, the number of woodworking

establishments from 21 to 30, and the number of textile firms leaped from 7 to 59.

Of all the manufacturing sectors that found a home in Trenton, however, none was more successful than the ceramic industry. The industry got its start in the 1850s, when a few potters from Great Britain came to the area because of its industrial prominence. Their success caused others to follow, and the whole thing snowballed until Trenton was the leading ceramics producer in the United States. The city was the home of hundreds of ceramic firms both large and small. It was in Trenton that such internationally famous companies like Lenox and Boehm got their start.

Trenton roared into the twentieth century in fine fettle, proud of its past and full of confidence in its future. The city's factories were humming day and night, the people had jobs and money, and life seemed good. The famous slogan "Trenton Makes—the World Takes" summed up the city's pride in its vital industrial sector, as well as the confidence that Trenton would always be an important and necessary manufacturing center.

It didn't work out that way, for reasons not totally within Trenton's control. The post–World War II suburban stampede from the cities (Trenton's suburbs grew by 40 percent between 1940 and 1950) coincided with the decline of manufacturing all across the northeastern United States. As the city's industrial lifeblood ebbed, Trenton was caught in a downward spiral typical of many big American cities, faced with the triple-whammy of an aging physical plant, shuttered factories, and a shrinking revenue base.

Today, however, Trenton is bouncing back. The decision by New Jersey officials not to move employees and facilities to the suburbs sparked a surge of office building in Trenton by the state during the 1980s. This in turn attracted developers, who began their own building spree of offices and service-oriented complexes. The town tried to lure back the shoppers who had once roamed the streets with package-laden arms by closing off

73 Aerial view of Trenton in the 1920s, during the city's industrial heyday. (Courtesy of the Trentonian Collection, Trenton Public Library)

74 The large fleet of delivery trucks from Hill's Bakery in Trenton, ready to fan out over the city. Trenton had a thriving bakery industry. (Courtesy of the Trentonian Collection, Trenton Public Library)

several blocks to vehicular traffic and turning them into a pedestrian mall, and aggressively courted businesses. The New Jersey State Museum, the state library, and the city's renown Chambersburg restaurant section continue to draw people to Trenton. The electric "Trenton Makes" sign, dark for so many years during the decline, was refurbished and relit, and now glows proudly, almost defiantly, once again, for all the world to see. It may not have the same meaning anymore, but "Trenton Makes—the World Takes" once again symbolizes the city's burning desire to be number one.

75 Trenton has been plagued by floods throughout its history. This scene shows a portion of the city's South Warren Street during the October 1903 flood. (Courtesy of the Trentonian Collection, Trenton Public Library)

CHAPTER ELEVEN

When New Jersey Was Hollywood

" C A M E R A S were everywhere, grinding out dramas. Burglaries and dynamite and fat men rolling down hills, and nobody even turned to look at them. Kindly old ladies didn't blink an eyelid when three galloping Mexicans were shot and killed at their very door."

Of course, this quote must be about Hollywood. Like Pavlov's dog, we are conditioned to make certain assumptions in life, and one of these is that movies are made in Hollywood. After all, where else would the sight of robberies, murders, and explosions be so commonplace that passersby stifled yawns at the sight of such mayhem?

The answer is: Fort Lee, New Jersey.

Today, Fort Lee is assumed to be merely the last exit in New Jersey before the George Washington Bridge. But like most other assumptions made in haste and ignorance, those about Fort Lee are wrong. There is a story to be told here, in this Hudson County community of 30,000, a fascinating story of heroes and villains, combining all the elements of classic cinema. It is a tale of the time when not just Fort Lee, but all of New Jersey, was the undisputed movie-making capital of the United States, and Hollywood was just an unknown town in California. So have a seat and pass the popcorn; the show's about to start.

There is no question that Thomas Alva Edison belongs on the roster of New Jersey's greatest citizens. The Wizard of Menlo Park was one of those rare people who moved humanity forward through the force of his own genius. His many inventions helped make the late nineteenth and early twentieth centuries an exciting and optimistic time, when wondrous new devices like the phonograph and the electric light seemed to spew forth from Edison's lab almost daily.

Edison's claim to the invention of motion pictures, however, is much more cloudy. Despite the popular perception that the concept of moving pictures sprang full-blown into his mind from nothingness, others had been pursuing this idea for years before Edison and his employee, William K. L. Dickson, began serious work on it at Menlo Park in the early 1890s. Although both were brilliant men, the two don't seem to have conceived of anything incredibly new in the development of motion pictures. Their real genius was in taking preexisting elements, such as nitrocellulose film, clock gears, and other mechanical parts, and arranging them into the proper components that would enable pictures to move.

That they did this, and more, is beyond dispute. In March 1893, Edison patented a machine called a Kinetoscope, which was a coin-operated device that was used by just one person to view moving pictures. Realizing the commercial potential of movies, Edison built the famous "Black Maria" at West Orange, the world's first motion picture studio. Within three years came the Vitascope, a machine that could project movies (which Edison bought from two men in Washington, D.C.) for viewing by an audience. Edison used these as the building blocks to swiftly forge a major role in the fledgling motion picture industry. Although it had competitors, particularly overseas, the Edison company was the dominant United States film manufacturing company in the early years of film.

Because it was Edison's home, New Jersey contributed many of the subjects and locations for early films. In the beginning people were astonished by the mere fact that pictures moved, and so most early films involved nothing more elaborate than the surf breaking on the beach or people dancing. However, audiences soon tired of the novelty and began demanding more sophisticated films. One of the first films to employ a story line was Edison's *A Morning Alarm, Starting for the Fire*, and *Fighting a Fire* (1896). These three short films were actually one long movie of the Newark Fire Department doing the things described in the titles. Because of their narrative structure, the films could be shown independently or in sequence. New Jersey also supplied the location for Edison's famous *The Great Train Robbery* (1903), which was shot on location in the Essex County Park reservation and on the Erie and Lackawanna Railroad near the Passaic River.

Still, audiences were not satisfied. Early movies were primarily made by businessmen who often didn't vary scenery, story elements, or camera angles from one film to another. In fact, movies became such a turn-off that theater owners showed them only at the end of vaudeville programs, knowing that the appearance of a film would make the audience leave.

Obviously, more variety in a movie's characters, plot, and scenery was needed. The day that filmmakers realized this was the day that New Jersey's Golden Age of Movies truly began.

Although the first films were shot indoors, movie-makers quickly realized the advantages of outdoor locations. The use of natural light and the ability to utilize various backgrounds, plus the availability of ready-made props, made outside filming superior to inside shooting. Freed from the confines of the studio, movie plots became more diverse, mixing drama, comedy, and romance all within a single film. Stories were no longer written by businessmen, camera operators, and directors, but by professional writers, who knew how to create coherent narratives.

New York City, which provided most of the actors and movie-making capital, was initially the most popular source for outdoor locations. The city's gritty streets became the source of reels of urban dramas.

The problem was that those same gritty streets were not very helpful when making westerns, Civil War films, sea stories, or numerous other types of pictures. While early audiences were unsophisticated, it's doubtful they could be convinced they were watching two cowboys shoot it out on the open range while a streetcar was rumbling past in the background. Filmmakers began searching for scenic vistas, open fields, and sparsely populated towns; they found it all in New Jersey.

New Jersey had everything the movies needed: beaches, mountains, farms, woods, and fields. In particular, the northern part of the state presented filmmakers with a smorgasbord of locations: not only were there sprawling urban centers like Jersey City and Newark, but also miles of unspoiled countryside, and plenty of sparsely inhabited towns, all within a relatively short distance of each other. (In 1910, the population of Jersey City was 267,779; just a few miles to the north and east, Fort Lee had just 4,472 people, while Leonia contained barely 1,500.) If you couldn't find the right location in New Jersey, you just weren't trying. Movie crews began packing up their cameras and casts and heading across the Hudson.

Before long, it seemed that you couldn't turn around in New Jersey without bumping into a movie crew. In those simpler times, it didn't require a small army of equipment and people to shoot a film. Often the director, cameraman, and crew would cruise around in cars until they found a location that suited their storyline. Everyone would pile out, the director would position the single camera, the cast would get a few perfunctory instructions, and movie magic would begin.

Long before the star system ruled Hollywood, the first real "stars" of the silver screen were New Jersey towns and locales. Asbury Park, High Bridge, Bayonne, Edgewater, Sea Bright, North Bergen, New Brunswick, Linden, and scores of other towns were used in everything from slapstick comedies to tear-jerking melodramas. Actors and actresses soon became intimately familiar with the New Jersey countryside. Actress Linda Arvidson, later to become the first wife of pioneer director D. W. Griffith, said that she was "made love to on every rock and boulder for twenty miles up and down the Hudson." In fact, the Palisades region was used so often in films that in 1910, a writer in the *Dramatic Mirror* complained about the repeated use of "Jersey scenery" in the movies.

However, of all the New Jersey locations used, nowhere topped Fort Lee. For an all-too-brief time, the tiny town along the Palisades was the cinematic capital of the world.

It's fitting that both Fort Lee and the movies were attracted to each other, for each was just taking its first tentative steps at the beginning of the twentieth century. The town, originally named Fort Constitution but changed to honor Revolutionary War general Charles Lee, was incorporated on March 29, 1904, just as the movies were coming into their own as public entertainment.

Fort Lee had several advantages for film companies: It was just across the Hudson from New York City; it was built-up enough to provide facilities such as restaurants and hotels that the movie companies needed, but still largely rural and thus ideal for filming many different types of pictures; and, most importantly, it had Coytesville.

Located in the northern part of Fort Lee, the Coytesville section looked exactly like a prairie town in the Old West. It had dirt roads, wooden frame buildings, and neither telephone nor telegraph wires. Best of all, it had Rambo's Roadhouse, which looked so much like a western saloon that one expected to see Wyatt Earp or Wild Bill Hickock come ambling out the front door any moment. Scores of cowboys were destined to come out of Rambo's, step onto the wooden front porch, hitch their fingers in their gunbelts, and walk out to the dirt street for a shoot-out.

Although Coytesville might not appear in Fort Lee's civic brochure, it delighted filmmakers. They were scouting near and far for authentic-looking western locations, and here was one practically in their backyard. And not only horse operas could be filmed in Fort Lee; the easy accessibility of forests, meadows, and the towering Palisades cliffs meant that the town could be virtually anything the director wanted it to be.

A trip to Fort Lee from New York City was relatively simple. Film people took either the train or subway to 125th Street, where they caught

76 Rambo's Roadhouse, circa 1910. (Courtesy Fort Lee Public Library Collection)

the ferry for the trip across the Hudson. Once in New Jersey, either a trolley or horse-drawn buggy would take them to that day's location.

Fort Lee had gotten a small taste of movie life in 1909, when Edwin S. Porter shot *Rescued from the Eagle's Nest* on the sheer cliffs of the nearby Palisades. The star of that adventure film was a young man named David Wark (D. W.) Griffith, who would soon make his mark on the young industry not as an actor, but as a director.

A short time later, when Griffith became the principal director at the American Mutoscope and Biograph Company, he remembered Fort Lee. Soon he was routinely bringing his cast and crew over from the city to make *The Man and the Woman*, *The Fatal Hour*, *Balked at the Altar*, *The Curtain Pole*, *A Tragic Love*, *Lucky Jim*, and dozens of other films.

Always a pioneer, by 1912 Griffith had moved on to California. However, he had blazed a trail to Fort Lee that others were quick to follow. Champion Studio, which specialized in westerns, had already settled in Coytesville in 1910. Now others came to town: Eclair (a French film

company), Peerless, Willat, Universal, Paragon, Solax, and Lincoln all built studio facilities in Fort Lee.

Suddenly tiny, sleepy little Fort Lee found itself in the spotlight. It took to its new role of film capital with gusto.

Virtually everything in the town was available for rent to the film companies, from a sturdy oak on someone's property that would make a good hanging tree for western ne'er-do-wells to an entire home. (Everything means *everything*—as evidenced by the youngster who would greet film people with the question, "Hey, you wanna rent me mudder?") The town boomed, as hotels, restaurants, garages, blacksmiths, stables, and just about every other business in Fort Lee benefitted from the needs of the movie companies.

Most importantly, the emergence of this new industry in Fort Lee meant jobs, and plenty of them. It's estimated that one-third of the town's population was employed by the studios in building sets, carrying scenery, painting props, and doing other odd jobs, while another third were extras. Wages were excellent; even the lowest-paid studio employee averaged be-

tween $100 and $150 per week—a veritable fortune during those times of low taxation and an even lower cost of living.

The demands of the studios were endless. Most averaged fifty-two pictures a year, and it wasn't uncommon to have several different film companies working within plain sight of each other. In one instance, crews from the Biograph and Reliance studios were shooting on opposite sides of the same fence. The needs of the studios might be as simple as renting a farmer's pasture for a day, or as complicated as constructing an entire German town and then destroying it. (This was done, on the site of present day Fort Lee High School, for the film *The Kaiser: The Beast of Berlin.*)

The most in-demand spot of all was Rambo's. The bottom floor appeared as a saloon, hotel, sheriff's office, and just about any other type of building that heard the jingle of a cowpoke's spurs in the Old West. Actors and actresses often dressed and put on makeup in the second-floor rooms. Behind the building was a cistern with a pump that performers used to clean off their makeup at day's end. Fort Lee residents looking for work as extras would congregate at Rambo's and wait for the film companies to arrive, hoping to be noticed.

Rambo's also became a gathering place for everyone connected with the movies. The hotel had a hundred-foot grape arbor on one side, and under this it placed a long plank table, with benches on both sides, to feed the hungry filmmakers. Although Rambo's menu never varied—ham and eggs, bread and butter, coffee, and homemade apple pie—everyone ate with the famished gusto that trekking around the New Jersey countryside all day provided. After dinner, everyone would sit around the long table trading stories and gossiping until it was time to either go back to work or go home.

With so many films in production simultaneously, Fort Lee became like some bizarre Disneyland, where a walk on the street could bring you face-to-face with an Indian, a cowboy, a sailor, a knight, a soldier, a southern belle, and dozens of other characters. In the evening, when darkness brought filming to a halt, many actors went in full makeup to parties and dinners at the homes of local residents.

Unfortunately, time has erased the names of most of those who made movies in Fort Lee. How many except die-hard film buffs recognize the names Mable Normand, Florence Lawrence, Irene Castle, Alice Brady,

77 Douglas Fairbanks (on horse) discussing an upcoming scene. This area is now the approachway to the George Washington Bridge. (Courtesy Fort Lee Public Library Collection)

and Stuart Holmes? All were stars during the early days of movies—all are forgotten today.

A few names, however, have survived throughout the years. Mary Pickford, "America's Sweetheart," made over a dozen films in New Jersey, while her former husband, Douglas Fairbanks, shot four films there. Lionel and Ethel Barrymore also made a handful of films in the Garden

State, as did Lillian Gish. On the other side of the camera, famous directors that plied their trade in New Jersey included D. W. Griffith (over eighty films, made mainly in the Fort Lee area), Raoul Walsh, and Mack Sennett.

New Jersey also gave rise to some modern film empires. William Fox (20th Century-Fox) and Lewis Selznick (father of David O. Selznick, who made *Gone With the Wind*) both got their start in Fort Lee. Fort Lee was also home to the remarkable Alice Guy Blache, who, through her Solax Studio, was the first female film director and studio executive.

DID YOU KNOW?

Of all the interesting people who made movies in Fort Lee, none is more fascinating than Alice Guy Blache. In an era when women were expected to be seen and not heard, Blache was the guiding creative and business force behind Fort Lee's Solax Studios.

Alice Guy began her filmmaking career in France in the 1890s, where she acted in and directed numerous pictures for the Gaumont Co. She married Herbert Blache in 1907 and came to the United States, where she became involved in the fledgling film industry. In 1910 Alice, her husband, and a partner founded the Solax Co. in Flushing, New York. Two years later the Blaches built a production facility in Fort Lee at a cost of $100,000 (an enormous sum for that time).

Although both husband and wife were equal partners in Solax, Herbert was still involved with Gaumont, so many of the business and artistic decisions fell to Alice. Widely recognized as the first female director in the history of film as well as the first person to actually call herself a "director," she helmed many of the Solax productions, which largely consisted of one- and two-reel comedies and adventure films. Even those pictures that she did not direct were under her artistic control, however, making her the dominant figure at Solax and one of the first female studio executives in history. Blache was involved in practically every aspect of the Solax films, from writing the story to selecting the props. Because of her astute business instincts and artistic ability, Blache commanded great respect among the hard-headed businessmen who ran the film companies.

But while she campaigned vigorously to break the shackles of home and

78 Fatty Arbuckle and Mable Normand getting set to shoot a scene. (Courtesy Fort Lee Public Library Collection)

hearth that bound women back then, ultimately Alice Guy Blache could not escape those confinements herself. The break-up of her marriage deprived Alice of the masculine presence needed to gain admittance into the boy's club of American movie-making, and she found herself isolated from the film community. Eventually she retired to France.

Of all those who achieved stardom in Fort Lee, however, none was more colorful (or more unusual) than Theda Bara. She burst to prominence in 1914 in William Fox's *A Fool There Was*, playing a "vamp" (short for vampire, and meaning a woman who sucked the life out of men). Scenes of her gloating over the fallen body of her male victim caused a sensation; the word "vamp" entered the popular lexicon, and Bara became an overnight success.

Sensing an opportunity, Fox threw his formidable publicity machine behind Bara. The press was swamped with accounts about how pleasant little Theodosia Goodman (Bara's real name) from Cincinnati was the most vile temptress in history, how no man could resist her, and how her lips burned like fire when kissed. Yarns were woven about her mysterious past as an exotic Arabian princess. Over a five-year period, Bara starred in more than three dozen pictures, many of them reprising her vamp characterization. By 1919 the public, growing either tired or bored, had turned their back on Bara, but she had been one of the first of a breed quite common today: the publicity-produced celebrity.

Another silent film star from the Fort Lee era, Pearl White, left us an even more enduring phrase than "vamp." In 1914, White made the Pathe Studio serial *The Perils of Pauline*, which featured the title character getting into all manner of precarious situations. Indoor scenes were filmed at Pathe's studio on Congress Street in Jersey City, and outdoor sequences were shot throughout the area (including on a hill behind Christ Hospital in Elizabeth).

However, the scene that grabbed the public's attention was shot on the Palisades cliffs near Fort Lee. It showed the lovely "Pauline" once again in danger, this time dangling from the sheer Palisades cliffs, holding onto nothing more than a spindly little tree jutting out from the rocks, while the Hudson rushed by below. The public was so enamored with that scene that they began calling such situations "cliff-hangers," and the term has remained with us to the present day.

Celebrities often went to Fort Lee to see what all the fuss was about, and sometimes, to make a film of their own. Harry Houdini arrived in town to make *The Man from Beyond*, a film about, remarkably enough, an escape artist. Baseball slugger Babe Ruth also came to Fort Lee to star in a picture called "Babe Comes Home," which had—surprise!—a baseball plot.

---

79 Pioneering director D. W. Griffith. (Courtesy Fort Lee Public Library Collection)

So did the years pass in Fort Lee, and the rest of New Jersey: women hanging off cliffs, shoot-outs in the street, heroes and villains fighting to the death, and tearful embraces between long-lost lovers. It was a time when the distinction between fact and fiction blurred, and sometimes even merged, such as when the citizens of one New Jersey town thought that the bank hold-up being filmed was real and began firing actual bullets at the "robbers."

Exciting, unpredictable times indeed. Yet by 1919, they were just about over. Many of the Fort Lee studios had either closed, or were in the process of shutting down, and heading west. By 1925, the once-burgeoning film industry in Fort Lee—and the rest of New Jersey—was virtually extinct. A number of different factors had combined to kill the golden movie goose.

The first occurred in 1913, when Cecil B. DeMille made *The Squaw Man* in a tiny California town called Hollywood. To his fellow producers back East, DeMille sent enthusiastic reports of long, warm days full of sunshine. Griffith was also firmly ensconced in California, and he probably added to the praises that the Golden State's temperate climate was receiving. In New Jersey, filmmakers who were struggling with frigid winters (Linda Arvidson would remember: "[In winter] our makeup would be frozen, and the dreary, cold damp rooms in the country hotels made us shivery and miserable") and humid summers must have read these reports with envy, and interest.

Not only were makeup and shooting schedules affected by the weather. Forced to shoot in the studio during the winter, directors had to turn up the intensity of indoor lights. The heat generated, combined with the extraordinarily flammable silver nitrate film stock, made fire a constant danger. (This was one of the causes of a fire in 1914 that virtually destroyed the Eclair studio.)

Transportation was also influenced by Nature's unpredictability. With so many filmmakers dependent on the Edgewater ferry to get back and forth across the Hudson, a storm or harsh weather meant that the boat ran on an irregular schedule—if it ran at all. More than once film companies got stuck on either side of the river because the water was too churned up to allow the ferry to operate.

"It was the rotten New Jersey weather that killed the movie business in Fort Lee," declared former movie stuntman Gustav Nelson in 1961.

---

80 The "Vamp," Theda Bara. (Courtesy Fort Lee Public Library Collection)

On top of the weather, filmmakers in New Jersey also had to deal with another problem: the Edison Company and its business allies.

Virtually from the beginning of motion pictures, the Edison Company sought to control the domestic film industry through its patents. For ten years Edison fought bitter court battles with its U.S. competitors (mainly the American Mutoscope and Biograph Co.) over patent infringement. After losing several court decisions, the Edison Company changed tactics and in 1908 was the guiding force behind the formation of an association with the other major filmmaking companies called the Motion Picture Patents Co. Through various schemes, such as charging exhibitors a weekly $2 licensing fee in order to show films and setting a strict production schedule, the Motion Picture Patents Co. sought to control the entire motion picture industry.

Today we would call the MPPC a monopoly. Back then the word was "trust," but it meant the same thing. Some filmmakers went along with the trust; others, calling themselves "independents," resisted, and continued to make movies in defiance of the MPPC. In response, the trust sent out

"THRILLS" IS THE MIDDLE NAME OF THE SERIAL WRITER, AND UNLESS YOU CAN DEVISE SITUATIONS LIKE THIS ONE FROM 'THE HOUSE OF HATE," IN WHICH PEARL WHITE APPEARED, YOU CAN'T WRITE THE 'CONTINUED NEXT WEEK" TYPE OF STORY

detectives to enforce their edicts—and their rough-house methods didn't include politely asking the independents to stop.

The result was much like a Mack Sennett comedy. An independent company would be filming somewhere, when word would come that trust detectives were prowling around the area. The cameraman would pick up the camera and dash away, leaving cast and crew innocently milling about in full costume and makeup, as if that was the sort of thing they did every day just for the fun of it. After a period of time, the company would reunite with the cameraman and filming would begin again, until the next time that the trust detectives approached, when the whole process would be repeated.

In the 1967 book *One Reel a Week*, pioneering cameramen Fred J. Balshofer described the difficulties of working with one eye always on the lookout for trouble:

> The towns of Fort Lee and Coytesville were so small it was a cinch for McCoy [the main trust detective] and his added assistants to hound us. McCoy and his cohorts appeared every place we went to photograph around Coytesville. Some in our company would spot one of the spies approaching and give me the signal. I folded the legs of the tripod, put the camera over my shoulder, and took off down the road or into the woods. . . . The continued nuisance had the effect of making it impossible to work since all of us had become too jittery to concentrate.

It would be difficult making a cake, much less a movie, under these types of circumstances. As filmmakers searched for ways to escape the trust's odious enforcers, California gestured once again. Not only was it 3,000 miles away from the trust, but it was larger, and full of unknown towns. A film company could vanish in the state's wide-open spaces and work unimpeded. As Balshofer said: "Los Angeles with its mild climate and sunshine beckoned as an escape both from the winter months of the East as well as the ever-present Patents Company detectives."

Already reeling from the twin evils of poor weather and the trust company methods, the New Jersey film industry was dealt a death blow by World War I. Government rationing deprived the studios of coal, which they desperately needed to heat their large, drafty buildings.

Finally, it all became too much; the exodus from New Jersey (and in particular Fort Lee) to California began.

---

81   Pearl White in a familiar "cliff-hanger" location—the Palisades cliffs. (Courtesy Fort Lee Public Library Collection)

Of course, no one in New Jersey could know that trickling away to California was an industry whose glamour and economic power would one day captivate the world. At this time there were no government commissions or politicians ready to bestow tax breaks on industries to keep them from leaving a state. Indeed, movie people were frowned upon back then as low-class entertainers, and it might well be that many people in Fort Lee and throughout New Jersey were glad to see them and their industry go. After all, what could all that gaudy makeup, extravagant costumes, and silly play-acting amount to anyway?

By 1925 the film industry had virtually vanished from New Jersey. Fort Lee caught its breath and settled down to become a thriving middle-class town. Changes came, of course; Coytesville could no more remain like a town in the Old West than Dodge City could remain a cowboy town waiting for the return of Wyatt Earp. Soon the streets were paved, telephone and electrical wires were erected, and newer, more modern buildings were constructed in the once-popular cowboy haven. Even Rambo's changed, although much later than the rest of the area. Progress spread its concrete and steel fingers throughout Fort Lee, irrevocably altering the town and wiping away the movie memories like a summer rain wipes away the dew. The open fields where Indians, cowboys, knights, soldiers, and lovers had cavorted before the camera became the approach to the George Washington Bridge.

"Thus passeth the glory of the world," proclaimed the *New York Herald Tribune* of Sunday, October 26, 1947, underneath a picture of an abandoned, dilapidated Fort Lee film studio. The newspaper might well have added: "And never to return this way again."

DID YOU KNOW?

Although the state's Golden Era of movies was almost three-quarters of a century ago, film cameras are still rolling in the Garden State.

Since 1978, thanks to the efforts of the New Jersey Motion Picture and Television Commission, approximately 4,300 film and video projects have been shot in the state. These have enriched state coffers by a total of $281,900,000. In 1993 alone, a record 448 projects were made in New Jersey, including all or part of 36 feature films, 85 television series and specials, and 180 commercials.

CHAPTER TWELVE

It's the Natural Thing to Do

SO FAR, every chapter of this book has exploded the myth that New Jersey is nothing more than macadamized highways and superfund sites. However, there are always a few hold-outs who cling to their repudiated beliefs until the bitter end.

For them, this is the bitter end. This is the story of the "natural" New Jersey—places like the Forsythe Refuge near Atlantic City and Great Swamp just past Morristown, where Nature has not been paved or cemented over and has instead been allowed to flourish in all its glory. It's the story of trees, flowers, animals, insects, and a host of other things having nothing to do with roadways and rest stops. (And this doesn't even include the Pinelands, which is so unique it deserves its own chapter.) From the seashore to the mountains, and everywhere else in-between, the "natural" New Jersey shines like one of Nature's brightest jewels—and all anyone has to do to find it is pull off the highway.

From numerous points in the Edwin S. Forsythe National Wildlife Refuge in Oceanville, you can look up and see the tall buildings and casino hotels of Atlantic City looming on the horizon. This is New Jersey's version of the Odd Couple: a major wildlife refuge that shuns development coexisting next to an urbanized metropolis that entertains millions of visitors each year.

The preserve was originally established in 1939 as the Brigantine National Wildlife Refuge. A second section, Barnegat, was founded in 1967.

The two were combined under the Forsythe name in 1984, in honor of the late Congressman Edwin B. Forsythe, a staunch friend of the refuge.

Over 200,000 people per year, many of them dedicated bird watchers, journey to Forsythe's Brigantine Division, which is one of the most heavily visited wildlife refuges in the United States. (Everyone visits Brigantine because that's where the public use facilities are located.)

Almost 90 percent of the Forsythe Refuge (Brigantine Division from here on, unless otherwise noted) is tidal salt meadow and marsh, interspersed with shallow coves and bays, which serve as resting and feeding habitat for water birds. Fish and shellfish use the calm tidal waters as nurseries, and also for spawning and feeding.

The refuge is located directly on one of the Atlantic Flyway's most active flight paths. Over 275 species of birds frequent the 24,000-acre natural area during the migratory season. Among these are a variety of ducks, geese, sandpipers, egrets, and bitterns.

Of all birds, herons are particularly well represented at Forsythe; nearly a dozen species nest at the refuge. Snow geese and the majestic Glossy Ibis are other birds that are frequently found there. Forsythe also has, at times, approximately 90 percent of the Atlantic population of brant, a small, dark goose whose extremely fussy eating habits limit it to a diet of just a few plants. (Brant are so picky that when a blight in the 1930s decimated its favorite food, eel grass, the population nearly died out due to starvation.)

During the migratory seasons, Forsythe practically bulges with birds. Tens of thousands of ducks, geese, wading birds, and shorebirds concentrate at Forsythe during these periods, stopping to feed and rest before resuming their journey. It's not uncommon during migratory periods to see massive squadrons of shorebirds flying in formation and practically blotting out the sun. When these groups of birds land *en masse* in one of the tidal pools, the roar they make upon hitting the water is like that of a colossal cannon being fired.

Once they arrive at Forsythe, some birds find that they like it so much that they don't want to leave. Black ducks remain there throughout the summer to nest and raise their young. If the weather permits, Atlantic brant and black ducks also overwinter at Forsythe.

The refuge plays an important part in providing undisturbed nesting habitats for several endangered and threatened species. Special nesting

82 Canada geese and their young in the marsh grass at the Edwin B. Forsythe National Wildlife Refuge. (Photo by Pat King-Roberts)

platforms have been erected for peregrine falcons and ospreys. Bald eagles are also seen on the refuge each year.

Although there are a few foot paths through the woods, the best opportunities for viewing birds and wildlife at Forsythe occur along the eight-mile Wildlife Drive. This one-way road loops around the refuge, and is wide enough to allow ample space for pulling over to the side of the road whenever desired. (This becomes particularly handy during gosling and duckling seasons, when the parents and their young think nothing of marching right across the road, often stopping traffic—and providing priceless photo opportunities.)

More than 6,000 acres of the refuge are designated as a Wilderness Area, including two of the few remaining undeveloped barrier beaches in New Jersey. This region provides essential nesting and feeding habitat for the rare piping plover, black skimmer, and least tern. The natural habitats of these species have been decimated by human development and increased recreational use of the beaches. The Forsythe refuge is one of the last places where the birds are guaranteed unimpeded use of beaches.

Even though Forsythe is largely wetlands, there are approximately 3,000 acres of woodlands there as well. These contain songbirds, deer,

turtles, raccoons, rabbits, muskrats, skunks, and other animals. Even the rare Pine Barrens tree frog sometimes hops over for a visit.

Like people, the Forsythe Refuge responds to the seasons: The natural ebb and flow of light and temperature throughout the year dictate the amount of wildlife activity at the refuge. During the depths of winter, when cold and snow lay heavy on the earth, the refuge is at its most quiet. However, with the coming of spring and the rebirth of the natural world, Forsythe explodes into life; waterfowl in particular are plentiful during this time, as thousands of birds stop there temporarily on their way to nesting sites further north. Summer finds life at the refuge again slowing down, although these are usually the months of peak duckling activity. (It's also the time of peak insect activity.) August is when the shorebirds reverse their springtime migration, responding not to clock or calendar but to ancient instincts that tell them that summer's warmth will soon be gone. The autumn brings another spectacular array of birds to Forsythe on their long journey south; over 100,000 ducks and geese have been known to gather in the pools at Forsythe at one time, frolicking in the water like swimmers out for one final fling on Labor Day.

Yet, even as the Forsythe Refuge once again falls under the dreamy spell of winter, it's comforting to know that within a few short months, the skies will once again be filled with birds, signaling yet another spring and another season of renewal at the Forsythe Refuge for all Nature's creatures—including us humans.

Despite the popularity of the Forsythe Refuge among the wings and feathers set, it isn't the only spot in New Jersey that migratory shorebirds frequent on their long journey northward. Each spring, from early May through the first week of June, over 1 million shorebirds stop for rest and relaxation along New Jersey's "other coast"—the Delaware Bay.

The migration of shorebirds every spring from Brazil, Argentina, and other South American countries to the far north, with a stop-over in New Jersey, is one of Nature's most reliable barometers. The concentration of birds along the Delaware Bay coast is the second largest gathering of

83   An egret in flight at Forsythe. (Photo by Pat King-Roberts)

shorebirds in the country. (Incredibly enough, the largest migration occurs in a wetlands section of land-locked Kansas!)

These birds are migrating primarily from South America to their nesting grounds on the Arctic Bay, a trip of about 7,000 miles. The Delaware Bay coastline is a half way point on their flight, and so nearly two dozen species have chosen the beaches there as the perfect place to rest from their arduous journey.

The Delaware Bay beaches that the shorebirds frequent bear little resemblance to those along New Jersey's ocean. To the birds, however, these small, rocky beaches are every bit as inviting as their Atlantic coast counterparts; without them, the birds would die.

Many birds fly nonstop from their winter homes in the south straight to the Delaware Bay, a distance of about 4,000 miles. Although, like long-distance runners, the birds fuel up before they start, by the time they reach New Jersey the exhausted creatures have hit the wall. Many of the birds lose up to 50 percent of their total body weight during the first part of their flight.

What attracts the shorebirds to the Delaware Bay coastline, besides the opportunity for a little R&R, is something near and dear to every trav-

eler's heart: food. For the shorebirds this means horseshoe crab eggs, a particularly tasty dish that makes their beaks water.

The Delaware Bay hosts the largest concentration of spawning horseshoe crabs along the Atlantic coast of North America. Although the crabs begin spawning in April, and don't stop until the summer is nearly over, May is their peak month for egg-laying. By a happy coincidence (unless you're a mama horseshoe crab, that is), this is also the time of peak shorebird activity. During these weeks, horseshoe crabs crawl up onto the beach by the thousands to lay their eggs, sometimes packing the sand so tightly that a person could literally walk on their shells and never touch the ground. After laying their eggs in the sand—350 tons worth, according to some estimates—the crabs head back to the bay. It's a good thing the crabs don't linger to see the results of their labors: Water and wave action, and activity by other crabs, unearths many of the eggs, leaving them to be eaten by the ravenous birds.

Thanks to the food and the rest, by the time the birds are ready to resume their trip they have undergone a remarkable transformation. The sleek and rested creatures that depart from the Delaware Bay bear little resemblance to the worn out, half-starved scarecrows that initially arrived.

After leaving New Jersey, most of the birds go straight to their nesting grounds in the Canadian and Arctic tundra, where they remain for about one month. In that short time they have to establish territories, find mates (obviously, long courtships are out), and start nesting. There's neither time nor the resources to feed—another reason why their stop-over at the Delaware Bay is so important to the birds.

The shorebirds stay at the nesting ground just long enough to mate. A few days after their eggs hatch, the adults begin the return trip south, leaving their offspring to fend for themselves. (Since they take a different route south, however, the birds don't stop at the Delaware Bay on the way back.) Over the next few weeks, the baby birds mature, learn to fly and feed, and then take off after their parents, using nothing more than instinct to guide them 7,000 miles.

Clearly, the Delaware Bay beaches play a critical role in the shorebird's life cycle. While residential development on these lands isn't likely due to severe erosion and general inhospitality, there is always the chance that commercial use could someday deprive the shorebirds of one of the few natural areas left on their flight path.

---

84 Shorebirds feeding on horseshoe crab eggs along the Delaware Bay. (Courtesy New Jersey Division of Fish, Game and Wildlife)

To forestall this, various state and federal agencies, as well as wildlife and conservation groups, have been acquiring this land and managing it for the use of shorebirds and other animals. Today nearly 100,000 acres of public land are administered by five agencies along Delaware Bay. Like an oasis in the desert, the rocky beaches of New Jersey's Delaware Bay will hopefully forever offer food and rest to the huge flocks of shorebirds that depend on them for their very lives.

DID YOU KNOW?

Did you know that the bald eagle, once nearly extinct in New Jersey, is making a remarkable comeback thanks to the state's Endangered and Non-Game Species Program?

Over ninety eagles, including nine nesting pairs, were spotted in New Jersey recently, the highest number in over two decades. During the 1970s, there was just one nest and less than a half-dozen eagles in the state, and the bird seemed headed for extinction in New Jersey. Pesticides that the eagles ab-

sorbed through the food chain had severely eroded the strength of the birds' eggs. The effect of the chemicals on the eagles caused the number of nesting pairs in New Jersey to plummet from two dozen in the first half of the twentieth century to just one pair by 1972.

Today, however, thanks to the Bald Eagle Restoration Program (part of the Endangered and Non-Game Species Program), the national symbol of our country is once again flying high in New Jersey. Eagle nests have been found in all the counties adjacent to the Delaware Bay, and even as far north as Hunterdon County. In fact, the program has worked so well that state officials have switched from a "restoration mode" to a "management mode" to help the existing birds thrive. Officials hope to have between ten and fifteen nesting pairs in the state by the end of the century.

The success of the eagle restoration program is another feather in the cap for New Jersey's Endangered and Non-Game Species Program, which is funded primarily through an income tax check-off and sales of the "conserve wildlife" license plate. The program has also restored populations of ospreys and peregrine falcons, protected and managed endangered beach-nesting birds, and protected habitats critical to the survival of rare species.

The front page of the December 3, 1959, *Newark Evening News* said it all: "Jetport in Morris Country" blared the headline. In the days that followed, as stunned local residents read about the massive new facility planned by the Port of New York Authority, they discovered that not only were they about to gain a new airport, but they were also going to lose an old friend: Great Swamp.

Born out of the dying gasps of the Wisconsin Glaciation some 25,000 years ago, Great Swamp was (in 1959) approximately 4,000 acres of swamp woodland, hardwood ridges, cattail marsh, and grassland. Populated by beaver, foxes, turtles, snakes, and dozens of varieties of fish and birds, the swamp was, like the Pinelands further south, a New Jersey anomaly: an area of unspoiled natural beauty harkening back thousands of years just twenty-five miles from humanity's ultimate monument to

---

85 A mass of ruddy turnstones during the spring migratory season at the Delaware Bay. (Courtesy New Jersey Division of Fish, Game and Wildlife)

concrete civilization—New York City. Thanks to the circumstances of its birth, Great Swamp for years had been able to survive the urban sprawl that had spread outward from the New York metropolitan area, engulfing farmland and small villages alike. Whether its luck would hold in the face of the Port Authority proposal, however, was anybody's guess.

Thousands of years ago, the massive Wisconsin Glacier moved across northern New Jersey like an invincible army of ice, crushing whatever soil and vegetation it encountered. Then, approximately 15,000 years ago, the mighty glacier began to melt and retreat northward. The water flowed into a natural basin surrounded by the Watchung Mountains to form what geologists call Lake Passaic. This ancient lake was estimated to be from 160- to 240-feet deep and thirty miles long by ten miles wide. After the passage of another few thousand years, Lake Passaic began to slowly empty into the Passaic River. Eventually the entire lake drained away, except for some low-lying areas, one of which was Great Swamp.

When the Europeans arrived in North America and began to explore the region that would someday be called New Jersey, they found the Lenni-Lenape or Delaware Indians living in and around Great Swamp. Besides animals for food and clothing, Great Swamp provided the Native Americans with many items that they used in everyday life, such as berries, the juice of which was used to make colored dyes; grasses for covering, roofing, and sweeping; and bird feathers for ornamental and ceremonial jewelry.

On August 13, 1708, Great Swamp was included as part of a land purchase by British investors from the Delawares. For thirty pounds Sterling in cash, as well as ten blankets, fifteen kettles, twenty axes, twenty hoes, four pistols, one hundred barrels of lead, twenty shirts, one hundred knives, and other assorted goods, the British bought 30,000 acres of land (about eighteen square miles) in northern New Jersey from the Indians, including Great Swamp.

The Delawares had been content to take what Great Swamp had been willing to give them. The Europeans, as well as the Americans who followed them to the area, tried to bend Great Swamp to their will, with predictable results: Most attempts at farming failed due to the mushy ground, while attempts to exploit the forests resulted in excessive chopping down of trees, which exacerbated the problem of excess water. As people abandoned their efforts to make Great Swamp into something that

86 A baby bald eagle, about two months old. (Courtesy New Jersey Division of Fish, Game and Wildlife)

it could never be, the land reverted to its former appearance: The woods returned to the uplands, while the low areas became even more swampy. As the years rolled by, and bustling communities like Morristown, Summit, and Madison sprang up all around it, Great Swamp remained a marshy, tree-filled expanse more suited for animals than people.

All this changed, however, with the Port Authority's jetport proposal. To be fair, it wasn't as if the authority suddenly dreamed up the idea to destroy Great Swamp on a whim. Armed with statistical projections that showed almost twice as many passengers and more than twice the cargo tonnage passing through the region's four airports (Idlewild [now John F. Kennedy], LaGuardia, Newark, and Teterboro) in 1965 as passed through in 1958—and even more in the 1970s and 1980s—the agency saw a clear need to head off overwhelming congestion. After evaluating fifteen sites for a possible new airport, the Port Authority concluded that only Great Swamp met all the requirements: "There is no other practicable site that would meet the criteria of an airport that the people of northern New Jersey and the metropolitan region must have," said the Port Authority in a report outlining its plans.

Historically, the Port Authority had always gotten its way with proposals such as the one they were now suggesting. This time, however, a group of residents took umbrage at the idea of an airport being dropped right into the middle of peaceful and bucolic Morris County, destroying Great Swamp in the bargain. They quickly united to fight the proposal.

Thus began what has become an old story today, but what at that time was a very new tale indeed: the saga of the environment versus the economy. Proponents of the jetport argued that it would bring jobs and business opportunities to the area, and create a virtual economic gold mine out of land that, in the case of Great Swamp, was lying around useless. Opponents countered that the land wasn't useless: It was home to scores of animals, fish, birds, and plants. Furthermore, the proposed airport would wipe out 700 homes, as well as churches, schools, and small businesses,

87 An adult bald eagle watches over its nest. (Courtesy New Jersey Division of Fish, Game and Wildlife)

88 Great Swamp National Wildlife Refuge. (Photo by Pat King-Roberts)

and completely transform the character of the region from small-town sleepy to big-city bustling.

For several years the two sides fought it out in New Jersey's own version of David and Goliath: the powerful Port Authority, with its vast wealth and political influence, against a citizen's group of environmentalists, with their coffee klatsches and neighborhood meetings. As the pendulum swung to and fro—sometimes the Port Authority would seem on the verge of gaining the necessary approvals, and sometimes the citizen's groups would seem to be riding an overwhelming tide of public support— the fate of Great Swamp hung in the balance. It had survived thousands of years of natural forces, but could it survive humanity?

The answer was yes; just like in the Bible, David slew Goliath. The public pressure and attention focused on Great Swamp's unique environmental characteristics were too much for the Port Authority to overcome. The Great Swamp Committee of the North American Wildlife Foundation raised more than $1 million to buy over 3,000 acres of land, which were then donated to the federal Department of the Interior for a Great Swamp Wildlife Refuge. More than 6,000 private citizens and 422 organizations representing 286 towns and 29 states contributed to the fight to save Great Swamp from extinction. On May 29, 1964, Great Swamp was

officially dedicated as a national wildlife preserve, at ceremonies attended by U.S. Secretary of the Interior, Stewart Udall. Four years later, on September 30, 1968, President Lyndon Johnson signed a bill that made Great Swamp the first wilderness area in the federal national wildlife refuge system. People power had won.

Today, thanks to additional land acquisitions, Great Swamp totals over 7,000 acres. Over 220 species of birds, dozens of mammals, and a large variety of reptiles, amphibians, and fish call the refuge home. Animals found at Great Swamp run the gamut from common creatures like the white-tailed deer and rabbits to the rare blue-spotted salamander and bog turtle. Wood ducks, which some call our most beautiful waterfowl, thrive at Great Swamp, producing more than 4,000 ducklings every year. The area also contains a fascinating variety of botanical species, such as ferns, mosses, wild lilies, orchids, and primroses.

A visit to Great Swamp is very different from most other natural areas. The purpose of the federal Wilderness Act is to let "an area of undeveloped federal land, retain its primeval character and influence . . . where the earth and its community of life are untrammeled by man." Here, in these "outdoor laboratories," the action and evolution of natural life can be studied and observed without the heavy-footed intrusion of humanity. Thus at Great Swamp there are no picnic areas, playgrounds, barbecue grills, or any of the other conveniences found at a park or recreation area. Human involvement is meant to be kept at a minimum.

There are, however, eight miles of hiking trails, winding through picturesque, serene landscapes that seem to have come just off an artist's brush. Alone on a path, with just the sky overhead, the trees alongside, and the faint song of a distant bird for company, it's easy to understand why Henry David Thoreau once said: "I enter a swamp as a sacred place . . . [here] there is the strength, the marrow of nature." He could easily have been talking about Great Swamp.

In this modern age of steel and concrete, its takes determination to help Nature and its creatures survive in an increasingly hostile world. An example of such dedication can be found at the Marine Mammal Stranding Institute in Brigantine.

89   Great Swamp National Wildlife Refuge. (Photo by Pat King-Roberts)

The institute rescues and rehabilitates stranded or otherwise stressed marine mammals, such as dolphins, whales, and seals, as well as sea turtles. Over 1,000 animals have been helped so far by the center, which, at this point, is financed solely through donations, memberships, gift shop sales, and fundraising efforts. Except for a tiny staff, all institute personnel are volunteers.

The institute, begun in 1978 by Robert Schoeklopf, was initially located in Gardners Basin in Atlantic City. Today Schoeklopf and his wife, Sheila, form the backbone of the institute, which is the only organization in New Jersey authorized to rescue and rehabilitate stranded marine animals and sea turtles. These can range anywhere from a small, five-pound Kemps Ridley sea turtle to a twenty-five-ton Humpback whale.

Schoelkopf's interest in marine mammals began three decades ago, when he saw how intelligent and playful dolphins were at an aquarium in Philadelphia at which he worked. When the aquarium moved to Atlantic City Schoelkopf, who had become the dolphin's trainer, moved with it. One cold March day, a friend told him that a whale had been beached. Schoelkopf went to the beach, and was moved by the animal's struggles and suffering. In his street clothes he waded into the surf and remained there for several hours, trying to comfort the whale. Schoelkopf remained with the animal for the next five days at a nearby Coast Guard station where it had been towed, trying to nurse it back to health. Although the whale died, Schoelkopf was so moved by the experience that he shortly thereafter began the Marine Mammal Stranding Institute.

When the institute gets a call about a stranded animal—which can come at any time of the day or night—they immediately head out to the site to determine the creature's condition. Often the animal is either sick or injured and in danger of dying. Institute personnel bring it back to their facilities at Brigantine, where it lives in one of the holding areas while it is nursed back to health. Doctoring a sick sea animal usually entails a lot more than just giving it a shot of medicine. Dolphins, for example, are voluntary breathers (unlike humans, who breathe involuntarily), so institute personnel have to physically get into the holding area pool with them and help them remain conscious until they stabilize. (If they become unconscious, they'll cease breathing and die.)

Eventually, if all goes well, the creature is released back into the wild. If it can't be returned to its natural habitat, then the stranding center looks for a suitable home for the creature.

---

90 One of the boardwalk trails through Great Swamp. (Photo by Pat King-Roberts)

Although it might not be apparent, even to someone who takes frequent coastline strolls, sea animals are getting stranded on New Jersey beaches in ever-increasing numbers. In 1978, there were nineteen strandings in the state; by 1993 that figure had leaped to 123.

One of the animals most likely to get stranded are seals, which often visit New Jersey waters in the winter from as far away as the Arctic circle. Sickness, becoming entangled in fishing nets, or being struck by boat propellers are just some of the injuries that can cause seals to become injured and disoriented and seek the shelter and safety of a beach. Harbor seals and gray seals are the most common varieties that get stranded, although harp seals, hooded seals, and ringed seals have also been found on the state's beaches during the past few years.

In the summer it's the dolphins' turn to sometimes wind up as un-expected guests at the stranding institute. The Atlantic Bottlenose dolphin often swims just off the coast in the summer, and, like seals, can run afoul of a number of man-made or natural occurrences that cause it to strand on the beach. Fortunately, Schoelkopf has not seen a return of the terrible summer of 1987, when hundreds of dead and dying bottlenose dolphins washed up on beaches up and down the eastern seaboard, with lesions on

their skin, burned lungs, and signs of pneumonia. The Marine Mammal Stranding Institute responded to ninety dolphin strandings that summer.

Other animals that may become stranded on the state's beaches are sea turtles and whales. The institute stresses that stranded animals are not to be pushed back into the water, petted, or otherwise interacted with. Such animals are often sick and in pain and may lash out at anyone who approaches. The institute should be called as soon as a stranded creature is spotted.

As both recreational boating and development increases, bringing with them more pollution and loss of natural areas, strandings are likely to also increase. Fortunately, the dedicated volunteers and staff of the Marine Mammal Stranding Institute stand ready to assist these sick, defenseless creatures, in the process proving once again that the "natural" New Jersey is truly a thing of beauty and wonder.

DID YOU KNOW?

New Jersey has over forty-five state parks and forests, where you can get in touch with the natural world in many pleasant ways.

New Jersey State Parks and Forests

Abram S. Hewitt Forest, Hewitt (Passaic County)
Allaire Park, Farmingdale (Monmouth County)
Allamuchy Mountain Park, Stephen's Section, Hackettstown (Warren County)
Barnegat Lighthouse Park, Barnegat Light (Ocean County)
Bass River Forest, New Gretna (Ocean County)
Belleplain Forest, Woodbine (Cape May County)

91 Part of the Marine Mammal Stranding Center facility in Brigantine. (Photo by Pat King-Roberts)

Bull's Island Section, Stockton (Hunterdon County)
Cape May Point Park, Cape May Point (Cape May County)
Cheesequake Park, Matawan (Monmouth County)
Corson's Inlet Park, South of Ocean City (Cape May County)
Deep Cut Park, Middletown (Monmouth County)
Delaware and Raritan Canal Park, Belle Meade (Somerset County)
Fort Mott Park, Salem (Salem County)
Hacklebarney Park, Off Rt. 24, Long Valley (Morris County)
High Point Park, Sussex (Sussex County)
Hopatcong Park, Landing (Sussex County)
Island Beach Park, Seaside Park (Ocean County)
Jenny Jump Forest, Hope (Warren County)
Lebanon Forest, New Lisbon (Burlington County)
Liberty State Park, Jersey City (Hudson County)
Monmouth Battlefield Park, Freehold (Monmouth County)
Mt. Mitchell Overlook Park, Atlantic Highlands (Monmouth County)
Norvin Green Forest, Sloatsburg Ringwood (Passaic County)
Parvin Park, Elmer (Salem County)
Penn Forest, New Gretna (Burlington County)
Princeton Battlefield Park, Princeton (Mercer County)
Prospertown Lake, Freehold (Monmouth County)
Ramapo Mt. Forest, Oakland (Bergen County)
Rancocas Park, Westampton Twp. (Burlington County)
Ringwood Manor, Ringwood (Passaic County)
Ringwood Park, Ringwood (Passaic County)
Round Valley, Lebanon (Hunterdon County)
Seven Presidents Oceanfront Park, Long Branch (Monmouth County)
Shepherd Lake, Ringwood (Passaic County)
Skylands Section, Ringwood (Passaic County)
Spruce Run Park, Clinton (Hunterdon County)
Stokes Forest, Branchville (Sussex County)
Swartswood Park, Swartswood (Sussex County)
Voorhees Park, Glen Gardner (Hunterdon County)
Washington Crossing Park, Titusville (Mercer County)
Washington Rock Park, Plainfield (Union County)
Wawayanda Park, Highland Lakes (Sussex County)
Wharton Forest, Hammonton (Atlantic County)
Worthington Forest, Columbia (Warren County)

CHAPTER THIRTEEN

Roads, Bridges, and Tunnels

CRITICISM of New Jersey frequently centers on its roadways and, through guilt by association, its other transportation aids such as bridges and tunnels. It's as if the Garden State somehow has more of these than any other state in the country, and thus is a fair target for ridicule and abuse.

Such mockery, however, is extremely short-sighted. Because of its dense population and corresponding need to move all of the vehicles that pour out onto the roads at something other than the proverbial snail's pace, New Jersey has frequently been the site of many transportation innovations. The Turnpike, for example, which has been the butt of more corny jokes than the audience at a cheap Las Vegas lounge act, was widely hailed when it first opened as a pioneering achievement in the fine art of highway development, a road that sped vehicles on their way so fast that it had propelled the science of highway engineering to the next level. The Pulaski Skyway was also considered something of a miracle for the engineering skill involved in its construction that enabled it to tower over the roads below, like a runway heading off into outer space.

More importantly, however, the story of roads, bridges and tunnels in New Jersey is the story of people—resourceful, dynamic people with vision and daring, such as the bespectacled engineer who dared to dream that he could build a tunnel under the Hudson River from Jersey City to New York, or the New Jersey family that paid a tragic price for their desire to show the world that suspension bridges could span even the greatest gaps between towns and cities.

This is the story of some of the most memorable New Jersey roads, bridges, and tunnels—and of the people who made them so.

"He builded better than he knew."

This phrase, awkward in its pronunciation but elegant in its sentiment, is on a plaque near the New York City entrance to the Holland Tunnel. The plaque and nearby bust commemorate Clifford M. Holland, the man who designed and oversaw the construction of what was then the first underwater tunnel strictly for automotive traffic. The story of the Holland Tunnel is an old one: a desire to conquer Nature's barriers for the convenience of humanity. And, like many similar endeavors, the price to achieve this desire was high.

The idea of a tunnel between New Jersey and Manhattan had long been a dream of far-thinking people. In the nineteenth century Hoboken's John Stevens, frustrated by the delays and unpredictability of ferry service between the two points, suggested building a stone tube under the Hudson

River to expedite wagon traffic between New Jersey and New York. The idea went nowhere, simply because it was considered impossible.

The problem, however, persisted, and with the dawning of the automobile age, accelerated into a crisis. Ferries remained the only way for cars to move across the Hudson, but most had been built to hold horse-drawn carriages and wagons and not the larger and bulkier autos. Consequently, only a few vehicles could make the crossing each time. Cars backed up for miles at Hudson River ferry depots, and it was not uncommon for motorists to have to wait several hours to make the thirty-minute trip across the water. Other vehicles were also at the mercy of the ferries and the weather, a point that was brought home quite clearly when a seven-day freeze of the Hudson caused a food shortage in Manhattan.

Obviously, a quicker mode of travel between New Jersey and New York was needed. After studying various alternatives, in 1919, a bi-state commission recommended building a tunnel under the Hudson River that would connect Jersey City and New York City.

Many reacted with laughter and scorn to this proposal. After all, they pointed out, in order to reach bedrock wouldn't the tunnel have to be dug nearly 100 feet below the surface of the Hudson? And wouldn't the tunnel have to be almost two miles long—a distance never before attempted? Finally, and most significantly, how would air circulate in a tunnel that long and that deep? Wouldn't it just fill with lethal carbon monoxide fumes and become a death trap for motorists?

All of these were valid objections. However, the skeptics hadn't reckoned with the ingenuity and determination of the man hired by the New York State Bridge and Tunnel Commission and the New Jersey Interstate Bridge and Tunnel Commission to do the job: a thirty-six-year-old civil engineer and Harvard graduate named Clifford M. Holland.

Born on March 13, 1883, in Somerset, Massachusetts, Holland was no stranger to building tunnels: He had previously worked on both the Battery and the East River tunnel projects and was recognized as a leader in the field. However, he had two strikes against him when he was interviewed by the tunnel commissioners for the project: Not only would the proposed Hudson River Vehicular Tunnel be more difficult than anything he had ever attempted (in fact, it was more difficult than any tunnel *anyone* ever attempted before), but the panel had already tentatively selected Gen. George W. Goethals, builder of the Panama Canal, as the man for the job.

92 Artist's conception of the building of the Holland Tunnel. (Courtesy the Port Authority of New York and New Jersey)

However, the slim, slightly built Holland blew away the famous canal builder with his visionary and well-thought out plans for the tunnel. A main feature of Holland's design was to use smaller-sized tubes lined with both cast iron and concrete for extra strength, rather than larger tubes lined only with concrete that Goethals had proposed. On July 1, 1919, Holland became the chief engineer in charge of building the tunnel, at a salary of $12,000 per year.

Because of the uniqueness of the project, Holland was forced to do things no one else had ever done before. To test the emissions of motor vehicles—a revolutionary concept back then—he sealed off an abandoned coal mine near Pittsburgh and measured the exhaust emitted by many different varieties and sizes of motorized vehicles traveling at various speeds. To measure the effects of carbon monoxide on living organisms, blood from student volunteers from Yale University who had inhaled a mixture of air and carbon monoxide was tested. A miniature tunnel was built to the exact scale of the proposed one to gather additional information on emissions and air circulation.

From the data gathered, Holland developed a brand-new method of ventilation called a "vertical transverse flow." This system utilized two ventilating stations on each side of the Hudson, housing a total of eighty-four huge fans that would pump 3,600,000 cubic feet of fresh air per minute into the tunnel. Forty-two fans would suck fresh air in and then force it through special chambers below the roadway, from where it would enter the tunnel through vents in the curbing, mix with the exhaust fumes and rise to the ceiling, where it would be removed by forty-two suction fans. This would provide a complete change of air every ninety seconds.

Although severely criticized, Holland's plan was adopted. On October 12, 1920, a ground-breaking ceremony for the new tunnel was held in New York. Within a few days, work began on the New Jersey side as well. Crews began tunneling toward each other from opposite sides of the river. sometimes making as much as fifteen feet a day and sometimes advancing just a few inches.

To design the tunnel, Holland had been working around the clock. Once the actual digging began, his workdays became even longer. Each laborious foot that the workers dug seemed to bring new problems, and Holland was constantly on-call to solve them. Even the few hours of sleep he got each night were frequently interrupted by problems that required his immediate attention. A myriad of decisions both large and small consumed every moment of his life. His wife, Anna, and their four daughters hardly ever saw him. For four years he ate, slept, and breathed the tunnel.

Finally he broke down. On October 8, 1924, it was announced that Holland was taking a one-month vacation from his job due to his "continuous devotion, night and day, during the past five years." With his health rapidly failing, Holland left for Battle Creek, Michigan, to rest so that he could return for the historic joining of both sides of the tunnel, now just weeks away.

He never made it back to New York. On October 27, 1924, Holland suffered a heart attack and died in Battle Creek. His untimely death canceled a special celebration commemorating the "holing through," in which President Calvin Coolidge was supposed to push a button in Washington setting off the final explosion.

Two days later, workers from each side broke through the final barrier of rock between them and shook hands, a moment that Clifford Holland had literally killed himself to accomplish.

(The tunnel was not yet through exacting its terrible price. Holland's replacement, Milton Freeman, also died five months later, a death that was also widely attributed to overwork. A third engineer, Ole Singstad, finished the tunnel, but not without regrets. In later life, he lamented the number of cars he had allowed to come into New York City.)

On November 12, 1927, New Jersey governor A. Harry Moore and Jersey City Mayor Frank Hague, along with officials from New York, officially dedicated the tunnel. Then, for the next several hours, thousands of people (20,000 within the first hour!) celebrated this engineering marvel by walking through the long tube from one side of the river to the other. (The tunnel connects Canal Street in Manhattan with Twelfth and Fourteenth streets in Jersey City.) For the pedestrians, it was strictly a party atmosphere; they laughed, shouted, sang, knelt down to feel the fresh air flowing through the roadbed vents and talked about establishing restaurants along the tunnel's sides.

Promptly at midnight, the tunnel was closed to pedestrians forever; a few moments later the first cars came rumbling through. On the New Jersey side, more than 1,000 cars had been lined up, seven abreast for four blocks, waiting to make the historic trip. The first driver through from Jersey City (not counting dignitaries) was J. Frank Finn, an attorney. He was the first "unofficial" New Jerseyian to enjoy the fact that the trip across the Hudson River had been reduced from thirty minutes to eight.

In honor of the man who gave his life so that it could become a reality, the Hudson River Vehicular Tunnel was renamed the Holland Tunnel. Because of its historic importance, the U.S. Department of the Interior designated it a National Historic Landmark in 1994, making it the first vehicle tunnel to gain that status. Thanks to the genius of Clifford Holland, a structure that was built to accommodate eight million vehicles a year today handles double that amount with no problem.

He had indeed "builded better than he knew."

DID YOU KNOW?

Just in case you're ever on a game show where winning the grand prize depends on knowing some real obscure information about the Holland Tunnel:

Width of the roadway: 20 feet
External diameter of the tunnel: 29 feet, 6 inches
Maximum depth from mean high water to roadway: 93 feet, 5 inches
Length of tunnel, portal to portal: 8,558 feet (north tube) 8,371 feet (south tube)
Initial construction cost: $48 million

Even as the Holland Tunnel was being dug, it was becoming obvious that it alone would not solve all the commuting problems between New Jersey and New York City. The tunnel was downtown; something else was needed closer to midtown Manhattan, the daily destination for thousands of New Jerseyians. That something, it was decided, was to be a suspension bridge from 178 Street in Manhattan to the rocky basalt cliffs of the Palisades in Fort Lee, New Jersey.

The announcement brought out all the nay-sayers who had been in hiding after their dire predictions about the Holland Tunnel had gone up in smoke. This time, the skeptics zeroed in on the great distance that the

93   Some of the workers who helped build the Holland Tunnel. (Courtesy the Port Authority of New York and New Jersey)

94   Life-sized sections of the Holland Tunnel (then called the Hudson River Vehicular Tunnel) and the Hudson & Manhattan Tunnel for trolleys, showing the great difference in size between the two. (Courtesy the Port Authority of New York and New Jersey)

proposed bridge would have to cover: 3,500 feet. No suspension bridge had ever reached that far; the only one even close was under construction at Detroit, and that was a "mere" 1,850 feet.

But again, the doubters had failed to consider the iron will of the man hired to build the bridge, a dour but brilliant Swiss engineer named Othmar Hermann Ammann. As single-minded as Clifford Holland in his pursuit of excellence, Ammann plowed ahead with engineering and topographical studies that showed the only way for the bridge to be feasible was to build massive towers from which to hang the suspension cables. In October 1927, ground was broken for the new bridge.

The bridge transformed the tiny town of Fort Lee, once home to the nation's movie industry (see chapter 11). The fields where Douglas Fairbanks, Fatty Arbuckle, and Mary Pickford had once cavorted for the cameras were paved over in order to build the roadway approaches to the new bridge. Even the great cliffs of the Palisades, where starlets had once hung in death-defying terror in order to make another of the popular "cliff-

hanger" films, were transformed through the building of the bridge's giant supporting towers and cable anchoring supports.

Ammann and his crew labored daily to build what many had said would be impossible. To answer those doubts, the Swiss engineer built two 595-foot-high steel towers (the height of a sixty-story skyscraper) to hold his suspension cables. Each tower was composed of 20 thousand tons of steel erected in single-story sections for twelve successive stories.

The four cables themselves were spun, strand by individual strand, by the Roebling Company of Trenton. Each fifth-of-an-inch thick wire had a strength of 98 tons per square inch. Each cable was 36 inches in diameter, and was composed of 61 strands, or 26,474 wires apiece. In all, the bridge used 105,000 miles of this spaghetti-thin wire, or enough to circle the Earth four times.

The major controversy during construction was whether or not to en-case the great steel towers in concrete, as was done on the Brooklyn Bridge and many other suspension bridges. Ammann opted not to, and to this day, people argue whether or not the naked steel towers of the George Washington Bridge are architecturally attractive or not.

Ammann, however, was more interested in results than lofty debates about beauty, and in this he was spectacularly successful. On October 25, 1931, the great bridge was opened, one year ahead of schedule. It was, at the time, the largest suspension bridge in the world, and immediately pro-vided the traffic relief that New Jersey commuters were seeking. Four and one-half million cars traveled over it during the first year.

Exuberance in Fort Lee knew no bounds on the day of the bridge open-ing. The town pulled out all the stops for the gala event, including a con-cert by the 310 Infantry Band of Englewood, speeches by various dignitaries to a celebratory crowd of 4,000, and even a night-time block dance on the bridge plaza.

Today, however, the mood in Fort Lee over the George Washington Bridge has turned decidedly chilly. Angered over the Port Authority of New York and New Jersey's policy of not sharing any of the estimated $140 million that the agency collects from bridge tolls, Fort Lee authori-ties announced in October 1994 that they would begin setting up barri-cades to block access to the bridge from borough streets when police or other emergency vehicles needed to get by. Obviously, this could create gridlock of epic proportions for the 250,000 vehicles that use the bridge

95 The first cars come through the Holland Tunnel on November 13, 1927. (Courtesy the Port Authority of New York and New Jersey)

daily, but Fort Lee authorities said they're tired of watching the Port Authority rake in the cash and not contribute anything to the city for road repairs, police time to handle traffic-related crimes, and the like.

"To the people of Fort Lee, you are an enemy occupying power," said a former councilman to the Port Authority, illustrating quite vividly how sixty years of relentless traffic can change your perception of things.

DID YOU KNOW?

Names considered for the new bridge were: Gate of Paradise, Bridge of Prosperity, Noble Experiment, Pride of the Nation, Peoples' Bridge, and Bi-State Bridge. Finally, because George Washington had commanded forts on both sites—Fort Lee in New Jersey and Fort Washington in New York—it was decided to name the bridge after the Father of Our Country.

Because you never know what quiz shows are going to ask:

Length of the bridge: 4,760 feet
Width of the bridge: 119 feet
Width of the roadway: 90 feet
Height of towers, above water: 604 feet
Water clearance of bridge at mid-span: 212 feet
Cost of initial construction: $59 million

At first, it may seem that the only thing the George Washington Bridge and Green Sergeant's Bridge, New Jersey's last remaining covered bridge, have in common is the word "bridge." After all, the Hudson River bridge, with its fourteen lanes and wide roadbed, dwarfs the one-lane, twelve-foot-wide bridge in Sergeantsville (Hunterdon County). But when you look a little closer, you'll find that both bridges exist today primarily because of the determination of people who wouldn't take "no" for an answer.

96   The New Jersey toll plaza of the Holland Tunnel. (Courtesy the Port Authority of New York and New Jersey)

It was on January 14, 1960, that the *Hunterdon County Democrat* first carried the story that was soon to captivate not only all of Hunterdon County, but the entire state of New Jersey as well: "Fate of Covered Bridge in Precarious Balance" read the headline. Either decay, or the vibrations from a large vehicle, had caused the nearly 100-year-old Green Sergeant's Bridge to slip off one of its massive supporting oak timbers. As a result, the bridge was sagging dangerously over the Wickecheoke Creek below, looking like it would topple into the water at almost any moment. Initially the county tried to fix the bridge by jacking it up and slipping the supports back into place, but the work was halted when rotting wood was discovered at the base of the bridge. Other components of the bridge, such as iron plates and rods, were also found to be unsafe because of their age.

Repair costs were estimated at between $12,000 and $15,000, and

some thought it not worth the money. The county engineer urged that a new bridge be built for safety's sake. "I've got as much sentiment as anyone," he said. "But if someone gets killed there, people will blame me for permitting such an antique, narrow bridge to remain in use. It's a wonder to me that there never has been a serious accident there."

Others agreed, pointing out that half-a-dozen schoolbuses used the bridge each day, as well as a large number of other vehicles. Since the bridge could only accommodate traffic heading in one direction at a time, it put drivers in the precarious position of hoping that no one else would come barreling into the span when they were crossing it. Although the Hunterdon County freeholders made no decision at the time, the prevailing mood seemed plain: Green Sergeant's Bridge was a relic of the past that had outlived its usefulness. No one would be sorry to see it go.

The error in that thinking was quickly revealed in the next issue of the *Democrat*. The newspaper was filled with letters urging that the quaint old structure be saved. "It sometimes happens that an undertaking of this sort is pushed thru by a few people of limited vision before the general public is aroused," one Stockton resident wrote. "If it goes we will all lose something of charm and beauty and be much the poorer in spirit." Another letter-writer said, "I deplore the destruction of such landmarks. In so many cases there is an utter disregard of the intrinsic value of them. Some parts of these [landmarks] should be preserved, not only for sentimental value, but [so] that the younger generations can see for themselves the methods and arts of former years." From far-away Essex County came a letter from students and teachers at Livingston High School summing up the prevailing mood: "Your idea of tearing down the covered bridge may be good materialistically, but as far as sentiment goes it should not be considered."

Almost overnight, the old bridge became a *cause celebre*. Swarms of people visited the ailing structure, some to take photos, others just to view a part of history whose days seemed numbered. Pressure steadily mounted on the freeholders to save the bridge. Even members of Governor Robert

97 Building the George Washington Bridge. (Courtesy the Port Authority of New York and New Jersey)

98 Building the giant towers of the George Washington Bridge came first. This is the view from New York City, looking toward New Jersey. (Courtesy the Port Authority of New York and New Jersey)

Meyner's cabinet got into the act; Salvatore A. Bontempo, commissioner of the state Department of Conservation and Economic Development, opined that "New Jersey's last covered bridge has a particular appeal not only for camera enthusiasts, travelers and historians, but for all those who appreciate the scenic beauties of New Jersey and strive to preserve them."

At the next freeholders' meeting, a citizen's group who favored saving Green Sergeant's Bridge offered to pay for their own survey of the structure, to see if preservation was feasible. One of the leaders of the effort, calling the bridge "a link between today and yesterday," said that replacing the bridge would be like tearing down the Leaning Tower of Pisa and replacing it with a straight tower.

But the pressure on the freeholders was not all one-sided. Others pushed for the bridge to be replaced by a newer and wider modern span better able to handle the modern traffic load. Eighty-one signatures opposing the restoration of the bridge were gathered and presented to the freeholders.

All the while, the fate of Green Sergeant's Bridge hung in the balance.

The bridge was built in 1872, after a meeting at Jacob Wilson's hotel in Sergeantsville had produced a resolution to place a wooden bridge over the stream, with "timbers of white oak and rock oak," and to have it "inclosed [*sic*] with pine boards." Its curious name came from a man named Green Sergeant, a well-known resident of the area who had also given his name to nearby Sergeantsville.

Back then, the only traffic the one-lane bridge had to worry about was horse-drawn, and it was fairly easy for a wagon or carriage coming one way to pull over to the side to let another pass. With the dawning of the Automobile Age, however, the bridge became more and more inadequate. It had already been repaired once, in 1932, by John W. Scott of Flemington for $500. Could it be saved again?

For months the preservationists, who had organized into the Covered Bridge Association, and the freeholders struggled to see if Green Sergeant's Bridge could be saved. Finally, with help from the state, a solution was found: a new bridge would be built next to the wooden bridge, to carry eastbound vehicles, while Green Sergeant's would be repaired and made one-way in the opposite direction.

Work began in May 1961. As Green Sergeant's Bridge was taken apart, each piece was marked—A, B, C, etc.—and stored in the county garage in Flemington. Then, like a giant jigsaw puzzle, the span was put back together, using as much of the original materials as possible.

On September 15, 1961, a dedication ceremony was held at the rebuilt bridge, now with a reinforced concrete deck slab in place of the old wooden timbers. "Here it is, mended a little, some new timbers on its east side, but just as lovely as ever, just as beloved as ever," said Mrs. Edward M. Stone, president of the Green Sergeant's Covered Bridge Association.

Today Green Sergeant's Bridge is listed on the state and national historic registers. The bridge is a natural tourist attraction (artists and photographers are drawn to it like bees to honey), particularly in the autumn, when the changing leaves of the surrounding woods drape it in a colorful mantle of Nature's finery. At any time of the year, however, Green Sergeant's Bridge is a beautiful symbol of days past—and of the wisdom of preserving that past for future generations to enjoy.

99   The George Washington Bridge today. (Courtesy the Port Authority of New York and New Jersey)

DID YOU KNOW?

New Jersey once had over two dozen covered bridges. However, today, with the exception of Green Sergeant's Bridge, these quaint reminders of yesterday have vanished into history.

All of the state's counties except Bergen, Monmouth, Atlantic, and Morris had at least one covered bridge spanning a public highway. Some of the more memorable are:

Crosswicks. This bridge in Crosswicks (Burlington County) over the Crosswicks Creek was near the scene of heavy fighting between British and colonial troops during June 1778, when the English were moving through New Jersey on their way to Sandy Hook. The bridge, built in 1833, was adorned with eagles and the United States flag.

Dividing Creek. Built in 1841 to cross Diving Creek in Cumberland County, the bridge carried a warning that anyone traveling over it at a gait faster than a walk would be fined $10. Cattle would often spend the night inside the bridge (which must have been quite a surprise to anyone using it after dark!).

Stockton. This bridge spanning the Delaware River and linking Stockton and Centre Bridge, Pennsylvania, was first opened in 1814, and had to be rebuilt several times until being destroyed by fire in 1923. When the Delaware was flooded in 1841, George B. Fell of Lambertville was on the bridge when it broke into two pieces. Fell climbed on top of the bridge and was swept down the raging river. He passed underneath two other bridges that collapsed seconds after he went by (New Hope and Yardleyville—now Yardley) before struggling ashore at Trenton—just as the debris of the other bridges came barreling past him.

Raritan Landing. Located about one mile north of New Brunswick (Middlesex County), this was the first covered bridge in New Jersey. Built in

---

100 Green Sergeant's Bridge, the last covered bridge in New Jersey. (Photo by Pat King-Roberts)

---

101 Although Green Sergeant's Bridge may not be very long, its beauty is great indeed. (Photo by Pat King-Roberts)

1772, it was partially destroyed by the retreating Continental Army in 1776 to slow the British pursuit of Washington's troops.

South Branch. This bridge across the Raritan River was featured in a Ripley's "Believe It or Not" segment in 1941 that claimed it was over 200 years old. In reality, the bridge wasn't erected until 1820.

No chapter on transportation innovations in New Jersey would be complete without the Roeblings of Trenton.

It would be wrong to call John A. Roebling the father of the suspension bridge, since such structures had been used in China, Japan, India, Tibet, and other countries since ancient times. What Roebling did, however, was move the suspension bridge light years ahead, and show a disbelieving nation—and world—that they could be used to span great distances.

Before Roebling, the roster of failed suspension bridges was lengthy: a 408-foot bridge over the Schuylkill River in Philadelphia collapsed under the weight of snow and ice; the Lewiston-Queenston bridge over the Niagara River went down in a gale in 1855; the Wheeling Bridge over the Ohio River flipped completely over before plunging into the water; and, worst of all, the Menai Strait Bridge in Wales was destroyed by wind three times (1826, 1836, and 1839).

Roebling, however, had a better way. Born on June 12, 1806, in Muhlhausen, Germany, Roebling had emigrated to the United States in 1831. After trying his hand at farming, Roebling, who had studied engineering at the Royal University of Berlin, got a job as assistant State engineer in Pennsylvania. Before long he was building dams, aqueducts, and bridges. Soon he had graduated to constructing suspension bridges at Pittsburgh, Cincinnati, and over the Niagara River, spanning gaps that most people thought impossible.

Roebling knew that part of the problem with suspension bridges had been that their roadbeds were too flexible and that the force of all that

---

102   Part of the gigantic Roebling Works in Trenton, in the late nineteenth century. In the foreground is the Delaware & Raritan Canal and the Pennsylvania Railroad. (Courtesy of the Trentonian Collection, Trenton Public Library)

weight being swung back and forth by the wind was too much to bear. "That bridge," he wrote about Wheeling, "was destroyed by the momentum acquired by its own dead weight." To rectify this, he devised a truss system to stiffen his own bridges and keep the road in place. Even more importantly, he perfected a method of twisting strands of wire together into extraordinarily strong, yet flexible, cable. In 1848, on the advice of his friend Peter Cooper, Roebling opened his own wire mill in Trenton, where he produced the cable and perfected techniques to make it even stronger and safer. By 1867, when Brooklyn came calling, he was the undisputed master of the suspension bridge.

Brooklyn, however, might never have sought Roebling's services if the winter of 1866–67 hadn't been so severe. Huge ice floes dotted the East River, making ferry travel (the only way to get from Brooklyn to Manhattan) all but impossible. Finally, when Brooklynites realized that people coming from Albany were arriving in Manhattan faster than they were, they gave Roebling the go-ahead for his suspension bridge.

Roebling was delighted. Here was the ultimate challenge; a bridge from Brooklyn to Manhattan had long been considered a fool's errand. Feverishly he got to work, planning it so that the length of the span (1,600 feet) and its weight (5,000 tons) would assure the bridge's stability. To this Roebling intended to add massive stone towers, carved as corniced walls and pierced with gigantic Gothic arches. The total effect would be a spectacle to behold. "The contemplated work . . . ," Roebling wrote, "will not only be the greatest Bridge in existence, but it will be the greatest engineering work of this continent, and of the age. The great towers . . . will be entitled to be ranked as national monuments."

Charged with enthusiasm, Roebling began the preliminary engineering work. But Fate had other plans for the master bridge-builder. On June 28, 1869, as he was standing on a cluster of piles on a ferry taking some measurements, the boat crashed into a slip. The wood moved, crushing Roebling's right foot. Long ago Roebling had decided that conventional medicine and doctors were not necessary and that a person could use the power of his mind to vanquish disease and injury. Now he held firm to this belief, even going so far as to order a surgeon to amputate his damaged toes without an anesthetic.

But John A. Roebling, conqueror of every obstacle Nature had ever thrown at him, had finally met his match. Tetanus set in and moved quickly through his body. Racked with pain, Roebling spent his last day on earth inventing an apparatus to help him move around in bed. On July 22, 1869, the famous bridge-builder died.

Work on the bridge, however, barely slowed, because appointed to replace Roebling was his son and assistant, Washington A. Roebling. Cast in the same determined mold as his father, the thirty-one-year old Roebling was not about to let the bridge that his father had given his life for come to naught. Like his father, Roebling was everywhere, personally supervising every aspect of the construction, which began in 1870.

Two years later, in the summer of 1872, Washington Roebling was carried out of an underwater chamber barely alive. He had suffered an attack of what was then called caisson disease, but is now known as the bends. The illness left him permanently, painfully paralyzed at age thirty-five.

Still, work on the bridge did not stop. Although now an invalid, Roebling oversaw construction every day from his apartment window through powerful field glasses. With his wife, Emily, he devised a hand-tapping code so that he could communicate his orders to her. She, in turn, passed them on to the workers. In this manner was the Brooklyn Bridge ultimately built.

On May 24, 1883, the Brooklyn Bridge was officially opened. Dignitaries, including President Chester A. Arthur, gave speeches, bands played, and people looked up in awe at the massive brown towers. Looking down at all of it was Washington Roebling.

It had cost $13 million, killed John A. Roebling and crippled his son, and taken fourteen years of back-breaking labor, but the bridge that most people thought would never be built was now a reality—a reality achieved only through the incredible determination of the Roeblings of Trenton.

It is, arguably, not only the most famous road in New Jersey, but in the entire United States.

Mention the New Jersey Turnpike anywhere else in the country, and you're almost certain to get a nod or smile of recognition; if people haven't actually been on it they've heard about it. Now try that with the New York Thruway, and see how many blank stares you receive. Love it or hate it, the Turnpike is, as the *New York Times* once said, the "most American of highways."

The Turnpike has come to define New Jersey. No one thinks of the Garden State Parkway, the Atlantic City Expressway, or any of the countless other roads that criss-cross the state in the same way that they do the Turnpike. Some people hate the road; for them it calls to mind all the evils of urbanization, like big oil refineries belching stomach-churning fumes into the air and miles of concrete cloverleaves on which you can seemingly travel for days without ever straightening your wheel. Others, however, think of the kinder, gentler Turnpike that runs through the central and southern portion of the state, where the traffic melts away, the scenery becomes greener, and the road becomes a multilaned beeline to wherever you want to go in a hurry.

Speed, in fact, was the initial reason behind the Turnpike's existence. As the automobile became the dominant mode of transportation in the beginning of the twentieth century, it became obvious that roadway construction in New Jersey was not keeping up. There are still people who quake with terror at the memory of trying to get from Point A to Point B on such highways as Route 9, which contains more red lights than a bordello. By the end of World War II, stop-and-go travel in New Jersey had become a painfully familiar way of life. As more and more people flocked to the suburbs, and the American Dream was redefined as how many large cars a person had, New Jersey's roads began to groan under the strain: Route 46, built to carry 32,000 cars per day, was carrying 56,000; Route 1, designed to accommodate 30,000 vehicles, was clogged with over twice that number; and Route 22 was a virtual parking lot, with over 69,000 cars per day. The state's highways had the highest traffic density in the world. Plainly, drastic measures were needed.

Up to the rescue stepped Governor Alfred E. Driscoll. A strong and opinionated Republican governor who enjoyed the benefit of a Republican legislature, Driscoll knew the state was drowning in traffic. In his January 1947 inaugural address, Driscoll outlined his plans for the Turnpike.

Back then, there wasn't the inertia-creating cynicism about government that exists today; the United States had, after all, just swept to victory in the Second World War. The future was bright and full of promise, and there didn't seem to be anything that a country or state couldn't do. When Driscoll said that the state needed a superhighway running virtually its entire length, people nodded, rolled up their sleeves and got to work.

In October 1948, the state legislature passed the New Jersey Turnpike Authority Act and the road was off and running. To emphasize the sense of urgency to build the road, Paul Troast, the chairman of the Turnpike Commission, put a sign on his office door: "The Turnpike Must Be Done By November Fifty-One!"

This, of course, was only two years—two years to build a 117-mile road from scratch. Today, it would take two years for people to stop laughing at this kind of deadline, but times were different then; there was a will and a determination to get the job done, and to do it right.

To meet the deadline, the Turnpike Authority divided the construction into seven sections, each of which was to be built simultaneously. Another incentive to get the job done quickly was the $48,000 per day interest charge that was accumulating on the $235 million of thirty-five year bonds that had been issued to finance the project. The quicker the road was built, the quicker the revenues would begin and the bonds could be retired.

Construction began in September 1949 and proceeded at a blistering pace. Along the way, numerous problems that threatened to delay the project were discussed, analyzed, and resolved in record time: The muddy marshes of north Jersey were conquered by using sand to draw off the excess water; the towering Pulaski Skyway, which stood directly in the Turnpike's path, was dealt with by squeezing the road under the Skyway, rather than over; crossing the wide Passaic and Hackensack rivers was

---

103 Building the approachway to the Hackensack River Bridge during construction of the New Jersey Turnpike in 1951. (Courtesy of the New Jersey Turnpike Authority)

---

accomplished by building what were, at the time, the two longest bridges of their type (6,955 feet and 5,623 feet, respectively). To make up for the loss of manpower caused by the Korean War, everyone just worked harder and faster.

Incredibly, the Turnpike was finished on schedule. On November 5, 1951, the first 53-mile section from Deepwater (Salem County) to Bordentown (Burlington County) was opened. Three weeks later, after formal dedication ceremonies, an additional 40 miles was opened from Bordentown to Woodbridge. Twenty-three more miles were opened over the next few months. At a total cost of $277 million, the New Jersey Turnpike had indeed "been done by November fifty-one!"

Ironically, considering the abuse that the Turnpike takes today, the initial reaction to the road was euphoric. Widely hailed as the "Highway of Tomorrow," prestigious national magazines such as *Time, Fortune, Business Week,* and *The Saturday Evening Post* carried articles on the wonderful new road. Drivers used to highways filled with traffic signals and stop signs were stunned by how quickly the Turnpike whisked them to their destinations (it was estimated that a passenger car would save 70 minutes, and a truck 90 minutes, via the Turnpike).

But as we all know today, this euphoria did not last. As the years went on, the Turnpike was hammered for everything from its lack of roadside esthetics to just being "ugly." All a comedian looking for a quick laugh had to do was mention the New Jersey Turnpike, and the guffaws came rolling down the aisles.

These criticisms, however, miss the point: The Turnpike was never meant to be pretty, or fun to drive, or an architectural wonder. As Angus Gillespie and Michael Rockland point out in *Looking for America on the*

New Jersey Turnpike, the Turnpike was simply meant to be a road that got you where you wanted to go as quickly and efficiently as possible. There are no sweeping curves to maneuver, and no rolling hills to admire, because the whole point of the Turnpike is that a straight line is faster.

So, while we may never come to terms with it, we might still want to take a moment and reflect on the New Jersey Turnpike: It may be all that its critics say it is, but you won't find a better example of the spirit of hope and optimism that once infused the United States than this "most American of highways."

DID YOU KNOW?

Turnpike Trivia

- Names of the Service Areas: Clara Barton, James Fenimore Cooper, Grover Cleveland, Thomas Edison, John Fenwick, Alexander Hamilton, William F. Halsey, Joyce Kilmer, Vince Lombardi, Molly Pitcher, Richard Stockton, Walt Whitman, and Woodrow Wilson.
- Length: 148 miles
- Most Common Vehicular Problems: mechanical trouble (49,000), flat tires (5,800), out of gas (4,300), battery failure (2,200)
- Busiest Toll Interchange: #16E/18E, Lincoln Tunnel and George Washington Bridge
- 1951 traffic volume: 787,195
- 1992 traffic volume: 184,385,900

The Garden State Parkway was designed to be the complete opposite of the Turnpike. Whereas the Turnpike is a no-nonsense, let's-get-where-we're-going-right-now type of road, the Parkway is more of a leisurely Sunday drive. Even the name "Garden State Parkway" conjures up images

104   Lifting girders into place for the Passaic River Bridge in January 1952. (Courtesy of the New Jersey Turnpike Authority)

of men with handlebar mustaches and linen dusters, and ladies with parasols and hoop skirts enjoying an outing in the park, while the word "Turnpike" calls to mind sweaty, grimy, two-fisted driving. The Parkway, with its tree-lined vistas and wide, grassy medians with bushes and flowers, was made to be visually enjoyed as well as traveled. (In fact, the road's forestlike appearance was once considered so inviting to deer that special reflectorized pieces of metal were installed in wooded areas to scare away the animals before they leaped out onto the roadway. It didn't work.)

In the beginning, the Parkway was hailed as a liberator, come to rescue the Jersey Shore from its isolationism and bring about an age of unparalleled prosperity to the entire region. In August 1954, the *Asbury Park Press,* with all the feverish optimism of post–World War II America, raved about the new road that had just opened: "One trip over the parkway will convince any motorist that it measures up to the bright promises with which it was built." The paper went on to laud the road's "smooth, broad roadways . . . carefully planned approaches . . . [and] beautiful vistas."

Prophetically, the newspaper also noted that one result of the Parkway would be "a vast increase in the number of people who move into this area . . . with this growth in population will come serious social and economic problems, upon the successful solution of which the preservation of the Shore as an attractive residential and recreational center will depend."

The Parkway delivered on all that and more. The road ushered in a tidal wave of people and problems that the Jersey Shore is still dealing with: Open space was gobbled up by ravenous development that seemed intent on placing a strip mall on every corner; pollution fouled waterways that had been clean for centuries, not only harming the vital tourist trade but putting fishing boats and related businesses in jeopardy; and, local property taxes skyrocketed as communities struggled to build schools and other facilities for the sudden flood of new residents.

Worst of all was the traffic. Suddenly driving on formerly quaint one-lane highways with ancient drawbridges became a nightmare, as gridlock strangled the Shore and threatened to turn it into the urbanized

---

105 The New Jersey Turnpike today. (Courtesy of the New Jersey Turnpike Authority/Thomas A. Suszka)

---

106 One of the infamous Turnpike toll plazas. (Courtesy of the New Jersey Turnpike Authority/Thomas A. Suszka)

community that many had come there to escape. Even the mighty Parkway itself wasn't immune to the automotive influx: Survivors of Sunday-night traffic jams on the Parkway would talk about them around the water cooler the next day like veterans swapping war stories.

Today the Parkway is just as much a lightning rod for criticism as the Turnpike. What particularly incenses drivers are the ubiquitous toll booths that seem, like crabgrass, to spread each year. Just as happened to its cousin the Turnpike, the Garden State Parkway is discovering that the days of hailing a roadway are long gone.

DID YOU KNOW?

Parkway Trivia

Average miles between tolls: 15
Mowable acres of land: 3,000
Number of homes and buildings acquired for original right-of-way: 2,000
Amount spent to acquire land for original right-of-way: $49 million
Length of the Parkway: 174 miles
Cost of original construction: $330 million

Traveling the Pulaski Skyway is not for the faint-of-heart.

Towering, at its highest point, a sky-scraping 135 feet above the Passaic and Hackensack rivers far below, the Pulaski Skyway is like a launching pad for a trip to Mars. When it was built, the road was the most spectacular highway in the United States, a 3.7 mile viaduct whose black steel latticework made it instantly identifiable from miles away.

Before the Skyway was built, the trip between Jersey City and points north, such as Newark and Elizabeth, was a grueling journey marked by innumerable traffic lights and two drawbridges that were open more than they were closed. The Skyway, built at a then-record cost of $7 million per mile, reduced the travel time between Jersey City and Newark to five minutes. Building the roadway took 88,461 tons of structural steel, more than was used in the construction of the George Washington Bridge.

The road is named for Gen. Casimir Pulaski, a Polish native who fought on the side of the United States in the Revolutionary War. Pulaski was considered one of the finest and bravest men on either side during that war, seeing action in engagements at Haddonfield, Egg Harbor, and Camden, among others. Pulaski died on October 11, 1779, after being shot while (typically) leading a charge in the Battle of Savannah. Both sides mourned his passing.

DID YOU KNOW?

New Jersey was one of the most active states in the Underground Railroad, a network of people and homes that helped Southern slaves gain their freedom in the years before the Civil War. Fleeing slaves would be moved primarily at night from station to station on the railroad, going city by city and state by state, until they reached their final destination in the north.

In New Jersey, one spur of the railroad crossed from Philadelphia to Camden, then wound its way north through Burlington, Bordentown, Princeton, New Brunswick, Perth Amboy, Rahway, and Jersey City, and then to points further north. A second spur began around Salem, then traveled through Woodbury, Eveshamn, and on to Bordentown, where it hooked up with the line going north. A third track crossed the Delaware River at Greenwich, then went to Swedesboro, Evesham Mount, and Mount Holly, and then joined with the northern route at either Burlington or Bordentown.

CHAPTER FOURTEEN

The Call of the Pines

T H E very first thing that must be understood about the New Jersey Pinelands is that their very existence is one of Nature's great jokes on humanity.

Think of it: 337,000 acres of virginal woods and unpolluted water in the middle of the most densely populated state in the union. Mile after mile of nothing but pine forests, sand roads, and a few tiny towns in the center of a state routinely dismissed as nothing more than an urban overflow of concrete and asphalt between the urban complexes of New York and Philadelphia. Over 1 million acres of woods, rivers, bogs, and open space—an area larger than Rhode Island—that occupies approximately 30 percent of the fifth-smallest state in the country.

The more you talk about it, the more the miles and acreages add up, the more incredible it sounds. Having the Pinelands in the middle of New Jersey is like turning a corner in Manhattan and finding yourself in the midst of Sherwood Forest. It just shouldn't be.

But it is. In a state full of surprises for the depth of its natural beauty, the Pinelands is New Jersey's ultimate prank. And, if you look deeper into the mysteries of this strange and fascinating land, you'll find that the New Jersey Pinelands is more than just a pretty face.

By now, the Pinelands shouldn't be a surprise to anyone. During the last few decades the region has received more warm and fuzzy publicity than a litter of kittens playing with a ball of string.

It all started in the mid-1960s, when John McPhee's insightful *New*

Yorker essays on the Pinelands culminated in his 1967 book *The Pine Barrens*, which introduced the region to the country for the first time. Since this coincided with the "back-to-the-land" movement spawned in the wake of hippies and flower power, the Pinelands suddenly became a media darling. Magazines tripped over themselves publishing breathless accounts of the joys of wandering through this "primordial" wilderness that, to them, had seemingly appeared out of nowhere in the middle of urbanized, mechanized New Jersey. "Piney Power" hats and T-shirts began popping up faster than crocuses on a spring lawn.

All of this praise was not only a welcome change for the Pinelands, but an astonishing reversal of public opinion. For decades before that, the region had the reputation of a worrisome place, since it was considered to be filled with demented backwoods people and their families, who would hide behind trees and shoot at passersby with their squirrel guns all day. According to popular belief, a "Piney" was unfamiliar with both soap and work. Like a clan of degenerate hillbillies, Pinelands residents were thought to spend their days drinking, smoking, sleeping, and having sex with anything that happened to walk past.

The impetus for this extremely unflattering view of the Pinelands came from a report published in 1912 by Elizabeth Kite, a psychological researcher at the Vineland Training School. While Kite bore no ill-will toward the people of the area, her depiction of them and their woodland lifestyle was notoriously harsh. Besides painting vivid portraits of imbecilic men, women, and children, Kite depicted Pinelands residents as having no more regard for life than most people do when they step on an insect. "They was all insured. I'm still young and can easy start another family," said one woman in Kite's report after finding out that her husband and children had all been killed in a fire.

This report incited a storm of public outrage. The United States' work ethic—shoulder-to-the-wheel, nose-to-the-grindstone—was never stronger than it was during the early years of the twentieth century, when it was practically a mantra for workers of every class. New Jerseyans were outraged that lurking in their midst was a group of shiftless, lazy people who ignored society's rules.

Politicians then were no less adept at jumping onto the bandwagon of public opinion then they are today. New Jersey Governor James T. Fielder toured the Pinelands to assess the situation firsthand. He returned a shaken man.

"I have been shocked at the conditions I have found," Fielder announced. "Evidently these people are a serious menace to the State of New Jersey because they produce so many persons that inevitably become public charges. They have inbred, and led lawless and scandalous lives, till they have become a race of imbeciles, criminals, and defectives." To keep New

Jersey free from the odious Pineys, the governor suggested that the region somehow be cut off from the rest of the state.

With friends like that the Pinelands didn't need enemies, but soon the residents had even more reason to retreat into the deep woods and let the rest of the world spin on its merry way without them. Kite's supervisor at Vineland, H. H. Goddard, took her findings and used them as the basis for a report on a family he dubbed with the fictional name of Kallikak. Boiled down to its essence, Goddard's proposition was that virtually everyone in the Pinelands was descended from one man, Martin Kallikak. Martin and a dim-witted barmaid supposedly conceived an illegitimate son, Martin Kallikak, Jr.—called the "Old Horror" by Goddard—who then proceeded to spawn all manner of drunks, prostitutes, imbeciles, and general cretins: "From him [Kallikak Jr.] have come four hundred and eighty descendants," wrote Goddard. "One hundred and forty-three of these, we have conclusive proof, were or are feeble-minded." He then went on to break down the more infamous Kallikak kin into thirty-three "sexually immoral persons," twenty-four alcoholics, three epileptics, three criminals, and eighty-two who died in infancy.

The overall message of all this negative publicity was crystal clear: the Pinelands were a place to be avoided at all costs, and avoid them most New Jerseyians did. (Ironically, Kite was subsequently forced to withdraw her report because of the firestorm that surrounded it. Although she admitted that her conclusions about the Pinelands being populated by sex-crazed morons were probably not representative of the region as a whole, the damage had been done.)

Even the residents themselves seemed ashamed of their heritage. In the 1930s and 1940s, when pioneering folklorist Herbert Halpert tramped through the woods collecting songs and stories of the Pinelands, he kept asking people he met where the Pineys were. Those in the north said they were further south, while those in the south told him to look in the north; no one wanted to be known as a Piney. Like an urban dark alley, the Pinelands became a sinister, dangerous place; walk down it, people would say knowingly, and you may not come back.

Today, the breeze of public opinion has sent the pine cone spinning 180 degrees. People flock year-round to the Pinelands for hiking, camping, canoeing, and other outdoor pursuits. The region is celebrated in story and song, and the residents are admired—even envied—for having the sense to live in the peace and serenity of the woods, away from the constant concrete cacophony of the cities and suburbs. In fact, the same society that was once condemned as a bunch of lazy imbeciles was afforded a singular honor in 1983, when the Library of Congress's American Folklife Center came to New Jersey to study and document the Pinelands way of life.

Everywhere the folklorists looked, they found something special about the Pinelands. They found it in the way grandparents would tell children stories around a fireplace at night, and in the method used to catch snapping turtles. They found it in the way some folks gathered spaghum moss, prepared food, or decorated their yards. They found it in the way loggers cut trees, trappers caught game, and crafts-workers made decoys and embroidered dollies for their tables. In short, what they found was an incredible body of life-affirming wisdom and knowledge, passed down through generations, that gave the Pinelands a unique cultural identity. In this increasingly hectic world of faxes, super computers, and information highways, the Pinelands still run according to the ancient and much more important laws of the human spirit.

"We often protect knowledge by making it tangible, binding it in books with acid-free pages which are then housed in monumental buildings of marble and granite," said the Folklife Center's final report on the Pinelands, entitled *One Space, Many Places*. "Yet local knowledge has its own life, a life lived independently and dynamically, and which must be monitored at its source if we are to keep up with it at all."

One of the stories that has undoubtedly been passed down from generation to generation in the Pinelands is that of the Jersey Devil. Another, however, concerns the indisputably real-life exploits of a man named Joe Mulliner.

Mulliner's place in Pinelands lore is open to dispute. Some depict him as a Robin Hood–type character, robbing mainly from the wealthy, tipping his hat to women, and generally behaving in a charming and civilized way. Others, however, claim he was a cold-blooded killer, a man who terrorized the countryside, stealing, pillaging, and burning anything and everything in his path. As usual when there are two widely divergent portraits, the truth lies somewhere in-between.

Joe Mulliner was the head of a large gang of robbers that operated in the Pinelands at the time of the Revolutionary War. The gang was dubbed "refugees" because of their supposed loyalty to England during the war, but since they preyed on both Tories and Continentals alike, it's likely that their only allegiance was to enriching their own wallets.

Mulliner himself was a tall, handsome Englishman who almost always had a brace of pistols tucked into his leather belt. A bit of a dandy, the outlaw chief loved to dress up in fancy uniforms and attend lavish parties, where he would dance with the bejeweled, petticoated women until the wee hours of the morning.

Since most of the men in the area were involved in the war, Mulliner's gang usually faced no more than token opposition. The group rampaged through the Pinelands for years, virtually without fear of the law.

According to legend, however, one time even Mulliner's conscience got

the best of him. The gang—minus Mulliner, who was probably off dancing somewhere—robbed the home of a widow named Bates. When she tried to stop them, they tied her to a tree and burned her house down. Mulliner supposedly felt so bad about this that, several weeks later, Mrs. Bates received an anonymous gift of several hundred dollars. It was whispered with certainty that the donor was Joe Mulliner.

For a long time Mulliner and his gang ran the Pinelands as their own little fiefdom, but once the war was over and the men came home, the countdown to justice began for the robber chief. Mulliner, however, ignored the changing circumstances, and this led to his undoing. One night in the summer of 1781, as he was dancing at a tavern in present-day Nesco, a group of men who had been searching for Mulliner surrounded the building and took the outlaw prisoner.

Mulliner was taken to Burlington to stand trial. There was little doubt of the verdict, as *The New Jersey Gazette* of August 8, 1781, reported:

> At a special court lately held in Burlington, a certain Joseph Mulliner, of Egg-Harbour, was convicted of high treason. . . . This fellow had become the terror of that part of the country. He had made a practice of burning houses, robbing and plundering all who fell in his way, so that when he came to trial it appeared that the whole country, both whigs and tories, were his enemies.

The sentence was death by hanging. According to the Rev. G. A. Raybold, an eyewitness to Mulliner's incarceration, the always-arrogant outlaw became alarmed at how he would fare in the hereafter, and tearfully admitted his "baseness" in the presence of three members of the clergy.

Since so many tales sprang up about Mulliner's life, it was perhaps inevitable that another began on the day of his death. According to local lore, Mulliner was taken back to the Pinelands, where he was hung from a tree on the banks of the Mullica River. Some even embellished the story further by claiming that his ghost can occasionally be seen riding along the road near the hanging tree.

However, Raybold's on-the-spot account of Mulliner's death proves that the bandit met his end very near to where he was tried. "Thousands of people, it was computed, were there from all parts of the country," the clergyman wrote.

---

107 Joe Mulliner, legendary outlaw of the Pinelands. (Interpretive drawing by William A. Herbert, Jr.)

The music sounded doleful as a wagon approached containing Mulliner [and] his coffin. . . . The procession passed out of Burlington . . . to a place called Gallows Hill. Mulliner rose and gazed upon the crowd. His countenance seemed unchanged. He spoke at some length. He acknowledged his gilt [sic] and begged the people to pray for him. Then closing his eyes he sat down and appeared to be in an agony of prayer.

A few moments later, the criminal career of Joe Mulliner was over for good. Some said that he was brought back to the Pinelands, where he was buried along Pleasant Mills-Nesco Road. For years a simple tombstone marked the site. The state even put an historical marker there. However, the gravestone disappeared in the 1960s, and has not been replaced. If it is indeed Joe Mulliner buried there in the soft Pinelands soil, he sleeps the lonely sleep of the anonymous dead.

It would be wrong, however, to assume that the Pinelands does *not* contain ghosts. If a ghost is a phantom of things past, a memory of what was but is not anymore, then the Pinelands could be the most haunted place in the United States. There are indeed ghosts in the Pinelands— ghost towns, that is.

These are not the typical, garden variety ghost towns like those found

in western movies on the late show; you won't find any wind-blown tumble-weeds or swinging saloon doors in the Pinelands. (If you do, it's advisable to run away as fast as possible.) Like everything else about the Pinelands, these towns are unique, primarily because almost all traces of them have vanished. There are no buildings, roads, or signs to indicate where they once were. In most cases, the only way to find any evidence of a town is to stumble across an outline of bricks half-buried in the ground, marking the place where a building once stood. These are the last indications of the era when the Pinelands was one of New Jersey's, and the nation's, most important industrial regions.

Many people are shocked to discover that the peaceful, bucolic Pine-lands once housed industry of any type. Yet for decades the sound of the breeze whispering through the trees was joined by the thunder and lightning of the hammer and the blast furnace from factories that produced glass, iron ore, lumber, and paper. Towns with quirky names like Martha Furnace and Atsion Forge sprang up to house those who worked in these factories. Each industry had its heyday, then, due to economic factors beyond their control, vanished. When the last factories closed down and the work disappeared for good, so did the people. The towns were abandoned, and a deep quiet settled over the Pinelands once again.

It is the iron ore industry, which existed in the Pinelands for nearly a century (1760–1850), that best illustrates the rise and fall of the region's industrial might. There were approximately two dozen "iron plantations" in the region during the industry's peak.

The Pinelands' iron industry played a critical role in the early history of the United States. Thousands of cannonballs produced in the New Jersey woods helped Americans win both the Revolutionary War and the War of 1812. (Batsto ironworkers were considered so vital to the Revolutionary War effort that they were exempted from military service.) Before sailing to fight the Barbary Pirates, Stephen Decatur's flagship was armed with twenty-four-pound cannons cast at Hanover Furnace. Decatur himself was at the site, checking things over, when he supposedly encountered the Jersey Devil (see chapter 8). The fence that once surrounded Independence Hall was made from Pinelands iron, as was the cylinder for John Fitch's steamboat and firebacks for George Washington's fireplace.

The iron found in the Pinelands was known as bog iron, because it was usually found in swampy ground alongside bodies of water. Bog iron is

108   The long-vanished grave marker of Joe Mulliner. (Photo by Michael Fowler)

created by the chemical reaction of iron salts in the area's numerous stream and marsh beds to pine needles and other decaying vegetable matter. As the iron rises to the surface of the water and hits air it oxidizes, forming brownish blue–colored patches that mix with the mud of stream and marsh beds.

Iron workers would dig up the ore and transport it by large boats to the furnace. There it was crushed into small pieces (called "stamping"), boiled to remove excess water, and cooked to separate the slag, or worthless material. The porous, impure, somewhat soft iron that was left was called pig iron and was used for products like stoves, kettles, and window sash weights. Most of the pig iron wound up at the forge, where it was re-smelted into metal of great strength called bar iron. Bar iron was used for items such as wagon wheels, tools, and horseshoes.

As might be expected, working at the iron forges was a difficult and demanding job. Men labored from sunup to sundown, usually in twelve-hour shifts with few breaks. Workers were usually sweat-streaked, dirty, and exhausted at day's end. Holidays were practically unheard of, and except for an occasional day off to go fishing or hunting, an ironworker's life was one of almost constant backbreaking labor.

The communities that sprung up around the iron works were company towns in the strictest sense. Workers and their families lived in small, sparsely furnished wood frame houses; luxuries were rare, and necessities often hard to come by. Women purchased practically all of the family's needs at the company store, which usually managed to ensnare most workers in a web of debt before too long.

As it was, many workers and their families never saw real currency. Many were paid either in credit slips or company-issued script that was only redeemable at the company store. Since competing businesses were frowned upon, and the towns were so isolated that there was nowhere else to go and spend actual money anyway, the company store was the hub of the town.

On the other hand, the ironmasters (those who supervised the iron-works and were responsible for production, much like overseers on southern plantations) lived in large, airy homes fitted out with nice furniture. Stories are told about the incredible luxury that the ironmasters lived in, compared to the abject poverty of most the workers. While many of these tales are probably the result of the natural resentment between the haves and the have-nots, there's no disputing the fact that the ironmasters had a much greater standard of living than the workers.

In the iron towns, the coming of spring meant the resumption of work. Once the temperature warmed enough to permit water to start flowing freely and turn the water wheels that powered the great bellows, the furnace was fired up. It would not go out until the return of winter froze the water once again. The furnace operated twenty-four hours a day, seven days a week, filling the town with its throaty roar, like an ever-present beast crying constantly for food. To feed the furnace, the woods for miles around an iron town were usually stripped bare of trees. (The perpetual need for wood was another reason why most iron towns were located deep in the forest.)

What destroyed the bog iron industry in the Pinelands was the discovery around 1840 of high grade anthracite coal and iron ore in the hills of western Pennsylvania. It was easier to extract the iron from this ore than it was from bog ore, which, coincidentally, had begun to be depleted. (It takes twenty years for Nature to renew exhausted bog iron beds.) Coal was also superior to wood charcoal as a fuel to fire the blast furnaces. The implications of the Pennsylvania discovery were not lost on those familiar with the Pinelands industry. *The Camden Mail and General Advertiser* of July 1, 1840, observed: "It is suggested that the recent application of anthracite fuel to the smelting of iron ore will be very injurious, if not fatal, to the iron works of New Jersey."

The newspaper was right. Once large-scale iron smelting began in Pennsylvania, New Jersey's bog ore industry was doomed. Death came fairly quickly to what had been a way of life for Pinelands residents for decades. The fires went out at mighty Batsto for the last time in 1848, and the rest of the furnaces followed in short order. Within twenty years not a single iron works remained in operation in the Pinelands.

When the furnaces shut down, the company store and all the ancillary businesses also closed. The workers discovered that living in isolation deep in the Pinelands made finding another job extraordinarily difficult. People suddenly found themselves with no money and no prospects. It was a time of desperation for many Pinelands families.

DID YOU KNOW?

Who was Charles Read? This forgotten man of the Pinelands can be rightfully called the Father of the region's Iron Age. In 1766, at age fifty-one, when other people are contemplating retirement, Read was consumed with building a business empire in the Pinelands through what he called his "iron works scheme." Within two years Read had built four iron forges: Etna, Taunton, Atsion, and Batsto. Unfortunately, he badly underestimated the amount of capital he would need for such an enterprise and was in financial trouble almost from the start. Beset by business troubles and personal tragedy, and in failing health, by 1773 Read had sold all his interests in his iron forges and went abroad. Sadly, financial trouble and ill health continued to plague him. On December 27, 1774, he died alone in North Carolina, without ever knowing that his "scheme" would shortly become a thriving industry that would help the United States win the Revolutionary War.

Some iron towns tried to shift their industrial focus when it became clear that bog ore was dying. Paper mills and glass factories were common attempts to fill the void left by the iron industry.

The town of Harrisville is probably the clearest illustration of the evolution of Pinelands industries. Beginning as the "Skit Mill," a lumbermill built in 1750, the town also operated a sawmill and then an iron forge before being converted to a paper mill by William McCarty in the early 1830s. By the time brothers Richard and William Harris took control in 1851, the little town—now called McCartyville—had a double paper mill in operation. The Harrises promptly changed the name of the community, enlarged the paper mill until it stretched to over 300 feet long, and built a gasoline plant to power both the mill and light the town.

The primary product at Harrisville was a heavy, coarse brown paper made from hay, reeds, rags, and waste paper called "butcher's paper." It is very similar to the type of paper steaks and other cuts of meat are wrapped in today. However, while this paper was great for pork chops, it was lousy for writing, which was where the money lay in the paper industry. The Harrises tried to tap this lucrative market by developing a high-quality writing paper, but failed. Yet, even with this handicap, for awhile Harrisville prospered.

At its peak, Harrisville was an ultramodern, sparkling clean city. One of its most distinctive features was a row of ornamental street lamps that lined the town's main road. The Harris brothers were benevolent landlords, who gave their employees rent-free homes, free ice, and other amenities almost unheard of for workers in that day and age. Richard Harris was a certified neatnik who would chastise adults and children alike if he saw them littering city streets and was constantly after the town's residents to close their gates and keep their properties looking orderly and tidy.

In the end, however, Harrisville failed like all the other Pinelands industrial towns. Perpetually undercapitalized, the Harrises' finances were stretched to the breaking point by numerous recessionary shocks that shuddered through the national economy. The final nail in the coffin came when the Raritan and Delaware Railroad decided to bypass Harrisville and build a line eight miles to the west of the town. The brothers and their partners were forced to sell their property at a sheriff's sale in 1891. After this, the town bounced from owner to owner. In 1910 a massive fire swept through Harrisville, destroying most of the buildings. Vandals took the rest, including the famous street lamps.

(Apparently, the Harrises had a hard time letting go. For years rumors persisted that the brothers had come back to live amidst the rubble of their town after its destruction. Although that scenario is unlikely, it is probable that the men returned from time to time to gaze upon the ruins and reflect on what once had been.)

The fate of Harrisville was a microcosm of what befell all industries and the communities they spawned in the Pinelands. By the second half of the nineteenth century, railroads had become the chief mover of goods in the United States, and the absence of rail service in the deep woods made it difficult to get Pinelands-produced products to the marketplace. Depletion of the wood supply—the iron furnaces used a thousand acres of pine trees each year—also helped to hasten the end of the industrial age, since it removed a chief source of fuel. Typically underfinanced, the owners didn't have enough capital to ride out rough business waters. The industrial focus of the United States was shifting to the cities throughout the nineteenth century, and the isolated Pinelands just didn't fit in. Gradually, all the towns were abandoned, and peace returned to the Pinelands once again.

Until well into the twentieth century, the industrial ghost towns of the Pinelands stood like silent sentinels of another era. Often tucked into the woods, they would suddenly just appear to hikers and campers as they turned a corner, looming stone and brick phantoms from another time and place. Well into the early 1970s, it was still possible to visit many of these abandoned communities.

Today, however, that opportunity is gone. The spotlight of attention thrown onto the Pinelands has led to a massive increase in visitors to the area, and not all of them care about preserving the region's heritage. Many of the abandoned buildings were shamelessly vandalized until they either fell down of their own accord, or had to be demolished for safety reasons. Opportunists, seeing the potential for a quick buck, stripped the buildings for material that they could resell, such as tin roofs. Others viewed the ghost towns as open-air building supply stores: stones were taken for fireplaces, cedar shingles for garages and basement family rooms, and bricks for outdoor barbecues.

Once the structures were gone, the relentless forest overgrew what was left. Now a hiker unaware of an iron town's location could walk right through the middle of what was once the company store, or a worker's home, and not even realize it. Michael Fowler, a Pinelands researcher who has extensively studied Harrisville, estimates that over 90 percent of the town has been destroyed since the early 1970s. To view the glory of what once was in the Pinelands, it is necessary to visit such restored villages as Allaire (formerly the Howell Iron Works) and Batsto.

DID YOU KNOW?

Everyone knows that towns in the Pinelands have some colorful names, such as Ong's Hat and Double Trouble. But how many people know the former names of some of these towns? On the left is the current name of some Pinelands towns; on the right is their former name or names. Try to match the past with the present:

1	Vincetown	A	Shamong
2	Retreat	B	Etna Furnace
3	Chatsworth	C	Worthless City
4	Pineworth	D	Shinntown & Nabo
5	McCartyville	E	Edgepollock, Shamong, & Brotherton
6	Pleasant Mills	F	Weepink, Brimstone, & Quakytown
7	Indian Mills	G	Harrisville
8	Medford Lakes	H	Two Bridges
9	Medford	I	Sweetwater

Answers:
1. F, 2. H, 3. A, 4. C, 5. G, 6. I, 7. E, 8. B, 9. D

When the industries failed, the Pinelands reverted back to what they once had been: quiet forests bisected by meandering streams and dotted with brackish bogs. The industrial collapse created a vacuum that others tried to fill with their own ideas of how best to utilize the Pinelands. One of these was Joseph Wharton.

Wharton was already a wealthy and successful Philadelphia businessman, poet, and artist when he began buying huge tracts of Pinelands prop-

109 The Batsto baseball team, circa 1860. (Photo by Michael Fowler)

erty. In 1876 he bought Batsto, although some probably wondered why. "The buildings were so dilapidated that there was much doubt as to whether they should be repaired or torn down," said Civil War general Elias Wright, who assisted Wharton with his Pinelands purchases.

Wharton spent a lot of money to rehabilitate Batsto, including an estimated $40,000 on the former ironmaster's mansion alone. Although he used some of his holdings to work on agricultural projects, such as raising sugar beets, it was really the region's unspoiled, crystal-clear water that Wharton was after. His native Philadelphia needed good drinking water, and Wharton thought that the pure, clean water of the Pinelands would fit the bill quite nicely.

Wharton planned to build almost three dozen reservoirs in the Pinelands that would flow, through a series of canals, to one gigantic reservoir in Camden. From here an aqueduct under the Delaware River would bring the water into Philadelphia. Fortunately, his scheme went for naught. The New Jersey legislature got wind of the plan, and passed a law in 1884 prohibiting the export of drinking water from the state.

To his credit, however, Wharton took the defeat philosophically. Instead of storming out of the Pinelands and letting his holdings deteriorate, he redoubled his agricultural efforts and was instrumental in developing

the region's cranberry industry. His Pinelands property ultimately became the 100,000 acre Wharton State Forest, with Batsto as its heart.

Besides water, the other main asset of the Pinelands following the industrial collapse was land. Unfortunately, where there was land, there was also likely to be dishonest land speculators.

Land speculation was a booming business in the Pinelands in the late nineteenth century. Millions of dollars were lost by people suckered by high-pressure salesmen into buying useless lots in the Pinelands. The typical victims were city residents, who had no knowledge of the area, and even less about how to get there. Many people bought, sight-unseen, worthless lots drawn out only on paper, and never actually visited their "holdings." Even if they did manage to find their way to the Pinelands, the lack of roadways and directional signs sent most of them home without ever having laid eyes on their so-called investment.

The most infamous land speculation scheme was called Magic City,

which was supposed to be located on 1,400 acres between Chatsworth and Tabernacle. Ads promoting the sale of the "finest" farming land began appearing in New York City newspapers in 1888. Investors were promised that for their money (home sites cost from $50 to $100 each, while a five-acre "farm" was priced at $175) they would be living in a community that contained such amenities as a college, a hotel, and a music academy. People responded to the ads enthusiastically. Over 10,000 housing lots and 200 farm plots were sold by 1895.

The Magic City that was finally built, however, was a far cry from the one advertised. It contained just twelve homes and a small factory. The speculation scheme collapsed, and those who had believed in the magic of Magic City joined the long list of others who had wanted so desperately to believe that the Pinelands was Paradise Regained.

Joseph Wharton is long gone from the Pinelands, as are, fortunately, the land speculators. Not all of those who came, however, wanted only to take something out of the Pinelands. Others wanted to give something back.

Elizabeth White, for example, spent years at Whitesbog developing the modern cultivated blueberry, finally succeeding in 1916. Just before she died, in 1952, this woman with hands stained dark blue from years of handling blueberries asked landscape architects for the new highway then being built called the Garden State Parkway to please consider planting blueberry bushes alongside the road. The architects looked at this tall, elderly woman with the long, old-fashioned dress and the years of knowledge in her eyes, and didn't know how they could refuse. When the time came, blueberry bushes were planted alongside the section of the Parkway that cuts through the Pinelands.

Then there were those for whom the Pinelands was merely a source of recreation, the pursuit of which reached a pinnacle in Chatsworth during the late nineteenth century. The membership roster of the Chatsworth

---

110 The grave marker of John Lynch. Lynch was a handsome carpenter building the Batsto church in 1808 when he broke his engagement to a local woman. Hurt, the woman wished Lynch dead before the church was finished. That very afternoon, Lynch fell off the church roof and broke his neck. On his tombstone, he left a message for his former sweetheart: "Reader behold as you pass by, As you are now so once was I, As I am now you soon must be, Prepare for death and follow me." (Photo by Michael Fowler)

Club contained names that one does not normally associate with the Pine-lands: Astor, Morgan, Gould, and Vanderbilt. Yet they, along with many other politicians, socialites, and captains of industry came to Chatsworth during the Gilded Age to relax from the pressures of being rich and pow-erful. When they weren't attending festivities at the Chatsworth Club, which was presided over by Levi P. Morton, vice-president of the United States under Benjamin Harrison, the *crème de la crème* of society could be found at the White Horse Inn (also known as the Shamong Hotel). Even-tually, the rich found other playgrounds in which to amuse themselves, and Chatsworth's brief moment in the spotlight was over.

Wharton, White, and Astor are names forever linked with the Pine-lands. Another is that of Emilio Carranza, "Mexico's Lone Eagle." He got the nickname because in June 1928, like Charles Lindbergh, Carranza was making a nonstop goodwill flight from Mexico City to Washington, just as Lindy had done in reverse the previous December. The young aviator was already a hero in Mexico, for his role in putting down a rebellion and for his incredible presence of mind in the air, including when he deliber-ately flew into a thunderstorm so that the rain could put out a fire on the plane's wing.

However, fog over North Carolina forced him to land, thwarting Car-ranza's initial nonstop attempt. Young, proud and determined, Carranza, after reaching New York City, announced that he intended to fly nonstop back to Mexico.

The day he chose—July 13—was a typical East Coast summer day, hazy and humid, with risk of thunderstorms increasing as the day wore on. Taking off from New York's Roosevelt Field in late afternoon, Carranza turned his plane south. Somewhere near Chatsworth, he met up with a thunderstorm. But this was not a benevolent storm like the one that put out the fire on his plane, and the storm tossed the small plane around like it was a child's toy. People in Chatsworth said they heard a plane in trouble that day, the noise audible but faint over the crash of thunder. Carranza's plane went down in a stretch of woods in Tabernacle Township.

Nearly twenty-four hours went by before the young man's body was found, thrown from the wreckage of his small plane, and disfigured so badly that it could only be identified through documents addressed to Carranza found in the pilot's pocket. The plane, according to the July 14, 1928, edition of the *New York Times*, "was half buried in the soft bog, and a few feet away was the Wright Whirlwind motor of the craft. The fuselage and the motor had crashed down into a small clearing in the midst of the pines and stunted oaks."

"I pleaded with him not to go," revealed Lt. Henry B. Clark, manager of Roosevelt Field. "I told him the weather was too bad and that it would be a miracle if he even got off the ground."

In Mexico City, three hundred thousand people accompanied Carranza's casket to its interment, and the entire nation mourned the loss of one of its best and brightest. Every year the Mount Holly American Legion post holds a memorial service at the crash site, which is now graced by a large, pylon-shaped stone monument. The inscription reads: "Messenger of Peace. The People of Mexico hope that your high ideal will be realized. Homage of the children of Mexico to the aviator Captain Emilio Carranza, who died tragically on July 13, 1928, in his goodwill flight." Although there is a green highway sign on Route 206 in Burlington County that points the way to the "Carranza Memorial," few visit the site today.

There are hundreds of stories like these in the Pinelands—tales of how people came to this vast expanse of sand and pine and met success and sorrow, disappointment and deliverance, triumph and tragedy. These stories began when the first human encountered the Pinelands, and they will continue for as long as the region exists. Like a magnet, the Pinelands will continue to attract those who see in it an opportunity.

This is the Pinelands that has existed since humanity first began exploring the region ten thousand years ago. It is the same place that once attracted men who dreamed of building an empire of iron, and the same place that cast cannon balls to defeat the British in the War of 1812. It is the same place that the *Atlantic* called "aboriginal in savagery" in 1859, and the same place that Governor Fielder found so frightening a half-century later. It is even the same place that McPhee wrote about in the mid-1960s, and considering how many other dramatic and profound changes have rumbled through the world since then, this is probably the most surprising of all.

Indeed, in many respects the Pinelands today are in better shape than they were when McPhee's book first alerted people to the existence of this culturally and environmentally unique region. Several proposals that were floating around in the mid-1960s that would have ripped the soul out of the Pinelands, including one to build a jetport in its heart and another to construct a new city for several hundred thousand people there (shades of Magic City), have been mercifully shot down.

These types of grandiose schemes led to 1978 federal legislation that declared the Pinelands the country's first national reserve, a partnership between the federal, state, and local governments to try and retain the region's singular character while not strangling development or economic opportunity. Under this plan, a core region of 337,000 acres is closed to traditional residential, commercial, and industrial development, thus preserving the Pinelands' pristine natural beauty for generations to come. The Pinelands Commission oversees activity within the entire 1.1 million acres of the reserve, trying to walk the fine line between not impeding development and not allowing it to run amuck.

So today, the Pinelands would seem to have the best of both worlds: preservation and carefully controlled development. However, if there's anything certain about life, it's that uncertainty is the only known constant in an ever-changing world. As New Jersey one day becomes "maxxed out" in terms of development, and there is no more land on which to build houses, roads, and shopping centers, will people not point to the Pinelands, with its clean water and miles of unbroken forests, and say: There. There is the next frontier of economic opportunity for New Jersey. We must seize it. And considering how many "budget crises" the state has gone through, and how many more the future promises to bring, who knows what could happen?

In 1967, John McPhee wrote that the Pinelands were "headed slowly toward extinction" because of development pressures. While that journey has been forestalled, even apparently derailed, it has not been canceled. Like a soldier tiptoeing through enemy territory, the Pinelands must always keep looking back, to make sure that something unpleasant isn't gaining on it.

DID YOU KNOW?

Pinelands Facts

- The Pinelands is home to 39 species of mammals, 299 types of birds, 59 species of reptiles and amphibians, and 91 various types of fish.
- Thanks to the Pinelands, New Jersey ranks second in U.S. blueberry production.
- The Cohansey aquifer contains over 17 trillion gallons of water—enough to cover all of New Jersey with ten feet of water.
- Seven species—the Pine Barrens treefrog, the carpenter frog, the ground skunk, the northern pine snake, the northern scarlet snake, the northern red-bellied snake, and the corn snake—are found in New Jersey only in the Pinelands.

111 The Carranza Memorial in the Pinelands, near the spot where the plane crashed. (Photo by Pat King-Roberts)

- Population density in the Pinelands ranges from 10 to 4,000 persons per square mile.
- The Pine Plains contains the famous pigmy pine forest, the most extensive area of its type in the country.
- Recently discovered in the Pinelands is monobactum, a substance that has the potential to revolutionize antibiotics.

CHAPTER FIFTEEN

Birthplaces and Burial Sites

A L T H O U G H a pessimist will tell you that we're born just to die, an optimist will retort that life is what you make it. All that is a rather roundabout way of introducing this chapter, which is a listing of the birthplaces and burial sites of many famous people that can be found in New Jersey.

Born in New Jersey

Abbott, William (Bud), comedian, born October 2, 1900, Asbury Park

Addams, Charles, cartoonist, born January 7, 1912, Westfield

Amos, John, actor, born December 27, 1941, Newark

Barnes, Priscilla, actress, born December 7, 1955, Fort Dix

Barry, Rick, basketball player, born March 28, 1944, Elizabeth

Basie, William (Count), band leader, born August 21, 1904, Red Bank

Bennett, Joan, actress, born February 27, 1910, Palisades

Blaine, Vivian, actress/singer, born November 21, 1924, Newark

Blake, Robert, actor, born September 18, 1933, Nutley

Bon Jovi, Jon, musician, born March 2, 1962, Sayreville

Burr, Aaron, politician, born February 6, 1756, Newark

Cauldfield, Joan, actress, born June 1, 1922, East Orange

Cleveland, Grover, U.S. president, born March 18, 1837, Caldwell

DID YOU KNOW?

Stephen Grover Cleveland, the only U.S. president born in New Jersey, is also the only man elected to two nonconsecutive terms as the nation's chief executive. He won his first term in 1884, lost to Republican Benjamin Harrison in 1888, then defeated Harrison in 1892 to become both the twenty-second and twenty-fourth president of the United States.

To illustrate what a different time it was, during his second term Cleveland underwent not one, but two operations for cancer of the mouth that were kept completely secret from the national media. Twice during July 1893, while the nation was in the midst of a financial panic, Cleveland had operations to remove cancerous bone and tissue from his mouth in a makeshift operating room on board a yacht. Worried that news about his health would throw the nation into an even worse panic, Cleveland kept both operations secret from the newspapers, passing off the rumors of his ill-health as merely "gout" and "dental trouble." The secret was kept so well that to this day some history books still don't mention these surgeries. (A complete medical analysis of Cleveland's illness is at his birthplace in Caldwell.)

Two weeks after he left the presidency for the second and last time in March 1897, Cleveland and his wife retired to Princeton. Here he spent the last eleven years of his life in a variety of pursuits. Although he enjoyed great honors, including being elected a trustee of Princeton University, nothing delighted him more than putting aside work to spend the day with his children. In March 1908, suffering from heart and kidney diseases, the aging former president celebrated a bittersweet seventy-first birthday in the Lakewood Hotel, one of his favorite spots, which stayed open an additional six weeks after the end of its winter season to accommodate its honored guest. Three months later, on June 24, 1908, after murmuring "I have tried so hard

112   Grover Cleveland, the twenty-second and twenty-fourth President of the United States. (Courtesy Special Collections and Archives, Rutgers University Libraries)

113   Grover Cleveland's birthplace in Caldwell.

to do right," Grover Cleveland died in his Princeton home. He was buried in Princeton Cemetery two days later.

Cooper, James Fenimore, writer, born September 15, 1789, Burlington

Copperfield, David, magician, born September 16, 1956, Metuchen

Costello, Lou, comedian, born March 6, 1908, Paterson

Cousins, Norman, publisher, born June 24, 1912, Union Hill

Crane, Stephen, writer, born November 1, 1871, Newark

Dancer, Stanley, harness racer, born July 25, 1927, New Egypt

Dee, Sandra, actress, born April 23, 1942, Bayonne

De Palma, Brian, film director, born September 11, 1940, Newark

DeVito, Danny, actor, born November 17, 1944, Neptune

Douglas, Helen Gahagan, congresswoman, born November 25, 1900, Boonton

Douglas, Michael, actor, born September 25, 1944, New Brunswick

Evigan, Greg, actor, born October 14, 1953, South Amboy

Ferrer, Mel, actor, born August 25, 1917, Elberon

Forsythe, John, actor, born January 29, 1918, Penn's Grove

Foster, Preston, actor, born August 24, 1900, Ocean City

Francis, Connie, singer, born December 12, 1938, Newark

Francis, Genie, actress, born May 26, 1962, Englewood

Garfunkel, Arthur, singer, born November 5, 1941, Newark

Ginsberg, Alan, poet, born June 3, 1926, Newark

Gore, Lesley, singer, born May 2, 1946, Tenafly

Gray, Barry, radio personality, born July 2, 1916, Atlantic City

Halsey, William (Bull), naval officer, born October 30, 1882, Elizabeth

Harris, Franco, football player, born March 7, 1950, Fort Dix

Hayden, Sterling, actor, born March 26, 1916, Montclair

Hobart, Garrett A., U.S. vice-president, born June 3, 1844, Long Branch

Houston, Whitney, singer, born August 9, 1963, Newark

Keith, Brian, actor, born November 14, 1921, Bayonne

Kilmer, Alfred Joyce, poet, born December 6, 1886, New Brunswick

Kirk, Phyllis, actress, born September 18, 1930, Plainfield

Kirsten, Dorothy, soprano, born July 6, 1919, Montclair

Kovacs, Ernie, comedian, born January 23, 1919, Trenton

114   Grover Cleveland's grave in Princeton Cemetery. (Photo by Pat King-Roberts)

Langella, Frank, actor, born January 1, 1940, Bayonne
Lewis, Carl, track and field athlete, born July 1, 1961, Willingboro
Lewis, Jerry, comedian, born March 16, 1926, Newark
Light, Judith, actress, born February 9, 1949, Trenton
Lindbergh, Anne Morrow, writer, born June 22, 1906, Englewood
Liquori, Marty, runner, born September 11, 1949, Montclair
McBride, Patricia, ballerina, born August 23, 1942, Teaneck
MacRae, Gordon, singer, born March 12, 1921, East Orange
Mailer, Norman, writer, born January 31, 1923, Long Branch
Mitchell, Thomas, actor, born July 11, 1892, Elizabeth
Moore, Victor, actor, born February 24, 1876, Hammonton
Murray, Kathryn, dance teacher, born September 15, 1906, Jersey
    City
Nehemiah, Renaldo, track athlete, born March 24, 1959, Newark
Nelson, Ozzie, actor, born March 20, 1906, Jersey City
Nelson, Ricky, singer/actor, born May 8, 1940, Teaneck
Nicholson, Jack, actor, born April 22, 1937, Neptune
Pangborn, Franklin, actor, born January 23, 1893, Newark
Parker, Dorothy, writer, born August 22, 1893, West End

Pollard, Michael J., actor, born May 30, 1939, Passaic

Previn, Dory, singer, born October 22, 1929, Rahway

Riddle, Nelson, composer, born June 1, 1921, Oradell

Robeson, Paul, singer/actor, born April 9, 1898, Princeton

Rovere, Richard, journalist, born May 5, 1915, Jersey City

Saint, Eva Marie, actress, born July 4, 1924, Newark

St. Denis, Ruth, dancer, born January 20, 1879, Newark

Schary, Dore, film producer, born August 31, 1905, Newark

Shero, Fred, hockey coach, born October 23, 1925, Camden

Simon, Paul, singer/songwriter, born November 5, 1942, Newark

Sinatra, Frank, singer, born December 12, 1915, Hoboken

Springsteen, Bruce, singer/songwriter, born September 23, 1949, Freehold

Stagg, Amos Alonzo, football coach, born August 16, 1862, West Orange

Stieglitz, Alfred, photographer, born January 1, 1864, Hoboken

Streep, Meryl, actress, born June 22, 1949, Summit

Swit, Loretta, actress, born November 4, 1937, Passaic

Symmes, Anna, wife of U.S. president W. H. Harrison, born 1775, Morristown

Theismann, Joe, football player, born September 9, 1946, New Brunswick

Terhune, Albert Payson, writer, born December 21, 1872, Newark

Travolta, John, actor, born February 18, 1954, Englewood

Valli, Frankie, singer, born May 3, 1937, Newark

Vaughan, Sarah, singer, born March 27, 1924, Newark

Von Stade, Frederica, mezzo-soprano, born June 1, 1945, Somerville

Warwick, Dionne, singer, born December 12, 1941, East Orange

Wheeler, Bert, comedian, born April 7, 1895, Paterson

Williams, William Carlos, poet, born September 17, 1883, Rutherford

Wilson, Edmund, writer, born May 8, 1895, Red Bank

115 Two famous birthplaces side-by-side in Burlington. On the left is the birthplace of author James Fenimore Cooper. On the right is the birthplace of Capt. James Lawrence, who uttered the immortal "Don't give up the ship" command when mortally wounded in a naval battle during the War of 1812. (Photo by Pat King-Roberts)

Wilson, Flip, comedian, born December 8, 1933, Jersey City
Woollcott, Alexander, writer, born January 19, 1887, North American Phalanx
Wyatt, Jane, actress, born August 12, 1912, Campgaw

Buried in New Jersey

Beach, Sylvia, first publisher of James Joyce's *Ulysses*, died 1962, Princeton Cemetery, Princeton

Berger, Meyer, journalist, died 1959, Riverside Cemetery, Saddle River

Bloor, Ella Reeve, labor organizer, died 1951, Harleigh Cemetery, Camden

Boehn, Edward, creator of realistic porcelain figures, died 1969, St. Mary's Cemetery, Trenton

Burr, Aaron, U.S. vice-president, died 1836, Princeton Cemetery, Princeton

DID YOU KNOW?

Another permanent resident of Princeton Cemetery is Aaron Burr, Jr., who served as vice-president of the United States in Thomas Jefferson's first term. However, it is as the man who killed Alexander Hamilton in a duel at Weehawken, New Jersey, on July 11, 1804, that Burr is best known. Most accounts of the affair claim that Hamilton didn't aim at Burr—supposedly he pointed his pistol up in the air or shot at a tree well over Burr's head—while the vice-president gets portrayed as the blackheart who deliberately murdered one of the country's Founding Fathers. That's history's portrait of Aaron Burr—but it might well be wrong.

As part of the nation's Bicentennial celebration, the Smithsonian Insti-

116 The almost indecipherable tombstone of Aaron Burr, Jr., in Princeton Cemetery. (Photo by Pat King-Roberts)

tution decided to restore the pistols (which had been supplied by Hamilton) used in the infamous duel. When they did, they found that the guns had been altered in several ways, including being able to use larger-size balls. However, the most significant "adjustment" was that the guns had a special hair-trigger; by secretly setting the trigger to fire after only a half-pound of pressure had been applied, rather than the normal ten to twelve pounds of pressure, a duelist could fire much quicker than his opponent. This could have been Hamilton's plan, and most accounts of the duel note that he fired first. Something caused him to miss, however, and Burr's shot found its target.

Aaron Burr, Jr., was no saint, as his sordid later career proves. (Among the "lowlites" are his involvement in a plot to have the western states secede from the United States, a trial for treason, and marriage to a former prostitute, whose considerable fortune he squandered in several months.) It does seem, though that he has been judged wrongly for his role in the most famous duel of all time.

Butler, Nicholas Murray, helped establish Carnegie Endowment for International Peace, died 1947, Cedar Lawn Cemetery, Paterson
Childs, Samuel, founder of the Childs Restaurant chain, died 1925, Cemetery of the Basking Ridge Presbyterian Church, Basking Ridge

DID YOU KNOW?

Buried next to Grover Cleveland in Princeton Cemetery is his daughter, Ruth Cleveland. Born in 1891, the little girl was so popular during her father's second administration that the Baby Ruth candy bar was named after her. Sadly, the happy child with the smile of gold was not fated to enjoy a long life; Ruth Cleveland died of diphtheria at age thirteen.

---

117 The graves of Thomas Edison and his wife, Mina, in the rear of Glenmont.

Cleveland, Grover, U.S. president, died 1908, Princeton Cemetery

Crane, Stephen, writer, died 1900, Evergreen Cemetery, Hillside

Edison, Thomas Alva, inventor, died 1931, Glenmont, West Orange

Edwards, Jonathan, Calvinist theologian, died 1758, Princeton Cemetery, Princeton

Gilder, Jeannette Leonard, early literary agent, died 1916, Bordentown Cemetery, Bordentown

Gilder, Richard Watson, founder of the Author's Club, died 1909, Bordentown Cemetery, Bordentown

DID YOU KNOW?

Two of the most enduring symbols of Americana—Leo, the M-G-M Lion, and Elsie, the Borden's cow—also claim New Jersey as their final resting place. Elsie is buried in Plainsboro (Mercer County) with a tombstone marked with her real name, Lobelia, while Leo rests in Long Hill Township (Morris County).

Lewis, Joe E., comedian, died 1971, Cedar Park Cemetery, Paramus

Lombardi, Vince, football coach, died 1970, Mount Olivet Cemetery, Middletown

McClellan, George, Union Civil War general, died 1885, Riverview Cemetery, Trenton

McGuire, Peter J., father of Labor Day, died 1906, Arlington Cemetery, Pennsauken

Marin, John, watercolorist, died 1953, Fairview Cemetery, Fairview

O'Hara, John, writer, died 1970, Princeton Cemetery, Princeton

Peterson, Thomas Mundy, first black man to vote, died 1904, St. Peter's Episcopal Church, Perth Amboy

DID YOU KNOW?

Thomas Mundy Peterson is known as the first black man to vote in the United States because he voted on March 31, 1870, in a Perth Amboy election to revise the city charter, one day after the Fifteenth Amendment to the Constitution barring race as a qualification for voting went into effect. In later years Peterson served on the charter commission, and was a delegate to the Republican convention.

Roebling, John A., bridge builder, died 1869, Riverview Cemetery, Trenton

Shahn, Ben, painter of social scenes, died 1969, Roosevelt Cemetery, Roosevelt

Whiteman, Paul, band leader, died 1967, Cemetery of the First Presbyterian Church of Ewing, Trenton

118   The memorial above the grave of George McClellan in Trenton's Riverview Cemetery. McClellan commanded the Army of the Potomac during the early years of the Civil War, until his proclivity for caution got the best of Abraham Lincoln and the general was relieved. He later ran for president of the United States against Lincoln in 1864, and served as governor of New Jersey from 1878 to 1881. (Photo by Pat King-Roberts)

Whitman, Walt, poet, died 1892, Harleigh Cemetery, Camden
Williams, William Carlos, writer, died 1963, Hillside Cemetery,
Lyndhurst

DID YOU KNOW?

Walt Whitman's castlelike tomb in Harleigh Cemetery in Camden is
quite impressive—but even more so after visiting the small, ramshackle house
on Mickle Street in which the poet spent the last years of his life. The story
behind the tomb illustrates the type of fierce determination that Whitman
possessed even when old and sick.

The Good Gray Poet's move to Mickle Street was not well received by
his friends and admirers, who felt the tiny house beneath a writer of
Whitman's stature. Accordingly, they raised money for Whitman to buy another home, possibly a retreat down by the seashore that he so loved.
Whitman, however, had his own ideas as to what to do with the money; instead of a vacation home, he used it to build his tomb.

On Christmas Day, 1890, Whitman went to Harleigh Cemetery, which
had offered to donate the land, to choose a site for his tomb. Aware that he
was dying, Whitman had thought a great deal about his final resting place;
inspired by a drawing by William Blake, Whitman designed a simple yet imposing structure that was meant to hold him and other members of his family.
Originally he had wanted a statue of himself on top of the tomb, but the cost
had been prohibitive. As it was, the total cost was $4,000 (later reduced to
$1,500 through his friends' influence).

*119   The impressive memorial to Peter J. McGuire in Arlington
Cemetery in Pennsauken. Known as the "Father of Labor Day" for his
devotion to establishing what has now become a national holiday
dedicated to labor, McGuire died penniless in Camden in 1906. (Photo
by Pat King-Roberts)*

*120   John A. Roebling's grave in Riverview Cemetery, Trenton. (Photo
by Pat King-Roberts)*

Needless to say, his friends were aghast when they heard that Whitman was spending his money on what they considered an ostentatious monument. The poet, however, blithely ignored the criticism. On several occasions Whitman journeyed to Harleigh to check on the tomb's progress, sometimes reading the workmen scraps of his poetry. As Whitman grew sicker, the project became a race against time.

It was a race that Whitman won. The brooding stone structure was completed just in time to receive the remains of the great poet after his death on March 26, 1892. Having gotten his own way in life, Whitman also had things his way in death; six other members of the Whitman family are interred with him.

121 Walt Whitman's tomb in Harleigh Cemetery, Camden. (Photo by Pat King-Roberts)

BIBLIOGRAPHY

General

Beck, Henry Charlton. *Fare to Midlands*. New York: E.P. Dutton, 1939.

Bishop, Gordon. *Gems of New Jersey*. Englewood Cliffs, N.J.: Prentice-Hall, 1985.

Brydon, Norman F. *Of Time, Fire and the River*. Self-published, 1970.

Brydon, Norman F. *The Passaic River*. New Brunswick, N.J.: Rutgers University Press, 1974.

Carruth, Gorton. *The Encyclopedia of American Facts & Dates*. New York: Harper & Row, Publishers, 1987.

Cohen, David Steven. *The Folklore and Folklife of New Jersey*. New Brunswick, N.J.: Rutgers University Press, 1983.

Cunningham, John T. *New Jersey: America's Main Road*. Garden City, N.Y.: Doubleday and Company, 1966.

Cunningham, John T. *The New Jersey Sampler*. Upper Montclair, N.J.: The New Jersey Almanac, 1964.

Johnson, Allen, and Dumas Malone, eds. *Dictionary of American Biography*. New York: Charles Scribner's Sons, 1927.

Kross, Peter. *New Jersey History*. Wilmington, Del.: The Middle Atlantic Press, 1987.

Lyght, Ernest. *Path of Freedom*. Cherry Hill, N.J.: E & E Publishing House, 1978.

McMahon, William. *Pine Barrens Legends, Lore and Lies*. Wilmington, Del.: The Middle Atlantic Press, 1980.

Mappen, Marc. *Jerseyana*. New Brunswick, N.J.: Rutgers University Press, 1992.

Roberts, Russell, and Rich Youmans. *Down the Jersey Shore*. New Brunswick, N.J.: Rutgers University Press, 1993.

Stockton, Frank R. *Stories of New Jersey*. New Brunswick, N.J.: Rutgers University Press, 1961.

1 New Jersey Firsts

Chris, Teresa. *The Story of Santa Claus*. Secaucus, N.J.: Chartwell Books, 1992.

"The Evolution of the Colt" and other miscellaneous materials supplied by Colt's Manufacturing Company, Hartford, Connecticut.

"The Father of American Cartoonists," in *TelNews*. New Jersey Bell, November 1991.

Haven, Charles T. and Frank A. Belden. *A History of the Colt Revolver*. New York: Bonanza Books, 1940.

Jones, E. Willis. *The Santa Claus Book*. New York: Walker and Company, 1976.

Michalsky, Barbara V. *Whitesbog—An Historical Sketch*. 1978.

"Negroes End Flight," *The New York Times*, July 29, 1933.

New Jersey Gold. New Jersey Bell Telephone Company.

One Hundred Years of Brewing. New York: The Arno Press, 1974.

Harry M. Potter. "The World's First Drive-In Theatre," *South Jersey Magazine* (October–December 1974).

Reilly, H. V. Pat. *From the Balloon to the Moon*. Oradell, N.J.: HV Publishers, 1992.

Segrave, Kerry. *Drive-In Theatres*. Jefferson, N.C.: McFarland & Company, Inc., 1992.

Tales of New Jersey. New Jersey Bell Telephone Company, 1963.

Weiss, Harry B., and Grace M. Weiss. *The Early Breweries of New Jersey*. Trenton, N.J.: The New Jersey Agricultural Society, 1963.

Winders, Gertrude Hecker. *Sam Colt and His Gun*. New York: The John Day Company, 1959.

2 The Geology of New Jersey

Burke, Gary, ed. *Yesterday Today in New Jersey*. Jersey City, N.J.: C&S Publications, December/January 1994.

Sattler, Helen Rodney. *The Illustrated Dinosaur Dictionary*. New York: Lothrop, Lee & Shepard Books, 1983.

Wacker, Peter O. *Land and People*. New Brunswick, N.J.: Rutgers University Press, 1975.

Wallace, Joseph. *The Rise and Fall of the Dinosaur*. New York: Gallery Books, 1987.

Widmer, Kemble. *The Geology and Geography of New Jersey*. Princeton, N.J.: D. Van Nostrand Company, Inc., 1964.

Wilford, John Noble. *The Riddle of the Dinosaur*. New York: Alfred A. Knopf, 1985.

Wolfe, Peter E. *The Geology and Landscapes of New Jersey*. New York: Crane, Russak & Company, 1977.

3   Interesting People

Biographical Sketch of Joseph Napoleon Bonaparte, Count De Survilliers. London: J. Ridgway & Sons, 1833 (No author; probably written by Louis Mailliard).

"Bordentown 1682–1976." Pamphlet by the Bordentown Historical Society.

Carlisle, Robert D. B. *Clara Maass Medical Center: Building Bridges for 125 Years.* Belleville, N.J.: Clara Maass Health System, Inc., 1993.

Clara Louis Maass: The Tradition of Caring. Booklet issued by the Clara Maass Foundation, 1 Franklin Avenue, Belleville, N.J., 07109.

Connelly, Owen. *The Gentle Bonaparte*. New York: The Macmillian Company, 1968.

Convery, Frank W. H. "The Life and Times of James Still." *Mount Holly Herald*, January 4, 1962.

———. "More on the Life of Dr. James Still." *Mount Holly Herald*, April 19, 1962.

Cunningham, John T. *Clara Maass—A Nurse, A Hospital, A Spirit*. Rae Publishing Co., Inc., Belleville, N.J., 1968

Daily Herald, Newbury Port, Mass. March 30, 1847.

Frankenstein, Alfred. *After the Hunt*. Berkeley and Los Angeles: University of California Press, 1969.

Greenhill, Ralph, and Thomas D. Mahoney. *Niagara*. Toronto: University of Toronto Press, 1969.

Hamilton, Rae. "Doctor James Still, Famous Negro Physician, Was Born Near Medford." *Mount Holly Herald*, July–August, 1938.

Irby, James B. *Black Heritage in Central Burlington County*. Self-published, 1975.

Johnson, Allen, and Dumas Malone, eds. *Dictionary of American Biography*. New York: Charles Scribner's & Sons, 1934.

Kralik, Marilyn, and Pauline S. Miller. *A Century of Art: 1850–1950; Ocean County Artists and Their Works Before 1950*. The Ocean County Cultural and Heritage Commission, 1992.

Macartney, Clarence Edward, and Gordon Dorrance. *The Bonapartes In America*. Philadelphia: Dorrance and Company, 1939.

"New Mystery In Hidden Vault In Bonaparte's New Jersey Estate," *The World Magazine*, March 22, 1914.

The New York Times, August 25–27, 1901.

Ross, Michael. *The Reluctant King*. New York: Mason/Charter, 1977.

The Saturday Evening Post: October 6, 1827, July 26, 1828, August 2, 1828, August 9, 1828, October 17, 1829, November 7, 1829, November 14, 1829, November 21, 1829, and December 5, 1829.

Stacton, David. *The Bonapartes*. New York: Simon and Schuster, 1966.

Still, James. *Early Recollections and Life of Dr. James Still*. New Brunswick, N.J.: Rutgers University Press, 1973.

Walsh, William S. "The American St. Helena." *Frank Leslie's Popular Monthly*, February 1894.

Wilmerding, John. *Important Information Inside*. New York: Harper & Row, 1983.

Woodward, E. M., *Bonaparte's Park and the Murats*. Self-published, 1879.

———. *Bordentown and It's Environs*. Self-published, circa 1890.

4 The Sporting Life

Briggs, Asa, ed. *A Dictionary of 20th Century World Biography*. Oxford, England: Oxford University Press, 1992.

Dempsey, Jack, *Dempsey*. New York: Harper & Row Publishers, 1977.

"Dempsey Knocks Out Carpentier in Fourth Round of the Bout." *Newark Evening News*, July 2, 1921.

DiClerico, James M., and Barry J. Pavelec. *The Jersey Game*. New Brunswick, N.J.: Rutgers University Press, 1991.

Durant, John, and Les Etter. *Highlights of College Football*. New York: Hastings House, 1970.

"The Football Match." *The Targum*, November 1869.

"Many Prominent Persons Will Witness Big Fight." *Newark Evening News*, June 30, 1921.

Mason, Nicholas. *Football!* New York: Drake Publishers, 1975.

Mayer, Ronald A. *1937 Newark Bears*. Union City, N.J.: William H. Wise and Company, 1980.

Nash, Bruce, and Allan Zullo. *The Baseball Hall of Shame 2*. New York: Pocket Books, 1986.

"New Jersey." *The New York Times*, November 9, 1869.

Overmyer, James. *Effa Manley and the Newark Eagles*. Metuchen, N.J.: The Scarecrow Press, 1993.

Peterson, Harold. *The Man Who Invented Baseball*. New York: Charles Scribner's Sons, 1969.

Roberts, Randy. *Jack Dempsey*. Baton Rogue: Louisiana State University Press, 1979.

Rogosin, Donn. *Invisible Men*. New York: Atheneum, 1983.

"Small Chance for Crooks at Fight." *Newark Evening News*, July 1, 1921.

Sobol, Ken. *Babe Ruth and the American Dream*. New York: Random House, 1974.

"The Start of It All." *Rutgers Alumni Magazine*, September 1969.

The Sunday World Magazine, September 21, 1930. (Article by John W. Herbert.)

Swinburne, Lawrence, and Irene Swinburne. *America's First Football Game*. New York: Contemporary Perspectives, 1978.

Weiss, Harry B., and Grace M. Weiss. *Early Sports & Pasttimes in New Jersey*. Trenton, N.J.: The Past Times Press, 1960.

Whittingham, Richard. *Saturday Afternoon*. New York: Workman Publishing, 1985.

The World, November 23, 1924

5 Away for the Day

Connor, Jack. *Season at the Point*. New York: The Atlantic Monthly Press, 1991.

Cooney, Patrick Louis, *Discovering the Mid-Atlantic: Historical Tours*. New Brunswick, N.J.: Rutgers University Press, 1991.

Hudgins, Barbara. *New Jersey Day Trips*. Green Village, N.J.: The Woodmont Press, 1993.

"Iches Dedicates Morristown Park." The *New York Times*, July 5, 1933.

Miscellaneous guides, pamphlets, and maps issued by the New Jersey State Division of Travel & Tourism.

Morristown. Washington, D.C.: The Division of Publications, National Park Service, 1984.

Scheller, William G. *New Jersey: Off the Beaten Path*. Chester, Conn.: The Globe Pequot Press, 1988.

Tourbook: New Jersey and Pennsylvania. Heathrow, Fla.: American Automobile Association, 1994.

Westergaard, Barbara. *New Jersey: A Guide to the State*. New Brunswick, N.J.: Rutgers University Press, 1987.

Zatz, Arline. *New Jersey's Special Places*. Woodstock, Vt.: The Countryman Press, 1990.

6   Celebrated Sons and Distinguished Daughters

"After the Laughs." by Acocella, Joan. *The New Yorker*, August 6, 1993.

Bacon-Foster, Corra. *Clara Barton, Humanitarian*. Washington, D.C.: The Columbia Historical Society, 1918.

"Clara Barton's Role In Bordentown's History." *The Bordentown Register*. September 6, 1956.

Clark, Barbara Louise, *E.B.* Philadelphia: Dorrance & Company, 1975.

Ehrlich, Scott. *Paul Robeson*. New York: Chelsea House, 1988.

Fishwick, Marshall W., *Illustrious Americans: Clara Barton*. Morristown, N.J.: Silver Burdett Company, 1966.

Frewin, Leslie. *The Late Mrs. Dorothy Parker*. New York: MacMillan Publishing Company, 1986.

Gibson, Emma Ghering. *Pioneer Women of Historic Haddonfield*. West Collingswood, N.J.: Varacomp.

Harwood, Michael. *In the Shadow of Presidents*. Philadelphia: J.B. Lippincott Company, 1966.

Meade, Marion. *What Fresh Hell Is This?*. New York: Villard Books, 1988.

The New York Times, January 24, 1976.

O'Malley, Michael. *Keeping Watch*. New York: Viking Penguin, 1990.

Paul Robeson: The Great Forerunner, by the editors of *Freedomways*. New York: Dodd, Mead & Company, 1965.

Robeson, Susan. *The Whole World in His Hands*. Seacaucus, N.J.: Citadel Press, 1981.

Ross, Ishbel. *Angel of the Battlefield*. New York: Harper & Brothers Publishers, 1956.

Tally, Steve. *Bland Ambition*. New York: Harcourt, Brace, Jovanovich, 1992.

This Is Haddonfield. Haddonfield, N.J.: The Historical Society of Haddonfield, 1963.

Whisenhunt, Donald T. *Elias Boudinot.* The New Jersey Historical Commission, 1975.

7   Great Storms

The *Asbury Park Press*, December 11–20, 1992.
The *Asbury Park Evening Press*, September 15–16, 1944.
Caplovich, Judd. *Blizzard!* Vero Publishing Company, 1987.
Ludlum, David M. *The New Jersey Weather Book.* New Brunswick, N.J.: Rutgers University Press, 1983.
New Jersey Courier, March 14–21, 1888.
The New York Times, March 12–15, 1888.
Newark Evening News, March 14–15, 1888.
Savadove, Larry, and Margaret Thomas Buchholz. *Great Storms of the Jersey Shore.* Harvey Cedars, N.J.: Down the Shore Publishing, 1993.

8   Ghosts, Tall Tales, and Legends

Beck, Henry Charlton. "Ghosts of 1800s Haunted Church in Jersey City." *Sunday Star-Ledger*, March 29, 1964.
Cohen, Daniel. *Phantom Animals.* New York: Pocket Books, 1991.
Cohen, David Steven, *The Ramapo Mountain People.* New Brunswick, N.J.: Rutgers University Press, 1974.
Halpert, Herbert. *Folktales and Legends from the New Jersey Pines.* Bloomington: Indiana University Press, 1947.
Jarvis, Sharon. *Beyond Reality: True Tales of the Unknown.* New York: Bantam Books, 1991.
McCloy, James F., and Ray Miller. *The Jersey Devil.* Wallingford, Penn.: The Middle Atlantic Press, 1976.
Quarrie, George. *Within A Jersey Circle.* Somerville, N.J.: Unionist-Gazette Association Publishers, 1910.
Weird New Jersey 4, Summer 1993. (Compiled by Mark Sceurman, Bloomfield, N.J.)

9   Historical Happenings

Asbury Park Evening Press, October 31, 1938.
Booth, Sally Smith. *The Women of '76.* New York: Hastings House, 1973.
Brady, Frank. *Citizen Welles.* New York: Charles Scribner's Sons, 1989.
Bridgeton Chronicle, November 13, 20, & 27, 1874.
Cantril, Hadley. *The Invasion from Mars.* New York: Harper & Row, Publishers, 1966.

Gilman, Col. C. Malcom B. *Monmouth Road to Glory*. Red Bank, N.J.: Arlington Laboratory for Clinical and Historical Research, 1964.

Koch, Howard. *The Panic Broadcast*. Boston: Little, Brown and Company, 1970.

Leaming, Barbara. *Orson Welles*. New York: Viking, 1985.

Lender, Mark. *The Battle of Monmouth*. Unpublished manuscript.

Mulford, William C. *Historical Tales of Cumberland County*. Bridgeton, N.J.: Evening News Company, 1941.

Newark Evening News, October 31–November 1, 1938.

Sickler, Joseph S. *Tea Burning Town*. New York: Ubelard Press, 1950.

Smith, Samuel Stelle. *The Battle of Monmouth*. Monmouth Beach, N.J.: Philip Freneau Press, 1964.

———. "The Search for Molly Pitcher." *Daughters of the American Revolution* magazine, April 1975.

Stryker, William S. *The Battle of Monmouth*. Port Washington, N.Y.: Kennikat Press, 1927.

Witcover, Jules. *Sabotage at Black Tom*. Chapel Hill, N.C.: Algonquin Books, 1989.

10 A Town Treasury

Asbury Park Press, June 29–30, 1994.

Baker-Carr, C. D. T. *Sand and Glass*. Garden City, N.Y.: Nelson Doubleday, 1960.

Baver, W. John. *William Carlos Williams, Stephen Crane, and Philip Freneau*. Trenton, N.J.: The New Jersey Historical Commission, 1989.

Daniels, Morris S. *The Story of Ocean Grove*. New York: The Methodist Book Concern, 1919.

Grover, Kathryn. *Hard at Play*. Amherst, Mass., and Rochester, N.Y.: The University of Massachusetts Press and the Strong Museum, 1992.

Harris, Howard. *The Transformation of Idealogy in the Early Industrial Revolution: Paterson, New Jersey, 1820–1840*. Ph.D. diss., 1985.

Herbst, John A., and Catherine Keene. *Life and Times in Silk City*. Haledon, N.J.: The American Labor Museum, 1984.

Hewitt, Louise. *Historic Trenton*. Trenton, N.J.: The Smith Press, 1916.

History of Ocean Grove. Ocean Grove, N.J.: The Ocean Grove Times, 1944.

Johnson, Virgil S. *Millville: 1802 to 1952*. Self-published.

———. *Millville Glass: The Early Days*. Millville, N.J.: Delaware Bay Trading Co., 1971.

McMahon, William. *Historic South Jersey Towns*. Atlantic City: Press Publishing Company, 1964

———. *South Jersey Towns*. New Brunswick, N.J.: Rutgers University Press, 1973.

Miller, John C. *Alexander Hamilton: Portrait in Paradox*. New York: Harper & Row, Publishers, 1959.

Millville, N.J. Centennial Souvenir, 1866–1966. The Millville Centennial Corporation.

The North American, October 11, 1908.

Norwood, Christopher. *About Paterson*. New York: E.P. Dutton & Co., 1974.

Osborn, W. B. *In the Beginning, God*. New York: The Methodist Book Concern, n.d.

Podmore, Harry J. *Trenton Old and New*. Trenton, N.J.: MacCrellish & Quigley Company, 1964.

Quigley, Mary Alice, and David E. Collier. *A Capital Place: The Story of Trenton*. Woodland Hills, Calif.: Windsor Publications, 1984.

Raum, John O. *History of the City of Trenton*. Trenton, N.J.: W.T. Nicholson & Co., 1871.

Stokes, Reverend E. H. *Ocean Grove: Its Origin and Progress*. Philadelphia: Fress of Haddock & Son, 1874.

Trenton Times, June 30, 1994

Tripp, Anne Huber. *The I.W.W. and the Paterson Silk Strike of 1913*. Urbana: University of Illinois Press, 1987.

Whittemore, Reed. *William Carlos Williams: Poet from Jersey*. Boston: Houghton, Mifflin Co., 1975.

11   When New Jersey Was Hollywood

Altomara, Rita Ecke. *Hollywood on the Palisades*. New York: Garland Publishing, Inc, 1983.

"American Bicentennial News," 1776–1976.

Balshofer, Fred J., and Arthur C. Miller. *One Reel a Week*. Berkeley and Los Angeles: The University of California Press, 1967.

Hendricks, Gordon. *Origins of the American Film*. New York: Arno Press & the *New York Times*, 1972.

New Jersey Motion Picture & Television Commission, "1993 Annual Report," pp. 3–25.

Jersey Journal, May 24, 1971.

New York Herald Tribune, October 26, 1947.

New York World Telegram, October 29, 1947.

Nye, David E. *The Invented Self*. Odense, Denmark: Odense University Press, 1983.

The Record, January 29, 1964.

Spehr, Paul C. *The Movies Begin*. Newark, N.J.: The Newark Museum, 1977.

Sunday Record, March 6, 1983

Sunday Record Call, July 6, 1969

12   It's the Natural Thing to Do

Cavanaugh, Cam. *Saving the Great Swamp*. Frenchtown, N.J.: Columbia Publishing Company, 1978.

Leck, Charles. *The Birds of New Jersey*. New Brunswick, N.J.: Rutgers University Press, 1975.

Niles, Lawrence, Kathleen Clark, and Sharon Paul. *Comprehensive Management Plan for Shorebirds on Delaware Bay* (Joint publication of the Endangered & Nongame Species Program & the Nature Conservancy).

Roberts, Russell. "Next Stop Delaware Bay." *New Jersey Living* (April 1987), p. 24.

Miscellaneous pamphlets, hand-outs, and data sheets from the Edwin B. Forsythe National Wildlife Refuge and the Great Swamp National Wildlife Refuge.

1992 Annual Report, Endangered and Nongame Species Program, New Jersey Department of Environmental Protection and Energy, Division of Fish, Game and Wildlife.

Riley, Laura, and William Riley. *Guide to the National Wildlife Refuges*. Garden City, N.Y.: Anchor Press, 1979.

13   Roads, Bridges, and Tunnels

Asbury Park Press, August 7–10, 1994.

Beaver, Patrick. *A History of Tunnels*. Secaucus, N.J.: The Citadel Press, 1973.

Cranmer, H. Jerome. *New Jersey in the Automobile Age*. Princeton, N.J.: D. Van Nostrand Company, 1964.

"Fort Lee to Block Access to George Washington Bridge," *Trenton Times*, October 14, 1994, p. A-10.

Gillespie, Angus Kress, and Michael Aaron Rockland. *Looking for America on the New Jersey Turnpike*. New Brunswick, N.J.: Rutgers University Press, 1989.

Hankins, Grace Croyle. *True Stories of New Jersey*. Philadelphia: The John C. Winston Company, 1939.

Miscellaneous materials provided by the Port Authority of New York and New Jersey.

The New York Times, October 28, 1924, November 13, 1927, and October 25, 1931.

Olney, Ross R. *They Said It Couldn't Be Done*. New York: E.P. Dutton, 1979.

Plowden, David. *Bridges*. New York: The Viking Press, 1974.

Shirley-Smith, H. *The World's Great Bridges*. New York: Harper & Row, Publishers, 1953.

Silverberg, Robert. *Bridges*. Philadelphia: Macrae Smith Company, 1966.

Steinman, D. B. *The Builders of the Bridge*. New York: Harcourt, Brace and Company, 1945.

Trachtenberg, Alan. *Brooklyn Bridge: Fact and Symbol*. New York: Oxford University Press, 1965.

14   The Call of the Pines

Carter, James H. *A Trip Through the Pines*. Self-published, 1969.

Goddard, Henry Herbert. *The Kallikak Family*. New York: Macmillan and Company, 1912.

Hufford, Mary. *One Space, Many Places.* Washington, D.C.: The Library of Congress, 1986.

McPhee, John. *The Pine Barrens.* New York: Farrar, Straus, & Giroux, 1967.

Moonsammy, Rita Zorn, David Steven Cohen, and Lorraine E. Williams. *Pinelands Folklife.* New Brunswick, N.J.: Rutgers University Press, 1987.

The New York Times, July 14, 1928.

Pierce, Arthur D. *Iron in the Pines.* New Brunswick, N.J.: Rutgers University Press, 1957.

Pinelands Guide, New Jersey Pinelands Commission

"Pinelands Collection," Pinelands Room, Burlington County College.

15   Birth Places and Burial Sites

Arbeiter, Jean, and Linda D. Cirino. *Permanent Address.* New York: M. Evans and Company, 1983.

Canby, Henry Seidel. *Walt Whitman: An American.* Boston: Houghton-Mifflin Company, 1943.

Cantor, George. *Historic Landmarks of Black America.* Detroit: Gale Research, 1991.

Chupack, Henry. *Walt Whitman in Camden.* Ph.D. diss., New York University, 1952.

Hoyt, Edwin P. *Grover Cleveland.* Chicago: Reilly & Lee Co., 1962.

Johnson, Otto, ed. *The 1992 Information Please Almanac.* Boston: Houghton-Mifflin Company, 1992.

Nigro, Dana. "Saving a Famous Mascot's Grave." *The Independent Press,* August 3, 1994.

Sarapin, Janice Kohl. *Old Burial Grounds of New Jersey.* New Brunswick, N.J.: Rutgers University Press, 1994.

Stetler, Susan L. *Almanac of Famous People.* Detroit: Gale Research, 1989.

INDEX

About the Author

Russell Roberts is a lifelong New Jersey resident currently living in Bordentown. He has written two other books (*Down the Jersey Shore* and *All About Blue Crabs and How to Catch Them*), and has had articles and short stories appear in over 150 national and regional magazines. In 1994 he won the Rutgers University/CIT Journalism Award for distinguished writing.